Paris and the Parasite

Paris and the Parasite

Noise, Health, and Politics in the Media City

Macs Smith

The MIT Press
Cambridge, Massachusetts
London, England

This book was set in Stone Serif and Stone Sans by Jen Jackowitz. Printed and bound in the United States of America.

Library of Congress Cataloging-in-Publication Data

Names: Smith, Macs, author.
Title: Paris and the parasite : noise, health, and politics in the media city / Macs Smith.
Other titles: Paris and the parasite (M.I.T. Press)
Description: Cambridge, Massachusetts : The MIT Press, [2021] | Outgrowth of the author's thesis (doctoral)—Princeton University, 2018, under the title: Paris and the parasite : the politics of noise in the mediatic city. | Includes bibliographical references and index.
Identifiers: LCCN 2020022995 | ISBN 9780262045544 (hardcover)
Subjects: LCSH: City planning—France—Paris. | Architecture and society—France—Paris. | Architecture—Human factors—France—Paris. | Parasitism (Social sciences)
Classification: LCC NA9198.P2 S55 2021 | DDC 711/.40944361—dc23
LC record available at https://lccn.loc.gov/2020022995

10 9 8 7 6 5 4 3 2 1

For my mother, who taught me that a healthy body doesn't mean anything, that love is what matters

Contents

Acknowledgments

I completed this book while under lockdown because of Covid-19. When I had to leave my room in Oxford, my partner's family took me in, not knowing how long my stay would be. In the end, I spent over one hundred days in their home. I am conscious of how much hospitality has been shown me since I began work on this project seven years ago.

Paris and the Parasite emerged from my doctoral research at Princeton University. The people who shaped and nurtured my development as a scholar all contributed to it in some way. This book would not exist were it not for André Benhaïm. André was the first person to ask me if I thought absolute hospitality was something you could practice or something hypothetical. His mentorship is the best argument for the former. Göran Blix, Katie Chenoweth, and Tom Levin gave me excellent feedback and encouragement. I especially want to thank Tom and Joseph Vogl for introducing me to McLuhan and Serres. I am grateful to Princeton University for generously supporting my work, and for its faith in and financial commitment to the creative power of its students and researchers. Thank you to the Department of French and Italian, the School of Architecture, and the Program in Media + Modernity for giving me a home and for fostering interdisciplinary research. I am indebted to Charlotte Werbe, Chad Córdova, Melissa Verhey, Emily Eyestone, Hartley Miller, Sarah Kislingbury, Molly O'Brien, and many others for our conversations and friendship.

The Queen's College, Oxford, has provided me a community and the time to write. I am grateful to my colleagues for pushing my thinking in new directions, and to the Hamilton family for their generous support for research in French studies. Thank you to Seth Whidden, Jessica Stacey, and Holly Langstaff in particular. Additionally, thank you to Sophie Marnette and Michael Sheringham for facilitating my first research visit to Oxford, and to Emma Claussen, Gemma Tidman, Olivia Tolley, and Sarah Jones for making me want to return.

Thank you to the MIT Press, particularly to Doug Sery and Noah Springer, and to my copyeditor, Gillian Beaumont. My peer reviewers provided insightful comments that significantly improved this book. Thank you to all of my students, who inspire me with their courage, their vulnerability, and their determination to bring beauty into the world. Thank you to Julian, Celia, and Owen Iredale for welcoming me into their home. Thank you, Hope and Henry. And lastly, Ellen, I love you even more than Paris.

1 Introduction

In February of 2016, the municipal government of Paris published a "Plan de prévention du bruit dans l'environnement," or Plan for the Prevention of Noise in the Environment (PPBE). The document opens with two observations: first, that polls have shown growing levels of concern about noise among Parisians; and second, that noise represents "the second-most-important environmental influence on human health after air pollution."[1] The document lays out a five-year plan consisting of 39 measures to quiet the soundscape of the city. The PPBE acknowledges that the line between sound and noise is fuzzy. Noise is subjective. It is one person's experience of a sound "at a given moment." Music coming through the wall from my neighbor's apartment is sound if I'm in a mood to listen to it, and noise if I'm not. Traffic, birdsong, and voices in the street might be perceived as pleasant signs of a vibrant city, or they might not. There is nothing in the soundwaves themselves that can tell us how a sound will be perceived by a listener. Parisians might be increasingly worried about noise, but what each of them thinks of as noise might be different. By stating this, the PPBE undermines its premise right from the start. If there is no objective definition for noise, then what is there to regulate? If the meaning of "noise" can change for a given person from moment to moment, then the government seems to be taking on the task of imposing a normative aesthetic standard on the urban soundscape and policing citizens' personal experience of it.

The PPBE dodges this trap by turning to the International Organization for Standardization, which defines noise according to the "sensation" it produces. That word can be interpreted physiologically as well as emotionally, opening up the possibility of an objective definition of noise based not on the listener's mood or artistic tastes but on the effect the sound has on

Figure 1.1
Noise map of Paris created by Bruitparif (www.bruitparif.fr)

their body. A sound can therefore be defined as noise if it harms the listener's body in a detectable way.

With this definition in hand, the PPBE proceeds to argue that noise is a health issue and, indeed, that Paris is experiencing a public health crisis. Noise, the report states, raises stress levels, worsens cardiovascular health, and interrupts sleep, leading to a host of secondary health issues. Playing up the "environmental" part of its title, the PPBE repeatedly ties noise to air pollution, saying that vehicles that emit less CO_2 also emit less noise, and comparing the quiet of green spaces and parks to the clean air the trees provide. Readers are led to assume that reducing noise in the city will also indirectly benefit their lungs. In interviews conducted after the release of the report, Célia Blauel, the *adjointe* to the mayor in charge of the environment, cited the statistic that 10,000 deaths in Paris per year are caused by noise. "Beyond questions of comfort and quality of life," she said, "the acoustic environment constitutes a public health concern."[2]

Public health is not the only reason to care about urban noise. Noise also has a sociopolitical dimension, according to the PPBE. It is "an important factor in social segregation" as the rich buy homes in quiet neighborhoods while the poor are exposed to harmful soundscapes, disadvantaging them for life. How the government proposes to manage noise likewise directly concerns the social politics of the city. Many of the suggested interventions center around the commute, and in particular how residents of the *banlieue*, Paris's suburbs, get into and out of the city center. Reducing automobile traffic may reduce noise, but for people who rely on cars to access the city center, a reduction in traffic is a threat to what Henri Lefebvre calls their "right to the city."[3] This side of things is all the more fraught given the historic power and wealth imbalance between the center of Paris and the suburbs. The *boulevard périphérique*, Paris's ring road, features prominently in the PPBE. Because it marks the limits of Paris proper, lying in the footprint of the city's last defensive walls, the *périphérique* is a symbol of the difficult relationship between central Paris and the *banlieue*. The PPBE's proposals to quiet the highway, for instance by burying it underground, constitute symbolic renegotiations of the boundaries of the city. How the city proposes to manage noise thus opens questions of who is allowed into the city and who has a right to its resources.

I am not going to discuss the merits of the policies put forth in the PPBE. My interest lies instead with the discourses it deploys. The document begins with a question about the soundscape of the city, about what sounds are desirable and what constitutes noise. That quickly becomes a question about urban hygiene and about the sociopolitics of the city. The discursive overlap of noise, hygiene, and the sociopolitical that we see in the PPBE is exemplary of the pattern Michel Serres identifies in *The Parasite*. The word "parasite" in French (*le parasite*) has four meanings. The first is a vestigial meaning taken from the original Ancient Greek usage: a poor person allowed to eat at a rich man's feast, an unwelcome guest (from *para-sitos*, to eat alongside). The second is a sociopolitical meaning: the mooch who lives off another person's labor. The third is the biological sense of an organism that lives in and off a host organism. And finally, there is a mediatic sense: noise or interference in mediation. Serres sees these four definitions as deeply connected. To use one is to activate them all. We see this in the PPBE, where a discussion of acoustic noise—a mediatic parasite—cannot help bringing into relief two other kinds of parasite: the biological and the social. Serres argues that all of the various meanings of "parasite" are expressions of a single conceptual framework: the desire for order. A parasite is simply that which threatens the order of a system. The unwelcome guest disturbs the boundaries of the home, the mooch upsets the economic system, the organismal parasite erodes the bodily integrity of its host, and noise disrupts clarity in communication, thereby undermining the premise that rational thinking produces clear ideas and ordered systems of thought.

Serres's overarching argument is that Western modernity is founded on the privileging of order and the concomitant pathologization of anything that threatens it. Western modernity is anti-parasitic. It identifies parasites and purges them to create well-organized, efficient, high-fidelity systems. A parasite is always defined in relation to a host, so if Western modernity is anti-parasitic, it is also pro-host. It creates the conditions for rational and autonomous subjects, the owners of the property and knowledge from which the parasites are banished. This project is flawed, Serres writes, because parasites can never be purged from a system: "There are channels, and thus there must be noise. No channel without noise."[4] The argument is as austere as the second law of thermodynamics. There is no system immune to entropy. As Serres sees it, Western modernity is thus built on a mendacious promise, a kind of epistemological Ponzi scheme where debts are passed on but never paid, where parasites are continually displaced but never eradicated, where hosts think they've been made whole but never truly are.

My argument over the course of this book will be that Parisian urbanism and urban politics are dominated by just such anti-parasitism. The pathologization of acoustic noise that we find in the PPBE is but a recent example of a long-standing project to rid the city of its parasites. In this project, the politics of media overlap in complex ways with biopolitics and sociopolitics. Sometimes, as we will see, concerns about epidemic disease are used to justify interventions in media or politics; sometimes a social group is depicted as diseased outsiders or a cacophonous rabble whose demands don't make sense; sometimes mediatic clarity is presented as an unproblematic virtue, preempting debate about the social and political side effects of its pursuit. Consistent with Serres's argument, the eradication of Paris's parasites has never been realized and can never be realized—it is an unending dialectic. Through the identification and pathologization of endless parasites, the city's hosts are constituted and reconstituted. This is a violent process, and I will contend that its stakes need to be critically reevaluated.

Serres primarily associates anti-parasitism with the modern period, which for him roughly begins with the writings of Descartes in the seventeenth century, but he offers examples of hosts attempting to expel parasites going back to the origins of civilization. Anti-parasitism as an ideology is exemplified by certain systems of thought, but the gesture to expel parasites from a place or system can be found almost anywhere. The relationship between host and parasite is present at the founding of the first city; it is present in the basic principles of architecture. To speak about a city and its parasites is thus to speak about the city and parasites. I will consider the larger philosophical implications of my questions over the course of this book, and especially in the final chapter, "Underground." For the most part, however, I will restrict myself to a specific historical period. I will focus on Paris from the nineteenth century to today. At the end of the eighteenth century, France saw the emergence of the science of hygienics and the concept of public health. These ideas were immediately applied to cities, and played a major role in shaping the nascent field of urban planning. Over the course of the nineteenth and twentieth centuries, these concepts gradually became intertwined with thinking about new media and new technologies, leading to the informatic urbanist rhetoric we see today. While parasites of different kinds have played a role in Paris since its foundation, only since the nineteenth century do we find the full discursive nexus identified by Serres—the fusion of social, biological, and mediatic forms of anti-parasitism—applied to Paris in a comprehensive way.

This argument will build on a growing body of research that lies at the intersection of urbanism and media. In 1988, Friedrich Kittler published his essay "The City Is a Medium." In it he defines media as technologies that "record, transmit, and process information," and he argues that the city is just such a technology.[5] The city is a complex of communication systems whose information takes the form of data, goods, and bodies. Building on observations made by Lewis Mumford in the 1960s, he argues that walls and streets are channels comparable to the circuits of a computer. Kittler's notion of the city as medium has nourished two branches of urban studies. Researchers like Manuel Castells (*The Informational City*, 1989), Stephen Graham and Simon Marvin (*Telecommunications and the City*, 1995; Graham also edited *The Cybercities Reader*, 2004), M. Christine Boyer (*CyberCities*, 1996), and William J. Mitchell (who produced a trilogy on urbanism and virtuality) seized on the computational metaphor for the city. They built on the comparison between the city and the circuit board, and argued that cities have undergone a revolution brought on by new telepresence technologies and virtual reality.

The second research area Kittler's argument fed into was less interested in the computer or the digital and more interested in the mediatic. In the 1990s, scholars like Beatriz Colomina and Anthony Vidler examined how architecture and urbanism are intertwined with other media. In Colomina's *Privacy and Publicity* (1994), she shows how Le Corbusier and Adolf Loos engaged with photography, film, and home media in their reconceptualization of domestic architecture. In *The Architectural Uncanny* (1992), Vidler demonstrates how architecture, just like film, television, and literature, can mediate a concept like the uncanny. The book culminates in the essay "Transparency," in which Vidler compares the architectural façade to a screen. In the twenty-first century there has been an explosion of research in this area. Works include Scott McQuire's *The Media City (*2008) and *Geomedia* (2016); Simone Tosoni, Matteo Tarantino, and Chiara Giaccardi's edited volume *Media and the City*, and Myria Georgiou's monograph of the same name, both released in 2013; Shannon Mattern's *Deep Mapping the Media City* (2015) and *Code + Clay . . . Data + Dirt: Five Thousand Years of Urban Media* (2017); Martijn de Waal's *The City as Interface: How Digital Media Are Changing the City* (2014); and de Waal and Michiel de Lange's *The Hackable City: Digital Media and Collaborative City-Making in the Network Society* (2019). McQuire summarizes the core critical conceit of this area of scholarship thus: "Acceptance of the heightened role of media in the production of contemporary experience demands the critical embrace of McLuhan's insight that media constitute an *environment.* [. . .] Moving through the world at large now involves the ongoing negotiation of, and participation in, diverse media flows. Neither home nor street nor city can now be thought apart from the media apparatus which redistributes the scale and speed of social interaction in their domains."[6] Focusing on mediation instead of computing or some other fixed technological metaphor leads to a more fluid understanding of the city. Media shift constantly in response to other media, to the messages that pass through them, and to the uses people put them to. Media are inherently relational. They channel information from one person to another, from one place to another, from one system to another. To study media is to study the kinds of people they connect and the kinds of messages they communicate.[7]

Paris and the Parasite builds on this second area of scholarship—and is in many ways critical of the first, for reasons I will explain shortly. I will work on the premise that the city is a media system. Now, the breadth of writing on the media city can create terminological confusion. The term *media* is difficult to define, and different authors understand it in different ways. Some use the term to refer to Information and Communications Technologies like the telephone, television, and computer; others, like de Waal, to refer more specifically to so-called "new media" like the smartphone and digital platforms. Yet others, like Georgiou, use it to refer to "the media," meaning the industries that produce newspapers, television, films, and music. McQuire and Mattern use it in a more copious sense: any technology or system that carries and transforms information. As the title of Mattern's book suggests, clay can be a medium just as much as computer code. I will be using the term in this last sense. I am interested both in the phenomenon of screens being attached to walls, and in the wall itself in its limestone materiality as a media environment. I understand the city to be composed of many layers of channels, and imbricated with an array of other media like writing, painting, film, photography, and the computer. I also understand the media city to mean that the city is always mediated, that there is no direct knowledge of the city that does not pass through mediation, that there is no city prior to or outside of mediation. In "Apartment," I will discuss Michael Haneke's 2005 film *Caché*. In the first shot of that film, the audience sees the façade of a house in the 13th arrondissement of Paris. Several minutes go by without any action. Gradually the spectator discovers that he or she is watching not the house, but a taped recording of the house. When we thought we were looking at the city itself, we were actually seeing a mediated version of it.[8] This I take to be a general principle.

Thus, when I speak of the mediatic parasites of the city, I will not just be referring to the acoustic noise targeted in the PPBE or the interference on the telephone lines. The mediatic parasites of the city include the friction in the city's communication of bodies and goods from one point in space to another, the ambiguity in the speech and texts that are channeled through the city's forums and writing surfaces, and the unexpected meanings that emerge out of encounters between the urban media system and its users. Noise is not only passive either. Serres underscores the agency and, indeed, the power of the parasite who deliberately alters messages as they pass through a channel. Noise can be something an actor introduces to a system, either as a dissident move or to suppress dissidence.

I shall call the approach to urbanism that seeks to eliminate noise from the networks of the media city "informatic urbanism." This is an urbanism that conceives the media city along the lines of Claude Shannon's theory of communication, in which an emitter has a concept, encodes it in a message, and passes the message through a channel, where it encounters noise before arriving at a receiver, who deciphers the message to obtain the concept. In this theory of information, value is placed on the fidelity of transmission, on the concept arriving at its destination the same as it was when it left the emitter. Noise is the enemy. Mark Nunes defines the "ideology of informatic control" as the "[dream] of an error-free world of 100 percent efficiency, accuracy, and predictability."[9]

We can see an example of informatic urbanism in the Paris municipal government's recent push to transform Paris into a smart city. On May 26, 2015, the mayor of Paris, Anne Hidalgo, presented "Paris Intelligente et Durable: Perspectives 2020 et au-delà" ("A Smart and Sustainable Paris: 2020 and Beyond") to the city council. Whereas the PPBE focused on acoustic noise control, this document offered a broader five-year plan to cover Hidalgo's first term as mayor. In it she lays out a number of initiatives designed to make Paris into a smart city, or *ville intelligente*. Smart Paris is an intensely mediatic city. The government will embrace new technologies, transition the city's bureaucracy to digital interfaces, invest in data analytics, install tracking devices to monitor urban infrastructure, convert office space into start-up incubators to make Paris a center for the tech and new media industries, make technology available to a larger percentage of the population, and create online platforms for participatory democracy. The city is clearly thought of as a network through which information constantly circulates. The new initiatives, it is promised, will render that circulation ever more efficient. The installation of tracking devices in buildings will "enable the detection of malfunctions and the mobilization of users to reduce waste." Digital technologies will be "designed to simplify processes." The city will not just be connected, but "hyperconnected." Error and noise will be virtually eliminated, and citizens will enter an informatic utopia where all information is available on demand, anywhere and "at a moment's notice." This is informatic urbanism.

"Paris Intelligente et Durable" also shows how informatic urbanism plays into larger anti-parasitic ideologies. Like the PPBE, the plans to make Paris a smart city connect the desire to eliminate error from the city-as-information-processor to biopolitical and sociopolitical discourses. The document speaks of the need to cleanse the environment, and promises that this cleaner and more efficient Paris will bring health benefits to the whole population. The authors note the challenges posed by economic precarity and social exclusion, which likewise bear on public health, as "social and territorial inequality generates environmental and sanitary inequality." The three kinds of parasitism—mediatic, biological, and social—are all in play. Error has to be purged from the city's networks and disease and pollution from its body, and this will transform who is excluded from the urban community and who has access to its resources.

Many scholars have been critical of the smart city because of the authoritarian overtones of its promise of total surveillance and control, and because it locates too much power in private tech companies that are not accountable to the public. Some, like Mattern, have extended that critique to informatic urbanism in general. But even in criticism of informatic urbanism, the noise of the urban media system is seldom acknowledged, and almost never on its own terms. In de Lange and de Waal's *The Hackable City*, various modes of interference with the efficient functioning of the media city are discussed, but they are described not as forms of entropy but as an alternate kind of organization. They do not inhibit, much less break down, the informatic city; they offer "a new paradigm for smart cities, urban informatics and urban governance."[10] Informatic urbanism persists, but in a modified form. De Lange and de Waal's text is a good demonstration of the stakes of writing about the noise of the urban media system. The erasure of noise is a core ideology of informatic urbanism; by failing to listen to noise on its own terms, one accepts or reproduces the premises of informatic urbanism. The critic remains trapped within what Michel Foucault would call informatic urbanism's discursive field; consequently, even in the act of critiquing it, the critic reproduces it. To truly step outside of informatic urbanism and examine its values, fault lines, and power structures, one has to be attentive to noise. "Error," as Nunes puts it, "reveals not only a system's failure, but its operational logic."[11] Attention to noise is the starting point for genuine critique of informatic urbanism, and for conceptualizing alternatives to it.

The smart city is often presented as a rupture with previous modes of city planning, but informatic urbanism and the rhetoric of connectivity and efficiency that it deploys are not new at all. They have, as I will show, characterized Paris's engagement with other media from the nineteenth century to today.[12] What is at issue with informatic urbanism is not simply the recent phenomenon of city planners borrowing technologies and metaphors from computing. The problematics raised by informatic urbanism and the pathologization of noise concern the basic precepts of urbanism. Addressing them thus requires a new thinking of the city rather than a return to predigital approaches to urbanism.

While theorists of the media city have largely neglected noise, scholars working in other areas have been increasingly attentive to it in recent years. The emergence of sound studies has brought new attention to the acoustic noise of the city. Two recent texts particularly worth mentioning are Aimée Boutin's *City of Noise* and Ross Chambers's *Atmospherics of the City*, both published in 2015. Both books focus on the acoustic noise of Paris in the nineteenth century. At times both texts fall into the trap I mention above: of not reckoning with noise on its own terms. Boutin's text, though it traces the emergence of noise as a particular category of sound, frequently conflates sound and noise, and her task of reconstituting the soundscape of nineteenth-century Paris leads her to resolve cacophonous noise into its component sounds. She recovers the sound of the city at the expense of its noisiness. Chambers argues that Charles Baudelaire's poetry and his "fetish aesthetics" were shaped by his alertness to the noisiness of the city. Chambers's argument is especially relevant to mine in the way he connects the noisiness of the city to the noisiness of Baudelaire's poetry. His idea that a literary aesthetics offers a way to study noise as noise is an idea I shall discuss in "Underground."

Moving away from acoustic noise to noise in the informatic sense, there has been a growing interest of late in the parasites of media systems and the intersections between media and biology. This is unsurprising, given the spread through popular culture of terms like the computer virus, viral media, and the meme. Researchers like Jussi Parikka (*Digital Contagions*, 2007, and *Insect Media*, 2010), Tony Sampson (*Virality*, 2012), and Luciana Parisi (*Contagious Architecture*, 2013) have embraced Serres's notion that anomalies are fundamental to system function, and that we cannot study systems without studying their failures.

Work in this area, in asking why biological metaphors have such currency in digital cultures, at times crosses over into what Eugene Thacker calls biomedia, a media theory of biology in which the living organism is understood as a communication channel, an information processor, and a repository of coded messages. These texts do not treat biology as a simple metaphor for the digital. Life and technology are not neatly separable, much less opposed. Parikka adopts the Deleuzian concept of the assemblage. "An assemblage," he writes, is not "a collection of already existing elements (technology taking the animal as its model for example)." It is "more akin to becoming than expressing a solid being (the becoming animal of technology, the becoming technical of the insect)." An assemblage can take biological or technical forms depending on the context, meaning that "questions of naturality or artificiality are bracketed, and the focus is placed on the nonrepresentational environment and the machinic assemblage in which the entities act."[13] This idea helps to explain how anti-parasitism traverses the mediatic and biological: the parasite is not a metaphor but an assemblage that can take biological, technical, or social forms depending on the context.

An important feature of work in this area is that it often challenges the negative connotations carried by terms like virus. Tony Sampson argues that virality is the connective tissue of society rather than a threat to its survival. A similar reevaluation of the language of disease, and of disease itself, has been undertaken in research that straddles biology and political philosophy. Three prominent authors in this domain are Ed Cohen (*A Body Worth Defending*, 2009), Roberto Esposito (*Immunitas*, 2011), and Alfred Tauber (*Immunity*, 2017). They show how political concepts shape biological theories, and how those theories in turn naturalize political ideologies. All three apply ecological thinking to the human body, challenging the negative connotations of terms like *parasite* and arguing for a less hierarchical understanding of the human body's relationship to nonhuman organisms.

Both media theoretical work on biology and techne, and research on immunity and the boundaries of the human, are closely connected to the philosophical field of the posthuman. Thinkers like Donna Haraway and Rosi Braidotti have questioned the ontological boundary between the human and nonhuman, and with it the anthropocentric—and often androcentric—foundations of culture and politics. *Paris and the Parasite*, by critically examining the violent processes that lead some bodies—whether human or nonhuman—to be pathologized and excluded from the city, likewise calls into question the anthropocentrism of urbanism. While there are some points of divergence between this book and other works on the posthuman (discussed in "Underground"), this work can be read as a posthumanism of the city.

In summary, *Paris and the Parasite* takes the reassessment of parasites that is ongoing across media theory, biology, and philosophy, and applies it to the media city. It does this to one city in particular, and it is necessary to explain why I have chosen to do that. Most existing work on the media city focuses on multiple cities. Scholars borrow Saskia Sassen's notion of the "global city." Sassen coined the term to describe the nodes of the modern global network of goods, capital, and tourism. Such cities are, she argues, more like each other than they are like the countries surrounding them. The global city and the media city are interconnected concepts in her argument, and this has led scholars of the media city to treat it as a global phenomenon. There are, obviously, good reasons behind this approach. Few technologies are rolled out in one city alone. One of the most important effects of media like the telegraph, television, and internet is that they connect cities in new ways, allowing a resident of Paris to be virtually present in London or Tokyo. Focusing on a single city in isolation makes it difficult to account for that dimension of the media city.

However, the international, comparative approach also has its limitations. By treating the media city as transnational, researchers forgo rigorous historicization. Focusing on global trends, researchers can often miss how local cultures and traditions clash with globally deployed technologies to produce unique local media environments. Approaching the media city globally can at times serve as a hermeneutic shortcut: when a given technology or practice cannot be found in one city, the author can discuss it in the context of another city without unpacking what it was about Paris or Berlin that led it not to adopt that technology. As a result, work in this field can overstate the homogeneity of contemporary metropolises and can argue, sometimes despite promises to the contrary, for what Graham calls a technological determinism wherein media technologies frictionlessly impose their own logics on urban life wherever they are deployed. By focusing on one city, I hope to avoid that trap.

Why Paris and not London, New York, or Hong Kong? Paris, as Walter Benjamin put it, was the capital of the nineteenth century, owing to its role as an incubator for the development and urban integration of new technologies of transport, communication, and exchange. These days, the title is often invoked backhandedly, implying that Paris is not the capital of the twenty-first century. Contemporary Paris is often accused of being a museum city, obsessed with the preservation of its past to the detriment of its present and future. For these reasons, it seems an inapt subject for a study focused at least in part on the integration of new media and digital technology into urban life. And yet, today's Paris is a much more complicated machine than these stereotypes give it credit for. Setting aside the impossible task of guessing which cities will be the centers of the current century, Paris is one of the cities that has most eagerly taken on the challenges posed by new technological and mediatic paradigms. As detailed in the planning documents described above, Paris's planners have placed media at the heart of a radical rethinking of how cities should be structured and how life within them should look. That Paris should be one of the philosophical centers for new ways of thinking the city is not hindered by its attention to its past. While the "smart city" is usually portrayed as a rupture in the history of the city, this portrayal, as I have suggested, fails to account for the ways in which cities mediated long before the silicon chip ever came to market. Paris's legacy as a center for urbanist innovation throughout the nineteenth century, and its planners' continued reflection on that legacy, make it a particularly enlightening case study for understanding how mediatic changes currently taking place in the city will reshape community.

Paris is, moreover, a quintessential media city in the sense that few cities have been as mediated in books, film, photography, and art. In "The Eiffel Tower," Roland Barthes describes Paris as "an object virtually prepared,"[14] present to the entire world, but as an image. This is true of all cities. There is no city that we can have immediate knowledge of. We always encounter places in mediated forms. But artists' preoccupation with Paris means that there is an especially rich corpus for thinking the mediaticity of this urban space.

Focusing on Paris—and, by extension, the French context—is further motivated by my interest in the parasite. There is a certain amount of linguistic specificity to this term. "Parasite" is not used for noise in every language. Serres acknowledges that some of his analysis relies on wordplay that would not be possible in English. That is not entirely true, as the word is used in a mediatic sense in English-language speech act theory, a fact which did not escape the attention of Jacques Derrida, as discussed in the final chapter of this book. English, moreover, offers numerous examples of words that traverse the biological and the mediatic: the computer virus and viral media, the meme, noise (which comes from the same root as nausea). Serres's argument that the same pathologizing gesture traverses biology, mediation, and the social holds even outside of the French language. With that said, the parasite and related subjects like hospitality, communicational clarity, and the integrity of the body have been particularly prominent in French philosophy. And many of the philosophers who have written on these subjects were influenced by having lived in Paris. When, for instance, Derrida wrote about urban politics, his audience was global but his examples were mostly taken from Paris. When he tried to collaborate with an architect to intervene in the urban landscape, he did so in Paris. Focusing on this city thus gives an additional layer of cohesiveness to my study.

This is a book in the vein of Reyner Banham's *Los Angeles: The Architecture of Four Ecologies* or Robert Venturi, Denise Scott Brown, and Steven Izenour's *Learning from Las Vegas*. It is a case study of one city whose arguments and observations concern architecture, urbanism, and urban politics more generally. It explores what Paris and its parasites can tell us about cities in general, about the city as *polis*, the space upon which democratic politics is founded. Just as Paris itself, through its virtual and mediatized extensions, stretches beyond the geographic boundaries of Île-de-France, *Paris and the Parasite* will, I hope, deepen and complicate reflections on media and urbanism around the world.

The book is divided into six chapters. I think of the structure as a heat map. Each chapter is named for a media environment of the city, but each one's contents radiate out into its neighbors, reflecting the connectivity of the modern, networked city and Marshall McLuhan's dictum that the content of any medium is another medium. This structure also encourages disorderly reading, consistent with my criticism of informatics. The chapters are built around close readings of cultural texts—literature, film, architecture, photography, political demonstrations, aesthetic practices that make use of the city. These texts are a mixture of canonical and obscure, classic and contemporary. My corpus is not intended to be exhaustive but to offer stimulating new perspectives on Paris.

Following this Introduction, the next three chapters move from private space to public, performing the book's deconstruction of the hegemonic hermeticism of contemporary Paris. In chapter 2, "Apartment," I discuss the emergence of hygiene and public health in France at the end of the eighteenth century, and their effects on domestic architecture and urban planning. In the nineteenth century, hygiene became a bigger issue in domestic space. Toilets and baths increased in size and prominence, and new features were added to the home in response to the latest hygienic theories. This was also the period when domestic space became interiorized in Paris. The home was increasingly closed off to the outside world. This trend was connected to hygienic thinking: it reflected a growing suspicion of community as a vector of contagion. Isolation from one's neighbors and the outside world was necessary to protect one's health.

Through close readings of theoretical writings by Le Corbusier, I show how, in the twentieth century, the biological anti-parasitism of public health thinking became wedded to a mediatic anti-parasitism. Le Corbusier conceptualized the home as a media environment. He modeled elements of his designs on photography and cinema, and promoted the integration of media technologies like the telephone, gramophone, and television into domestic space. Le Corbusier applied informatic thinking to these technologies and to the home itself, defending a vision of domestic space as a silent space of private contemplation and machinic efficiency. He connected these values directly to the health of the resident. Indeed, Le Corbusier embraced hygienic thinking to an extreme degree. He was involved with France's eugenics movement in the 1930s and 1940s. I draw attention to the anti-semitism of Le Corbusier's private writings, as well as the rigid elitism of his urbanism, as examples of social anti-parasitism. These three kinds of anti-parasitism are inextricable from one another in Le Corbusier's thought, and were influential among Paris's urban planners in the decades following the Second World War. The chapter concludes with a close reading of Haneke's *Caché*, in which media are deployed as a defensive fortification around a bourgeois family's private space. The film shows how the parasites of those media counteract the hermeticism of the home. The banished other of the city, the social parasite cast out of the protagonist's family space, returns through mediatic interference.

Chapter 3, "Wall," moves from the building's interior to its membrane. It centers on the media environment of the façade, and in particular on the question of its visibility or transparency. The chapter is framed around Brassaï's observation that in the mid-twentieth century the walls of Paris were "discovered" by modern artists. Why did walls need to be discovered? In what way were they invisible? In the nineteenth century, Victor Hugo's *Notre-Dame de Paris* promoted the idea of the building as narrative medium. This text influenced architects like Henri Labrouste, who referenced Hugo in his Sainte-Geneviève Library in Paris. But Hugo's text is striking for its absence of references to the façade itself, with the author more focused on other media like sculpture, painting, and music. Hugo's text thus offers one way of understanding the blindness Brassaï describes.

Twentieth-century architectural theorists offer another way of understanding it. For proponents of the modern style, the building façade was all too visible, and it was necessary to make it disappear. They promoted a logic of what Jay David Bolter and Richard Grusin call immediacy, whereby the façade becomes an invisible conduit to the building's volume. Le Corbusier warned architects not to let the walls of their buildings be invaded by "parasites" that would break the illusion of immediacy. I connect this warning to Serres's account of how parasites in communication draw attention to the channel itself. In Brassaï's case, the parasites that alert artists to the mediaticity of the wall are graffiti drawings. The chapter proceeds to survey contemporary Parisian street art, laying out the various ways in which these artistic interventions act as parasites, and how they parasite one another. I look closely at the pioneering French artists Invader and Blek le Rat, both of whom invoke explicitly parasitic themes and imagery.

In chapter 4, "Street," I consider the relationship between the street and cartography. In the 1950s and 1960s the avant-garde group Situationist International theorized the *dérive*, or drifting, as a way of combating what they saw as the growing atomization and industrial utilitarianism of Paris. Members of the group would wander the city's streets at random to identify the subconscious forces governing their everyday movements. Participants would craft collages of maps in response to their experiences in the street. With the *dérive* as its point of departure, the chapter examines two recent examples of aestheticized urban exploration with cartographic elements: Jacques Réda's *Le Méridien de Paris* and Philippe Vasset's *Un livre blanc*. These books explore what the map cannot represent of the built environment. They draw out the parasites that plague the media environment of cartography. Vasset's book embodies Jacques Rancière's idea that politics is an intervention in the distribution of the sensible. Politics is an act by which those excluded from democratic society are enfranchised by being made visible. Correcting the map, eliminating its parasites, thus has an important democratic dimension.

The chapter then looks at the extreme sport of parkour, which originated in the suburbs of Paris. Parkour is a spectacular and transgressive mode of urban exploration in which practitioners use their athletic ability to chart new paths through the city. Parkour is often filmed, with the results posted on sites like YouTube. Globally practiced, it seems to accomplish the situationist dream of enlisting the masses in a *dérive*. Parkour brings together the body, media, and the boundaries of the city and, unsurprisingly, it is intersected by an especially rich variety of parasitic discourses. It has been described as viral media and a meme, terms that underscore the contagious nature of its transmission through digital networks. It is commonly represented in popular culture as pathogenic, and doctors have warned of the dangers it poses to the health of practitioners. Thanks to its *banlieue* origins, parkour is frequently associated with social parasites and has sometimes been read as a metaphorical expression of young *banlieusards'* yearning for social mobility. At the same time, parkour generates strikingly hygienic and even eugenic discourses. The practice was inspired by *Hébertisme*, a mode of obstacle course training adopted by the French military during World War I, beloved by French eugenicists in the 1930s, and enshrined as a national training method under Vichy. Elements of *Hébertisme*'s fascist legacy continue to be detectable in the ways some parkour practitioners speak about their activity today. Parkour's status as an inheritor to the antihegemonic urban exploration practices of the situationists is further undermined by participants' reliance on digital technologies implicated in what Shoshana Zuboff calls surveillance capitalism.[15] This raises important questions about the relationship between the movement of bodies through city streets and the representation of those streets in cartographic media. The chapter concludes with a brief analysis of the *Charlie Hebdo* terror attack of January 2015, which prompted the French government to seize new powers of surveillance, and of the *marche républicaine* that took place in the aftermath of the attack, the largest demonstration in the streets of Paris in French history. While these events led to the expansion of the surveillance state in France, they are both replete with examples of its failure. They demonstrate the intractability of parasites, the impossibility of eliminating noise from mediation, and the irreconcilability of the street and the map.

In chapter 5, "Bodies," the media environment in question is not an architectural typology. Instead I focus on the body as a site of negotiation between host and parasite. The chapter begins with a discussion of immunity, and how political ideologies about the autonomy of the individual subject fused with biological theories about the limits of the body over the course of the nineteenth century. I then look at two alternative theories of the body as both biological and political site from the turn of the twentieth century: the sociological theories of Gabriel Tarde and the philosophical poetry and novels of Jules Romains. Both thinkers promoted collectivism rather than the individualism of their contemporaries. Tarde and Romains's writings are notable for their ambivalent attitude to noise, which they see as a key trigger for collectivization. They evince a proto-ecological thinking of the body that problematizes the hierarchy of host and parasite.

In the second half of the chapter I consider the synecdochal relationship between voice and body. This means returning to Rancière, who argues that for a group to become politically actualized its members must produce a unified voice. The group must suppress noise and speak clearly so that it can be listened to by the wider democratic community. Nuit Debout, a 2016 protest movement sparked by labor reforms, is an example of a movement that was fastidious in its desire to speak clearly. Despite this, many commentators described the movement as confused or mute, and its demonstrations were repeatedly thrown into chaos by parasitic interventions by *casseurs*, hooligans, and black bloc groups. Drawing attention to the ways in which authoritarian governments have weaponized noise in the past decade to effectively silence dissident movements—and again to Serres's dictum that it is impossible to eliminate parasites from a channel—I argue that the democratic expectation that groups speak clearly represents an impossible demand that fosters political stasis.

In chapter 6, "Underground," I ask if there is any way out of anti-parasitism. Maurice Blanchot argues that the literary is distinguished from other modes of meaning-making by its refusal to differentiate between meaning and noise.[16] Literary space is space where everything signifies, where nothing is classified as a parasite. This argument has been developed in different ways by Gilles Deleuze and Jacques Derrida. I ask if literarity can serve as a conceptual framework for an urbanism that does not distinguish between hosts and parasites. Two case studies are used to explore this question. The first is Rachid Boudjedra's novel *Topographie idéale pour une agression caractérisée* (Ideal Topography for an Assault), about an illiterate migrant who wanders through the Paris metro because he cannot read the signs of the city. This novel shows both the ethical stakes of creating a city that does not pathologize its parasites and the dangers of an overly simplistic application of literary concepts to urbanism. The second is the failed collaboration between Derrida and Peter Eisenman at the Parisian park of La Villette. Derrida and Eisenman were commissioned to design a garden. In their conversations, we see Derrida trying to apply deconstruction—a hermeneutic that is often unfairly caricatured as being exclusively literary and linguistic in application—to the medium of architecture. The chapter concludes with a discussion of recent architectural interventions in Paris that demonstrate a more open and hospitable attitude to the parasites of the city.

What is at stake in *Paris and the Parasite* is more than a city's attitude to car horns and late-night parties. What is at stake is ultimately how we understand collective life. Thinking through the relationship between Paris and its parasites means reconsidering the status of the individual; how an individual becomes a group; what the limits of the body are and what kinds of relationships ought to exist among bodies; what the unit of communication is, if there is one, and if communication is ultimately possible. These questions concern the core assumptions of Western democratic politics: the sanctity of the voice, the equivalence of the voice and the individual, the right to property, the naturalness of boundaries. One of the originalities of McLuhan's media theory was his observation that media are not simply tools we use, they are environments we inhabit. This is especially true of the city. While the lexicon of parasitism is ubiquitous in many media domains, in the city the questions posed by parasitism find startlingly simple, ethical formulations. Who eats? Who is welcome here? Who can share my home?

%

I would like to close this Introduction with an image. My dominant framework for understanding an approach to media in which parasites are not pathologized will be literary, but one could also look at the question through the lens of music. This image comes from the end of Jean-Pierre Jeunet and Marc Caro's 1991 film *Delicatessen*. The film is set in a ruined Haussmannian apartment building that has, after some apocalyptic event, been cut off from the rest of the city. The building is ruled over by a butcher who lures victims in with promises of lodging and work before killing them. He grinds their bodies into meat and sells it to the neighbors. Jeunet and Caro depict a world of pure self-preservation, where individuals bar the doors to their homes to keep themselves safe. Shared spaces like the staircase are hostile—"it happens at night in the staircase," the butcher's daughter, Julie, says of the murders, "that's why no one goes out." But this is also a world in which survival—or at least eating well, to use Derrida's term—depends on sacrifice. Human sacrifice. The assimilation of the other's body.

The main character, played by Dominique Pinon, is a circus clown turned maintenance worker who upsets the system. His job requires him to pass in and out of the other residents' private spaces. His humor and innocence provoke a resurgence of conviviality in the building. This has revolutionary consequences. At the film's surreal climax, the butcher's daughter and an army of vegetarian mole people rise up from the dark underground networks of the city and upset the balance of power in the apartment. The sewer system is weaponized and water gushes through the building, forcing open doors and sucking all of the residents and their belongings out into the staircase. The site of nocturnal human sacrifices is restored as a shared space.

In the final shot of the film, two small boys who live in the building climb up onto the roof and pretend to play home appliances as instruments. The camera pans to the left, and behind a thick layer of smog we see the two protagonists atop the roof as well, playing a duet on the cello and saw. The scene quotes an earlier sequence in which the butcher's daughter practices her cello to a metronome. Jeunet and Caro edit her playing to match the rhythms of a variety of everyday noises produced elsewhere in the building. Sounds cross the boundaries of the apartment that the characters refuse to cross. The metronome syncs up with the squeaky springs of the bed on which her father is making love, the rhythmic scratch of a paint roller on the ceiling of the lobby, a bike pump being compressed, a rug beater, water from a leak dripping into a bucket, knitting needles, a drill. Periodically the residents look up from their activities, wondering what all the noise is. They react with annoyance and appear to keep time with one another out of a sense of compulsion. There is no joy in this collective musicality. They would rather work at their own speed.

In the final shot, after the boundaries of the building have washed away, Jeunet and Caro again show us the musicality of everyday objects. The smog begins to dissipate, and the film closes under a bright sky. Whatever

Figure 1.2
Final shot of *Delicatessen*, dir. Jean-Pierre Jeunet and Marc Caro, prod. Claudie Ossard

apocalyptic pollution has hung over the city is starting to disappear as the characters harmonize. The film anticipates the PPBE's promise that a noiseless city will be an environmentally clean one. But what is notable here is that if this sequence is without noise, it is not because of a change in the building's soundscape. The tools used to produce music at the end of the film are essentially the same as those used in the first musical sequence. The noiselessness comes from a change in the characters' attitude. It comes from a newfound refusal to hierarchize between the properly musical instrument and the noise-producing tool. Jeunet and Caro equivocate between the whisk and the cello, and their characters take pleasure in the harmonies possible between them. They are happy to be implicated in a shared rhythm rather than resentful of it. They listen differently.

2 Apartment

The word parasite comes from the Ancient Greek *parasitos*. Literally, it meant one who eats alongside or nearby. It was used to refer to poor people—musicians, entertainers—allowed to eat at the feasts of nobles in exchange for their entertainment. A parasite in this first meaning was an outsider admitted into the home. Admitted, but not welcomed.

One who eats nearby, the parasite is not far, etymologically, from the neighbor. Martin Heidegger appreciated the latter term for being one of the only words in English or German to still bear the traces of old notions of dwelling. The -bor of neighbor comes from the Old English *gebur*, dweller, a root whose influence in words like building and being is not usually noticed by modern speakers. For Heidegger, "neighbor" brings those concealed meanings back to the fore, reminding us that building of any sort, but especially of the home, is not simply a matter of producing structures for people to use or shelter in. It is an act of dwelling. What dwelling means to Heidegger is a question that cannot be fully discussed here without sidetracking the chapter before it has properly begun, but there are two elements of Heidegger's understanding of dwelling that can serve as an introduction.

The first is that dwelling is an act of place-making. Dwelling transforms inert space into assemblages, into places with form and boundaries. But the boundaries it gives these places are not simple. Heidegger describes them as horizons, as openings rather than as closures. There is a psychic dimension to dwelling. One can think oneself into a place. This complicates notions of nearness. He opposes a Cartesian concept of space, where the distance between two things is mathematically determined by comparing their positions in a grid. The seemingly distant can be brought into a space by thinking it, attending to it, dwelling on it.

What, then, is a neighbor? How do we determine who dwells near us when the act of dwelling cuts wormholes into space? The French word for neighbor, *voisin*, comes from the Latin root *vicus* meaning town, quarter, or street. On which of these scales does neighboring take place? How do we account for alterations in space caused by technology? Faster transportation and improved communication systems can change what we think of as far away, and make it easier to imagine oneself into a distant place. It is sometimes easier to enter into conversation with someone on the other side of the planet than it is with someone next door. Knowing this, how does one determine the horizons of the home? How does one determine who is a neighbor?

These questions lead us indirectly to the second dimension of Heidegger's thinking of dwelling I want to underline: it is not just building, but being, that has its roots in dwelling. This is a sign that dwelling is part of being human: "dwelling is the manner in which mortals are on the earth."[1] Heidegger defines man as a being who dwells. Dwelling makes the man. So dwelling produces not only the boundaries of a place, but also the boundaries of the human. And dwelling has to do with the self. By dwelling I embed myself in the world. I create links between myself, my identity, my subjectivity, and things and places.

In Heidegger's excavation of the etymology of neighboring, three boundaries come into play: those of place, of self, and of the human. These three boundaries are not fixed. They are horizons. Building—architecture—is one of the prime ways in which these boundaries are negotiated. In this chapter I am going to examine how these boundaries have been negotiated through one Parisian architectural space in particular: the home. The home is the place where these three boundaries overlap most. It is the place the self is most bound up in. It is from the starting point of the home that one's neighborhood is defined, no matter how far one is willing to let its boundaries stretch. It is at home that we are most pressingly asked how we relate to neighbors. Throughout this discussion I will be interested in the distinction between neighbor and parasite, between two kinds of others that lurk in the vicinity of the home. Though contact with one's neighbors can inspire a spectrum of emotions, including dread, words like neighborliness and *voisinage* connote a positive affective relationship to the boundary between self and other, public and private. The parasite is the other side of this coin. It is the truly unwelcome guest, the visitor one cannot get to leave. Whereas talk of being a "good neighbor" at least aspirationally expresses a will to be open to those who dwell at the horizon of the home, talk of parasites expresses an anxious attitude toward the instability of the home's borders, a feeling that such instability is a problem that needs to be dealt with.

Closing the Door: The Invention of Private Space in Paris

In 1990, a group started by Atanase Périfan held the first annual Fête des Voisins, or Festival of Neighbors, in Paris's 17th arrondissement. Eight hundred buildings participated, organizing small parties in common spaces. It was, for many involved, the first opportunity to meet the people stomping on their ceiling, the students up in the mansard rooms, the family behind the beautiful door on the second floor. In 2013, the number of participants is estimated to have reached more than fifteen million, half of them in other European countries. The festival was created in response to a widely held belief about Paris: that it is an isolating place which has lost the conviviality and local identity that characterized it in the past. The website of the Fête previously cited a 2005 IPSOS poll which showed that 76 percent of French people believed their compatriots were becoming more closed off to the world, despite 82 percent expressing the desire to get to know their neighbors better. Knowing the people who live nearby retains a positive value in the Parisian imagination. It bears the connotations of premodern, "village" life.[2] But while the Fête des Voisins appeals to people's ideas of what life in a village is like, the boundaries that constitute the neighborhood for the Fête are not so wide. The holiday is pointedly not an opportunity to get to know the people on one's street or in one's *quartier*. It's a festival of the apartment building.

The Fête crystallizes a number of trends and ideologies underlying Parisian domestic architecture. The first is that the walls of the apartment building (the *immeuble)* constitute the natural boundaries of a resident's community. The second is that Parisians have lost touch with those natural boundaries through an atomizing process that has trapped each resident in his or her own apartment, or through unnatural (technological) distortions of space and time that create disconnected communities scattered throughout the city, country, planet. From these assumptions follows a third: that the apartment community is something that existed in the past and has been lost, that it is not something to be invented but something to be rediscovered. In this section I will historicize these assumptions by tracing their origins in nineteenth-century texts and architectural thought. My contention will be that the pathologization of diverse parasites has played a key role in this process. Paris's urban planners have repeatedly conjoined the desire to expel unwanted others—parasitic guests—from the home to anxieties regarding bodily infection and noise, promoting what Roberto Esposito calls an "immunizing" individualism at the expense of urban community.

The participants are right in thinking that the earliest residents of apartment buildings would be surprised to hear these buildings described as places of loneliness and enclosure. As Sharon Marcus demonstrates in her 1999 book *Apartment Stories*, the first apartment buildings (which came to Paris in the late eighteenth century)[3] were places that upset the traditional organization of social life in the city. In an apartment building, residents of different social classes were mixed according to a system of social stratification. The ground floor was usually commercial. Above the shop was an *entresol*, a mezzanine floor with living accommodation for the shop owner. Above that was the first floor, the *piano nobile*, where the owner of the building lived. This was the most elegant floor, with the highest ceilings. The floors above increased in modesty and were typically divided among multiple residents, up to the mansard roof. While the class differences within a building were not enormous, the residents were nevertheless forced into contact with people from different financial and cultural backgrounds. In previous mixed-class living spaces, like the *hôtel*, interactions between the wealthy and their servants were carefully managed with secondary infrastructure like servants' stairs, allowing rich and poor to meet only under tightly choreographed conditions. In the apartment building, all residents were thrown into the chaos of a single lobby and a single staircase. Long-standing boundaries between private and public life were displaced or blurred, and power hierarchies of gender and wealth were complicated. "The increased size," Marcus writes, "of nineteenth-century buildings, and their incorporation of vestibules, lobbies, and elaborate stairways, meant that these edifices brought more strangers into contact, in more places, than earlier ones had."[4] These spaces were both private, because of their separation from the street, and public, because one could encounter other people there.

Marcus argues that in the middle of the century the tide turned against this social chaos: "Paris became interiorized after 1850."[5] She holds that Haussmannization, the massive urban renewal project that took place in Paris between 1852 and 1870, resulted in apartments that were much more private than those built in the previous decades. This is an appealing hypothesis, but it must be said that the relative introversion or extroversion of domestic spaces in Paris is in the eye of the beholder. Franco Moretti looks at the same corpus of Balzac novels as Marcus, but where Marcus interprets Balzac's ability to see into private spaces and share their contents with his readers as proof that these spaces were not yet closed off, Moretti interprets the preponderance of domestic interiors in these novels as evidence that the interior had already gained the upper hand during the July Monarchy (1830–1848).[6] Walter Benjamin is on Marcus's side, describing Haussmannian apartments as "cocoons" and "spider webs,"[7] but the Goncourt brothers, who actually lived through Haussmannization, felt that it was bringing about the end of privacy. They write, in the November 18, 1860 entry in their journal: "The interior is about to die. Life threatens to become public."[8] Anne Debarre and Monique Eleb put the transition later, arguing that the "invention of modern habitation" in Paris took place between 1880 and 1914.[9] Establishing a fine chronology of the claustration of domestic space is difficult, if not impossible, and any critic's attempt to pin down a single turning point in that history is doomed to elicit counterexamples. But while the relative claustration of domestic space at a given moment in history is debatable—and while considerations like class and gender surely nuanced an individual's sense of domestic privacy more than a discussion of overarching trends implies—the existence of these debates shows that the nineteenth century was a period where the boundaries of domestic space were open to contestation. In my view, Debarre and Eleb are right: a decisive move toward a different thinking of domestic architecture in Paris took place after 1880. It was in this period that the ideological nexus between health, mediatic purity, and privacy—a tripartite rejection of urban parasites—truly took shape, but this transition was undergirded by ideological groundwork laid during the preceding half-century.

In her recent book *Ideals of the Body*, Sun-Young Park argues that it was in the first half of the nineteenth century that new theories of hygiene first began to exert influence on architectural and urban planning thinking in Paris. Park points to two traumas that gave impetus to this nascent discourse. The first of these was the collapse of Napoleon's empire in 1815, which left France searching for ways to regenerate "the French race" and save the nation from the decline military defeat seemed to signal. The second was the cholera epidemic of 1832, during which hygienists used new statistical sciences to construct theories about the insalubrious effects of the built environment on the health of citizens. These two events motivated a new kind of *dirigisme* in urban planning. The state began expanding the sewer system, planting trees, and building urinals. It gave itself new powers of expropriation so that it could tear down private property where necessary for the public good. These measures were not simply immediate responses to a particular outbreak but, rather, reflections of a broader understanding on the part of the state that it had a duty to cultivate the health of French citizens. Architecture and urban planning were tools for doing that.

In the aftermath of the cholera epidemic we see the beginnings of an understanding of the city as a space beset by parasites. This is not to say that scientists defined cholera as a biological parasite—the bacterium would not be isolated until 1854, and the science of parasitology would not emerge as a full field of study until later in the century. I mean that in this period, during which the germ theory of disease was being articulated, city planners were beginning to pathologize a set of biological others, invasive nonhuman pathogens that had somehow found their way into the city and needed to be expelled. Parasites, carried by drinking water and spread by defecation, had made their way into the urban feast.

Park makes it clear that the pathologization of the biological parasites of the city was closely intertwined with a pathologization of social parasites. The "need to sanitize and aerate the stagnant, unhygienic streets of the city's core" was the flipside of a move to "mitigate the insurrectionary impulses fomenting in working-class neighborhoods."[10] Hygienic thinking naturalized the cultural values of the increasingly powerful bourgeoisie, pathologizing behaviors deemed socially and politically undesirable.

Two dimensions of the parasite were thus starting to be conjoined. But the intellectual groundwork laid in the early nineteenth century did not yet concern mediatic parasitism (noise), and it did not yet have a real effect on the home. Park sees the influence of this ideology primarily in public amenities like gymnasia, public schools, swimming pools, and parks. She does not see extensive evidence of hygienic thinking in domestic spaces. That would begin to change during Haussmannization.

Haussmannization is a frequent focus of studies of the nineteenth-century city owing both to the unprecedented scale of the projects and, less explicitly, to the fact that the projects can be traced back to one or two leaders who had coherent aesthetic ideas. David Harvey and T. J. Clark make it the centerpiece of their seminal studies on modernity and the city.

Partly motivated by Paris's second major cholera epidemic in 1849, Haussmann expanded the hygienic principles of the first half of the century. He undertook a massive refurbishment of Paris's sewer system, created vast new parks, and installed a large number of public toilets. He took advantage of the government's powers of expropriation to seize vast tracts of Parisian real estate so that he could create wide boulevards and avenues through congested neighborhoods. Haussmann used a medical vocabulary to describe his planning procedures. The two forests he created flanking the city were the "lungs" of Paris, and the new market of Les Halles was its "belly." The sewers "would be the organs of the metropolis and function like those of the human body."[11] The streets were "arteries" in an urban circulatory system, and acts of demolition were surgical "incisions" (*percements*).

Haussmannization's effects on the city's sociopolitical others are well documented. Improving the city's health and the speed and fidelity of its communication networks involved large-scale expropriation and demolition. The properties most often targeted were those of the working poor, who were priced out of central neighborhoods. Over time, the city's poorest residents concentrated in the *banlieue* or suburbs. Paris's social "parasites" were expelled from the host body, forced to eat outside.

In these ways Haussmann built on the marriage of social and biological parasites pioneered earlier in the century, but he departed from his predecessors by incorporating media into his hygienic urbanism. The city commissioned Charles Marville to photograph the old city and the new as a way not only of documenting the changes taking place but also of teaching a new way to see the city. Photography presented Haussmann's Paris as a "territory of images," a space that could not be experienced apart from its technological mediation.[12] The government laid new telegraph lines and created the pneumatic postal service, an underground network of metal tubes through which cylinders of mail could be propelled at high speed to accelerate the delivery of intraurban messages. These improvements reflected a growing sense of the city's function as a media system.

However, while they bore a tangential connection to public health initiatives (the pneumatic post was developed by Eugène Belgrand, the same engineer responsible for the redesign of the sewer system), noise was not yet framed in the pathological terminology of parasites. Aimée Boutin writes: "there was no clear policy against noise in comparison with intolerance for bad smells, smoke, mud and overcrowding, factors more closely associated with sanitation and health."[13] So while in Haussmann's Paris the biological, social, and mediatic—the three sides of parasitism—overlap in more ways than they did in the previous half-century, the three are not pathologized in the same ways. Moreover, while Haussmann's interventions in the city were transformational for domestic architecture—his name is synonymous with the style of apartment building on the new streets—hygienic urbanism in this period remained a citywide concept. The pathologization of parasites had not quite entered the home. Starting in the 1880s, however, a variety of theoretical movements in France converged to codify the parasite as the primary antagonist of domestic architecture. This led to a dramatic acceleration in the atomization of city life.

In the 1880s the government of Paris approved two changes to the building code, a first in 1882 and a second in 1884. Another set of revisions came in 1902. The changes were made in response to growing frustration from architects who felt that they had been stifled by the planning procedures put in place by Haussmann. The effects of the new building codes have at times been minimized by historians, but they represented a significant epistemological shift in how Parisian architecture was conceived. During the Second Empire Haussmann had instituted a hierarchical planning structure, where architects reported to an *architecte-voyer*, a supervisor whose job was to ensure that each building fit within the aesthetic of the street. The building codes were restrictive, reflecting Haussmann's doctrine of straight lines. Identical buildings with identical elevations and connected balconies emphasized the perfect linearity of the city's new long avenues. The aesthetic object was the street, or even the city as a whole, and Haussmann was its artist. The new building codes changed that. Now, decorative elements could protrude from the building. New materials could be used. Brickwork and iron began to mix with the austere limestone preferred by Haussmann's engineers. Sculptures and bas-reliefs appeared. The balcony and roofline became starting points for wild and innovative forms. Louis Bonnier advocated setting apartments back from the street at irregular intervals through the addition of private gardens.[14] The result was that the street lost its homogeneity. Each building could stand out from its neighbor. The new façade competitions, begun in 1897, encouraged architects in this regard. The winner of the first citywide *concours* in 1898, Hector Guimard's *art nouveau* scandal-maker, the Castel Béranger, was a building where, as André Hallays put it, "The same obsession is everywhere evident, from the main entrance to the eaves: breaking with all tradition and defying all convention."[15] The aesthetic object was no longer the street, but rather the individual building, and architects were the artists, not the central planner. It became standard practice in this period for an architect to sign the façade of each building they designed.

This shift in thinking was a major step in a long transition process, wherein Paris's urban planners increasingly viewed private space, rather than public space, as their primary point of intervention. Over time, domestic space would absorb the activities and benefits that previously were hallmarks of public space, resulting in a gradual inward turn of urban life. What is especially notable in this process, as Fabienne Chevallier has shown, is that the anti-parasitic hygienic discourse that had previously been applied primarily at the level of the urban infrastructure would increasingly characterize thinking of the home. This can be seen in the building code writing process itself. Following the timid building code revision of 1882, the city government appointed a commission, led by the hygiene-minded architect Louis Bonnier, to study further changes in the code. Bonnier would go on to play a significant role in the revision of 1902 as well. Throughout the report his commission filed, Bonnier turns to hygiene to justify the new rules he proposes. He puts aesthetics and hygiene on an equal footing: "After all, aesthetics is not a luxury for the people, but a need and a right on the same level as hygiene."[16]

From the 1880s on, hygienic principles were at the very core of Parisian architecture, from urban planning to interior design. In 1882 the Paris health council consulted Léon Poincaré, a professor of hygiene and contagion, to explain why typhoid outbreaks had been observed after major building projects. He concluded that upheaval in the earth released disease agents, leading to a health council recommendation that every new building site should be supervised by medical professionals. In 1887 the Prefecture of Police instituted a new requirement that architects apply for a certificate before demolishing an existing structure. Part of the certification process was a visit to the site by a team of doctors to establish what steps were necessary to sanitize the demolition and construction process.[17] 1887 also marked the first time that the city's planners formally consulted the health council for its advice on a construction project, the extension of the Avenue de la République. The council reported that though some healthy green spaces would be destroyed by the new road, so too would many unhealthy alleys and slums, and so gave its approval.

The differences between the response to tuberculosis outbreaks and cholera are especially telling in this regard. In 1906, Paul Juillerat put forth the theory, based on the observed overlap between slum housing and illness outbreaks, that "tuberculosis is first and foremost a disease caused by darkness."[18] Previous city planners had responded to observations like these by rebuilding the city's networks and public spaces (wider streets, new sewers, big parks). The planners of the early twentieth century intervened at a different level. They created a list of *îlots insalubres* or unsanitary blocks. These were city blocks where densification and *ad hoc* additions had resulted in stuffy courtyards. The policy was to correct these blocks one by one. Once again the metaphor was surgical, but the body being operated on was not the entire city but the single block.[19] Tumescent growths (what architects today call parasitic architecture) were excised from the interior of the block, leaving a single, hollow construction with a courtyard filled with light. The apartment was preserved, and indeed reasserted, as a unity rather than razed at the expense of the network.

The city's new building-by-building response to citywide problems was also on show in its reaction to housing shortages. In 1882 it began promoting the HBM (*habitation à bon marché*, or low-cost housing) as an option for workers who could no longer afford market prices. Rather than systemic fixes, the city promoted single-building solutions. Unsurprisingly, these buildings in which the city's poor were concentrated were also subjected to hygienic principles. Henri Sauvage and his partner, Charles Sarazin, founded the Société anonyme de logements hygiéniques à bon marché (Low-Cost Hygienic Housing Company) in 1903 to provide the city with new buildings for the working class. Sauvage's hygienic design principles were most on show in his 1914 apartment building at 26 rue Vavin. Each floor of that building was stepped back from the one below, providing each resident with their own private solarium. This innovation, which Sauvage heavily promoted for the remainder of his career, was a way of internalizing within each single home Bonnier's idea of insulating the apartment building from the street by giving it a private garden. The façade of Sauvage's entire building was covered with ceramic tiles, evoking the supremely hygienic space: the bathroom.

Sauvage's buildings were influential on later architects, and they are good demonstrations of how hygienic principles shaped the design of private space, not just urban planning. The latest theories associated good hygiene with ample light, greenery, and the use of lots of water to wash the body. The homes of the turn of the century responded with more and bigger windows, or semi-outdoor areas like Sauvage's solarium. The relaxed building code allowed architects to create covered bow windows, balconies, loggias, and verandas that gave the resident the benefit of the outdoors without having to leave the home. Plants were brought into private space as well. Winter gardens and greenhouses became standard features of the homes of the wealthy. And the bathroom went from a small, utilitarian room to a focal point of the home.[20]

What of mediatic parasites? During the Haussmannian period new communications technologies developed alongside new sanitary ones, but noise had not yet been pathologized. During the Third Republic that began to change. This was a period, Aimée Boutin argues, in which the soundscape of the city began to be hierarchized, with some sounds newly classified as undesirable and deleterious to health. She cites the hygienist Fonssagrives, who believed domestic space was inadequately sheltered from noise. He and other hygienists succeeded in changing "thresholds of intolerance" and making "noise control and abatement [. . .] more of a priority for citizens and city governments."[21] Noise over technological communications networks began to be pathologized as well, and in 1907 "electromagnetic perturbations" entered the Nouveau Larousse encyclopedia as a new meaning of the word "parasites."

Collectively, these transformations point to a new vision of domestic space. The apartment of the early nineteenth century occupied a chaotic mixed-use building where interior space was both public and private. A century later, the ambiguity and permeability of early apartments was identified as a problem. Architects mobilized to isolate domestic space and cut it off from urban networks. The apartment was redefined as a single, bounded work authored by a single artist that had to respond only to its own interior logic. It could be separate from the buildings bordering it, just as it could establish distance between itself and the road. It stood alone, with its own style and its own internal ecosystem. For Pierre Pinon, the turn of the twentieth century provoked "a rupture between habitation and the city, with the former becoming autonomous."[22] Eleb and Debarre likewise see this period as ushering in "the creation of an autarkic space."[23] This rupture between domestic and public space relied on new theories from hygienic science. While the early nineteenth century laid the groundwork for thinking the city as a biological organism whose health needed to be safeguarded from invasive diseases, at the end of the century we see the explicit marriage of that notion to an ideology valorizing privacy and the self-sufficiency of domestic space. Urban planning and hygiene became so closely intertwined between 1880 and 1914 that it was normal for a doctor to diagnose a building site before construction could begin. Finally, this ideology became wedded to new ideas about the city as a media space, as a space of images, sounds, and information. Noise joined the list of pathological parasites to be exterminated. With this change, Paris urbanism became properly anti-parasitic. The apartment had become the space where a Parisian could be protected from three kinds of parasites: biological ones threatening to infect the body, mediatic ones threatening to interfere with the peace and quiet of the home, and social ones threatening the stability of the political order.

The anti-parasitic architecture articulated over the course of the nineteenth century developed in new directions in the twentieth. The invention of new media technologies created new kinds of noise to be mastered. New medical theories reinforced hygienic urbanism. The rise of fascism in France gave a new impetus to the proto-eugenic subtext of nineteenth-century hygienics, which had originally been motivated in part by a desire to strengthen the French race, and racist thinking shaped the social side of anti-parasitism to an ever-growing extent. These various developments shaped the architectural and urban planning thinking of a wide variety of French theorists, but they were especially influential in the thought of France's leading modernist architect, Le Corbusier.

Breaking the Collective Phenomenon: Le Corbusier's Individualism

Le Corbusier's influence on the Parisian landscape is uneven. Throughout his career he had difficulty obtaining commissions in Paris. Despite that, he was able to develop a devoted following among young, avant-garde architects through his theoretical writings. The first of these texts was *Toward an Architecture*, a book largely drawn from Le Corbusier and Amédée Ozenfant's architectural journal, *L'Esprit nouveau*. In it, Le Corbusier makes repeated reference to Haussmann, calling for a total reimagining of urban life with attendant revolutions in water, transportation, and food infrastructure. The influence of nineteenth-century hygienic urbanism is strong, and Le Corbusier shared Haussmann's *dirigiste* approach to urban planning. But Le Corbusier responded to the basic premise of public health thinking—that my neighbor's health affects my own—in a way that reflected the turn-of-the-century preference to intervene in private space. He consolidated the preeminence of the building in the architect's toolbox as well as the architect's place at the top of the urban planning totem pole, and he dramatically expanded the fortifications separating private space from public. He advanced an immunizing ideology that sought to improve the health of the city by severing the links between its residents, cutting off transmission of disease and malign influence. He dreamed of "breaking the collective phenomenon."[24] At the same time, Le Corbusier brought the concept of architecture as media to a new level, and his informatic thinking, which vilified the noises that disturb communication, helped to establish parasites as the pathological other of Parisian architecture and urban planning.

Looking back on his career a few years before his death in 1965, Le Corbusier described his life's work as a form of biology: "Isolating my microbe, I watched how it developed. The biology of my microbe appeared in indisputable clarity. Certainties were acquired and a diagnosis. Then, by an effort of synthesis, I cleared the fundamental principles of modern urban planning."[25] Le Corbusier's diagnostics showed him where the parasites threatening the life of the city were located: public space. Walking down the street, he says, "the pedestrian could die at any moment."[26] He echoes the Haussmannian metaphor of the street map as a congested circulatory system, and worries that the heart will fail. But whereas Haussmann saw wider and straighter streets as the solution to this problem, and described his avenues as though they were the tip of the surgeon's scalpel, Le Corbusier is dismissive of the street in any form. Shops and restaurants that encroach on the street are described as a "mold eating into the sidewalk," and "commercial enterprises that take place on sidewalks or the street in the center of Paris are like the nodules of a cancer that we've allowed to grow on the heart of the city. The cancer will choke the city."[27] He wonders what effect gasoline fumes have on pedestrians, pointing to the sorry condition of roadside vegetation. Courtyards, too—liminal spaces between public and private—are unsanitary. Tuberculosis, he says, is a disease that can be combated only by a shift in urban policy, away from the street and toward his vision of the apartment.[28]

Private space would be the point of intervention for Le Corbusier's cure. In the introduction to the second edition of *Toward an Architecture*, he writes: "The architecture of today concerns itself with the house, with the ordinary and common house for normal and common men."[29] The house is the architect's "primary tool." Private space is where one can be sealed off from the parasites of the city. Le Corbusier put forward a set of simple architectural principles, his Five Points, that were necessary for healthy private spaces. (1) The home ought to be built on pillars, which would bear the load for the structure and allow it to be lifted off the ground. This support system would (2) liberate the internal floor plan, which would no longer have load-bearing walls. It would also allow (3) freedom in the façade, owing to the use of a curtain wall. That façade would contain (4) only horizontal windows. Finally, the roof would be flat, not gabled, since the structure would be strong enough to survive rain accumulation. This would transform it into an accessible space that would (5) be planted with a roof garden. These rules create a schism between private and public space. The pillars physically lift the building off the street. This is a symbolic distancing, but also a logistical one: the ground floor of the classic Haussmannian apartment building is a space for shops, where the private stairwell ambiguously mixes with public commerce. Le Corbusier erases this space of public–private cohabitation. His curtain walls are flat, bereft of the long balconies that created both horizontal and vertical spaces of commerce between street and home, and between one home and the next. His windows serve two purposes: they "are for admitting light—a little, a lot, or none at all—and for looking outside."[30] They are conceived of as filters rather than as bidirectional apertures that might allow people on the outside to also look in—a notion that will be discussed in more depth in chapter 3. Finally, rooftop gardens offer the possibility of no more unhealthy courtyards, no more shared, permeable space at the frontier of public and private.

Domestic space is thus consolidated as a unit independent of any external network, social or infrastructural. But for this space to be truly independent, it needs to be self-sustaining. By the end of *Toward an Architecture*, Le Corbusier imagines exactly this, developing his single house into a phalansteric complex capable of responding to all the needs of its residents. The rooftop garden evolves into fields, each attached to a housing complex: "Right outside the houses, vast playing fields (soccer, tennis, etc.) at a rate of 150 m^2 per house. In front of the houses (at a ratio of 150 m^2 per house) land for industrialized farming, intensive farming with substantial yield."[31] Both would improve the health of residents by providing them with exercise and a healthy diet. The residents themselves till the land after returning home from their standardized eight-hour work day (one wonders when they'll find the time to use the athletic fields). Both economy and leisure are subsumed into the realm of the domestic (economy thus rediscovers its etymological meaning of management of the *oikos* or home). These principles would find their practical expression in the *Unité d'habitation*. The first of these high-rise apartment complexes was commissioned after the end of the Second World War, in 1945. The first stone of the *Cité radieuse*, or Radiant City, as Le Corbusier baptized the Marseille structure, would be laid in 1947, and the building was completed in 1952. It embodied the architectural rules Le Corbusier had articulated three decades earlier: pillars, an accessible rooftop leisure center, a garden separating the building from the street. But most of all, it demonstrated how many supposedly public amenities could become part of private space. Le Corbusier called the hallways of the apartment building "indoor streets," and along them he placed shops, a restaurant, a hotel, as well as medical and educational facilities. Private space was no longer just set back from urban networks *à la* Henri Sauvage; it was separate, having absorbed all of the public amenities that previously necessitated movement from private space out into public.

But these displacements create a new risk: that the social character of public space will be grafted onto private space. Is this not the rendering-fully-public of private space, rather than its inverse? But Le Corbusier's vision is deeply antisocial, and hostile to any extroverted appropriation of his spaces. Consistent with his phalansteric inspirations, he offers as a safeguard a functionalist segregation of residents that homogenizes the interactions that occur within the shared spaces of any given complex. He proposes a series of mass-production houses: the Domino house; the small worker's house; the bourgeois Citrohan house; the endlessly repeatable Monol house; and the Villa Apartments. These structures are utilitarian expressions of their residents' identities—an identity reduced to *métier*. This can be read as an exaggeration of the different price points at different floors of the Haussmannian apartment building, but whereas Haussmann's buildings mixed all classes in their staircases and lobbies, Le Corbusier imposes strict segregation of his housing typologies (undergirded by a specious argument about aesthetics and class hierarchy). Each typology is part of its own complex, with no mixing and matching. "When we talk about mass-production houses, we talk about entire housing developments. Unity of structural elements is a guarantee of beauty."[32] The connection between different classes is no longer one of proximity or mixing; it is purely stylistic: Le Corbusier proposes to use the same poured concrete to construct the houses for the richest and the poorest.[33]

And yet the possibility for encounter, however neutered and choreographed, remains. No matter: Le Corbusier has faith that the residents of his homes will learn to avoid such dangers. He removes the sidewalk from his complexes, so that when residents leave their homes, they are less likely to walk the same path as their neighbors across the lawns. The French will learn the American "respect of other people's property," and will avoid setting foot on a neighbor's land.[34] Using a lexicon simultaneously botanic and carceral, Le Corbusier summarizes his view of the challenge of modern life: "When it comes to urbanism, one can consider the apartment like a cell. [. . .] In general, we feel free in our cell (and we dream of living in a detached house somewhere to guarantee that freedom); reality has shown that putting cells together is an attack on freedom."[35] If we want the urban organism to thrive, we have to stay in our homes and not interfere with one another. It is only by placing oneself in permanent quarantine that health can be guaranteed.

Le Corbusier's design principles mobilized the sciences of biology and hygiene in service of a social ideology organized around a phalansteric compartmentalization of society, supreme individualism, and the autarky of private space. He pushed the medical and interiorizing ideology of turn-of-the-century Parisian architecture to a new extreme, seeking to lock every person in a private cell. What is most original in Le Corbusier's thinking, however, is not the extremism of his individualism but his recognition of how new media technologies—indeed, how architecture as media technology—could participate in the quarantine of the individual. Le Corbusier put a strong value on mediatic fidelity and clarity. Noise was an enemy. It was a form of pollution. He called it a "sickness" when someone in one house could hear someone in another.[36] Noise was just as serious a threat to the healthy individual as disease: "In this deafening noise of our era, it is time to use powerful counterweights if one wants to prevent mankind being reduced to the existence of termites by the scourge of anti-personalism. Quiet work, away from interference and without aspiration towards the outward world, could make such a counterweight."[37] Noise embodied everything about urban life that inhibited the self.[38] Architecture's task was not just to keep out the other's body; it would also have to keep out their noises. It would have to create the perfect isolation required for true freedom.

Media, somewhat counterintuitively, enable this isolation. In his "Housing Manual," a guide to living in modern homes, he recommends: "the gramophone or pianola will give you accurate interpretations of Bach fugues and will spare you the concert hall, and colds [*rhumes*], and the frenzies [*délires*] of virtuosos."[39] This passage is an example of Le Corbusier's openness to the penetration of new technologies of mass media into the home, and also of his belief that such technologies would render the home hermetic. The homeowner with a gramophone need not risk the street, the metro, the concert lobby, and the crowded hall to experience Bach. He would consequently be spared two kinds of parasites: the noise of coughing that distracts from the music (to say nothing of the sick manner of playing implied by the delirious virtuoso), and the disease coughing communicates. In this way media, ostensibly technologies of communication, serve to eliminate face-to-face interactions and secure privacy, quiet, and health. Issue no. 28 of *L'Esprit nouveau* features an advertisement for the pianola with a complementary anti-parasitic message: it promises the device will free music from "foreign influence."[40]

Le Corbusier's embrace of media extended far beyond the incorporation of specific devices. Media, in particular the camera, served as important models for the way he conceptualized his architecture. Anthony Vidler has shown that one of Le Corbusier's major influences was the cinema of Sergei Eisenstein, and vice versa.[41] In 1929, Le Corbusier performed in a short film, *Architecture d'aujourd'hui*, starring as an inhabitant of his own Villa Savoye. His character returns home from a day at work, but without any of the conventional trappings of the "Honey, I'm home" scene. There is no dinner on the stove, no children rushing to greet their father, no family at all. Instead, Le Corbusier canters through the house, the camera hot on his heels. Each room is visited only long enough to capture a view of it, culminating with a panoptic scene in which the architect mounts the rooftop observation deck to look back on the terrain he has just traveled. The man is in motion because this is an architecture that can be perceived only in motion, a cinematic architecture.

For Beatriz Colomina, the camera is not simply a way of apprehending these spaces, nor is cinema montage just a reference point for their relation to time. Instead, "the house itself is a camera pointed at nature."[42] Look, for instance, at Le Corbusier's windows. He was adamant that windows should be horizontal and not vertical. In response to Auguste Perret, who told him that "a window is a man, it stands upright," Le Corbusier wrote: "This is fine if what you want are 'words.' But I have discovered recently in a photographer's chart these explicit graphics. [. . .] The table says this: . . . *The photographic plate in a room illuminated with a horizontal window needs to be exposed four times less than in a room illuminated with two vertical windows.*"[43] The vertical window corresponds to *logos* and anthropocentrism; the horizontal window corresponds to images and *techne*. Le Corbusier likewise encourages his potential residents to demand "blank walls in your bedroom, living room, and dining room" to make them reflect the greatest quantity of light, and suggests storing paintings in drawers when they aren't being contemplated so as not to reduce the reflective quality of the walls.[44] The interior is a kind of light box or *camera lucida*. Le Corbusier installed electrically controlled curtains that would close from each side of the window like the diaphragm on a camera.

Colomina writes: "everything [. . .] seems to be disposed in a way that continuously throws the subject toward the periphery of the house. The look is directed to the exterior in such a deliberate manner as to suggest the reading of these houses as frames for a view."[45] But this optical relation is not conceptualized as a point of contact with the outside world. Here, Le Corbusier's advocacy of pillars takes on a new significance. What is in question is not just a spatial distancing between private and public space, but rather a fundamental rupture between two spatial regimes. As the house rises above its surroundings it ceases to be part of the environment, it becomes an apparatus through which the environment can be framed, frozen, and classified: "The apartment itself is here the artifice between the occupant and the exterior world, a camera (and a breathing machine). The exterior world also becomes artifice; like the air, it has been conditioned, landscaped—it becomes landscape."[46] As the house bears no relation to its environment, it can be anywhere; environment becomes a kind of décor, akin to the paintings on the wall (or, as Le Corbusier frugally and tellingly suggests, photographs of paintings).

Colomina argues that "For Le Corbusier, 'to inhabit' means to inhabit the camera. But the camera is not a traditional place, it is a system of classification, a kind of filing cabinet. 'To inhabit' means to employ that system."[47] Le Corbusier was an obsessive of the filing cabinet, to the point that his own filing system is an exhibit in the museum dedicated to him. The image of the filing cabinet helps to explain the consequences and motivations of his mediatization of the domestic space. Le Corbusier's architecture is a way of processing the outside world, and sorting it into abstracted and digestible bits of information. It is a way of compartmentalizing the exterior, much as furniture, works of art, toys, and food must be kept in hidden shelves within the walls, to be extracted only when they are needed and for as long as they are needed. It is the apotheosis of his strategy of insulating private from public, a totalizing filter that protects the individual from unregulated outside influences. This informatic architecture is safeguarded from mediatic parasites so that it can process the world with maximum efficiency and fidelity. It also entails, in Marc Perelman's view, a mode of biological safeguarding to the degree that the mechanization of the home "removes the body from the interior, as a way of de-inhabiting the apartment."[48] The pathogenic human body disappears from the home as the resident transforms into pure gaze, pure data processor. The human subject finally achieves perfect hygiene through the elimination of the body that is the precondition for disease.

Le Corbusier tried the same trick with the walls of his buildings. As the wall is the membrane connecting sanitized interior to infectious exterior, it represents the weak point of the whole mediatic-medical-architectural machinery of isolation. While Le Corbusier was able to develop material innovations, like a proprietary system of double-paned, honeycombed glass tiles that he installed in his own studio to improve the noise resistance of his windows, these could not fully foreclose the danger of parasites seeping through the walls. Mastering this danger required all of an architect's talent: "it is the architect's task to bring the surfaces that envelop these volumes to life, without their becoming *parasites* that consume the volume and absorb it to their profit."[49] The ideal, he wrote, would be walls that could still separate inside from out while themselves disappearing. The perfect wall is like a soap bubble, both there and not there, liable to pop if you touch it. It is immediate, a channel become invisible, so perfectly does it process the whole world beyond it.

Le Corbusier's work brought the anti-parasitic ideological undercurrents of French architecture and urbanism to a new height. All three avatars of the parasite—disease, noise, and the other—were active, and played essential roles in structuring his approach to the city. The three aspects of parasitism overlapped and commingled in complex ways, making it impossible to disentangle one parasite from another. The task of the architect was clearly defined as the task of keeping out parasites, whatever form they might take.

Now, considered in a vacuum, Le Corbusier's anti-parasitic architecture is unproblematic, a natural if austere implementation of Western values like individualism, privacy, and rationalism. His principles might offend partisans of neighborliness and their open thinking of the boundary between homes, but a desire to keep out unwelcome guests does not preclude Le Corbusier from opening his door under the right conditions to the welcome ones. And yet, if we look at the original meaning of parasite, things are not as simple as that. In ancient Greece, in the primal scene of parasitism, the unwelcome guest or parasite at the feast was not one guest among others. Their relationship to the host was different. They were marked out by their class, beneath the other diners in status. The relationship between host and guest was ordered by a set of rules and duties that put them on equal footing, a reciprocity expressed in French by the use of the same word (*hôte*) for each. The guest could not be thrown out according to the whims of the host. The parasite was not entitled to such respect. It was not an unwelcome guest by choice, but because those with more power had classified it as such. What makes Le Corbusier's architecture anti-parasitic is not simply its valorization of privacy or its atomizing individualism; it is the inequality that characterizes the relationship between the host or resident and the others excluded from their property. It is the racism, classism, and sexism that are latent in Le Corbusier's desire to banish parasites from his homes.

During the Second World War, Le Corbusier had close friends in France's Nazi-sympathizing Vichy government. He was friends with Alexis Carrel, who created the Foundation for the Study of Human Problems, a eugenics institute devoted to perfecting the French race. Le Corbusier dedicated his 1941 book *On the Four Routes* to Carrel as well as to a number of French fascists.[50] In the book he would praise both Hitler and Maréchal Pétain for understanding architecture's capacity to regenerate the race. Two years later Le Corbusier was appointed Technical Advisor for the Department of Bio-Sociology at the Carrel Foundation.[51] In the wake of the February 6, 1934 fascist riots in Paris, Le Corbusier used the vocabulary of hygiene to express his support for the rioters: he called it "the reawakening of cleanliness," and he elsewhere accused Jews of having "turned the country rotten."[52] A proposal Le Corbusier submitted for a new district in La Chaux-de-Fonds segregated the Jews in a ghetto. In private correspondence he referred to himself as an antisemite.[53]

As Marc Perelman argues in one of the three books published in 2015 that drew attention to Le Corbusier's fascist sympathies, the theorist's personal beliefs cannot be dissociated from his work.[54] On the contrary, his architectural and urbanist theories implement his political beliefs. Le Corbusier's "modulor" system of architectural proportions, which he came to treat as something like a personal religion, placed the "standard man" at the heart of design. The body in question was a six-foot-tall, athletic male. The modulor is but the most direct example of how bodily normativity, a fundamentally exclusive idea about the kinds of bodies the city is for, sits at the heart of Le Corbusier's designs. His obsession with the body, with the perfected and healthy body, and with the city and home as body, all have a certain kind of body as their starting point. His determination to insulate the standard man from the parasitic influences latent to collective life is inextricable from ethnic, cultural, and biopolitical questions about who is allowed to inhabit the city. Who lives here, who is a guest, and who is a parasite?

This is not just an issue with Le Corbusier personally. The eugenic beliefs into which Le Corbusier's hygienics often elided had widespread currency in French architectural circles, including after the Second World War. One of the most important texts in postwar French urbanism was Jean-François Gravier's *Paris and the French Desert* (1947), which advocated the depopulation of major cities and the redistribution of resources and industry to the provinces. Gravier describes big cities as parasites that "devour"[55] the resources and talent of the nation, and he calls Paris "*mortifère*" (bringing death). Urbanization is a public health crisis worse than alcoholism.[56] He, too, turned sanitary arguments into ethnonationalist ones. Gravier describes immigrants as barbarian invaders,[57] and those from the Middle East as "unassimilable and devoted to parasitism."[58] And like Le Corbusier, he had strong ties to the Vichy government. He was a member of the far-right political party L'Action Française (with which Le Corbusier was also associated); the editor of *Idées*, one of the most prominent Vichy newspapers; and an employee of the Carrel Foundation. Gravier's book was the bible of French planning doctrine throughout the De Gaulle and Pompidou presidencies, a span of over 25 years.

There are multiple ways to interpret the fascist ties of France's theorists of anti-parasitic urbanism in the mid-twentieth century. One would be, borrowing from Roberto Esposito, to say that fascism is the unavoidable, logical extreme of anti-parasitism. Esposito sees the hygienic/eugenic discourses of fascism and its violent hatred of the other as extreme expressions of a more fundamental biopolitical ideology of immunity. Immunity is the antithesis of community, and whether the term is deployed in the biological realm (the immune system) or the political one, it expresses a desire to be free of the other.[59] Following Esposito's logic, it is no accident that the "immunizing" anti-parasitic discourses of French architecture in the nineteenth and twentieth centuries were so consistently yoked to individualism and the valorization of privacy. Le Corbusier's dream of "breaking the collective phenomenon" is the very definition of Esposito's immunity, and his fascist sympathies are that dream pushed to its limit.

One could also give a more agnostic interpretation of Vichy's connection to Parisian urbanism. The point is not necessarily that the hygienic discourse of the late nineteenth century set Paris on the path to fascist dictatorship, nor even that twentieth-century European fascism bears some privileged relationship to the discourse of parasitism (though this question will come up repeatedly in this book). One could instead simply take fascism's compatibility with anti-parasitic urbanist ideologies as a reminder that calls to eradicate parasites are never uniquely biological or mediatic. They are always political, always ethical. The construction of thicker walls and soundproof windows, the demolition of "unsanitary" buildings to open light-filled courtyards, and the desire for greater privacy are, at their core, always expressions of how one relates to the other.

Critiques of Architectural Atomism

Le Corbusier's architectural thought exerted significant influence on French urbanism in the decades following the Second World War. His ideas about self-sustaining housing complexes with separation from the street pervaded residential construction. The most impactful expression of their success would come with the creation of the *grands ensembles* in 1954. These "mass housing developments of unprecedented cheapness" were intended to be constructed within a year, each one with eight to ten thousand units for thirty to forty thousand residents. The most famous was Sarcelles. A village of 8,000 before construction began in 1956, by 1965 it had more than that number of individual dwellings.[60] The complex was a Corbusian dream, as is apparent in Christiane Rochefort's description of it in her novel *Les Petits Enfants du siècle*:

> Now *that*, that was a housing complex, the true housing complex of the future. For miles and miles houses houses houses. Identical. Aligned. White. More houses. Houses houses houses houses houses houses houses, houses houses houses. Sun. Houses filled with sun, passing through them, coming out the other side. Enormous Green Spaces, clean, superb, carpets, and on each one a sign saying Respect the Lawns and Trees, which seemed to have more effect than they did where I lived, doubtless because the people here were more civilized, just like the architecture.[61]

This is an immense, homogenized space stripped of any relation to the outside world, a place where equality is expressed through the endless tessellation of identical concrete buildings containing identical industrial living quarters. A place of lawns with that beautiful Disneyland quality of being natural without looking it, lawns that we must learn not to share.

Sarcelles was a jewel of the period, the apotheosis of the mass-produced, utopian housing Le Corbusier had theorized for many years. But shortly after residents moved in, something surprising happened. In the 1960s journalists began writing about Sarcellitis, a pop-psychological disease characterized by "juvenile delinquency, bored housewives, nervous breakdowns and a rocketing suicide rate."[62] The epidemic was certainly exaggerated by the tabloids, but a public health crisis was hardly what planners had in mind when they freed housing from the pestiferous influences of the street and city center. The peak of hygienic architecture had created a new disease.

The attention brought to the negative qualities of life in the *grands ensembles* by the media frenzy over Sarcellitis provoked a reassessment of the stakes of residential architecture. Jane Jacobs, writing in roughly the same period about New York, accused modern housing complexes of bringing about the collapse of community. Using the language of plant disease, she said that modern cities suffered from "The Great Blight of Dullness."[63] Critics in France began to question the monotony of life in the disconnected spaces into which the government had poured resources. The avant-garde artistic group Situationist International loathed Le Corbusier and blamed the *grands ensembles* for destroying city life. Ivan Chtcheglov wrote in 1953: "His cretinizing influence is immense. A Le Corbusier model is the only image that arouses in me the idea of immediate suicide. He is destroying the last remnants of joy. And of love, passion, freedom."[64] In 1967, Jean-Luc Godard released his feature-length essay film on life in the Paris housing projects, *2 ou 3 choses que je sais d'elle* (*2 or 3 Things I Know about Her*). The film was partly adapted from an exposé Godard had read about housewives in the suburbs who engaged in prostitution to supplement their husbands' income. The film makes a mockery of the term *grand ensemble*, punning on the sartorial ensembles the protagonist buys with the money she makes from prostitution and emphasizing the chasms that keep the inhabitants of the project from living *ensemble*.

The film opens on a construction site. In the front of frame, a wheelbarrow sits on the still-glistening asphalt of an unfinished highway on-ramp while a man in the background watches construction equipment rumble through the dirt. Godard then cuts to a view from the underside of an overpass, where support pillars both frame the factories in the background and obscure the cars passing through. The third shot is of another highway ramp, this one flanked by a few freestanding towers (see figure 2.1). On the right, an older building presents a bare party wall to the camera, an unmet invitation for another building to adjoin it. This structure is probably marked for demolition. Future construction and future ruins mingle indiscriminately. On the left of the highway, a tower in the modern style. The viewer's eye is directed to the focus of the shot by the highway, but what he or she finds there is a void, a vanishing point. The road leads nowhere. The slight upward tilt of the camera makes it difficult to see how

Figure 2.1
One of the opening shots of *2 ou 3 choses que je sais d'elle* (1967), dir. Jean-Luc Godard, prod. Anatole Dauman and Raoul Lévy

the towers connect to the road, if they do at all. Perhaps one can neither get to them nor leave them.

The total disconnect between living space, pedestrian space, and the road is reinforced by the final shot of the film's brief preface: the pedestrian shopping area of the *grand ensemble* in which the film is set. Pedestrians amble in darkness, cut off from the sky by a raised esplanade and from the street by the shops installed in the housing development for their convenience. Godard cuts to Marina Vlady, whom we see on the balcony of her apartment. The sharp cuts in the first five shots accentuate the disconnect between the places of the ensemble. The view moves from one place to another with little motivation. It is not clear if this is a trajectory—a commute—or moments in time in the construction of the development. Perhaps the views are not related at all. The culmination of the sequence, the arrival at the balcony, the emergence of the protagonist at the position of the apartment which ought to present a coherent view of the region, instead results in a greater feeling of disconnection. The view behind Vlady is dominated by the other tower of the complex and by a vast expanse of greenery and highway, both lost in the blur of Godard's focus. Matthew Taunton states that "Godard uses perspective to emphasize the difficulty of forming a relation between the individual and such a vast hive."[65] A side effect of this series of disconnects is that Vlady herself is split in two: Godard introduces her both as the actress, Marina Vlady, and, viewed from a different angle, as the main character, Juliette Janson. In contrast to Le Corbusier's vision of a domestic cocoon that would protect the self, Godard sees an isolation that fundamentally breaks it.

Critiques of official housing policy came to a head in 1968. The protests of *Mai '68* led to sweeping reforms in the École des Beaux-Arts that changed the architecture profession. New schools began challenging the hegemonic status of the Beaux-Arts, and new faculty, with backgrounds in fields like ecology and sociology, challenged the abstract thinking about human behavior that had dominated architectural training in France dating back to the nineteenth century. Critics like Henri Lefebvre drew attention to everyday life as an object of study, rather than something that should be blindly forced to adapt to new architectural exigencies, and advanced the idea of a collective right to the city. In the 1970s François Loyer began pushing for a return to Haussmannian principles of networked urbanism, with a focus on smaller buildings. By 1980, architects who had come of age in the aftermath of *Mai '68* were in the prime of their careers, and the election of François Mitterrand signaled a new phase in Parisian architecture.

However, while Mitterrand invested heavily in monumental architecture in Paris, the 1980s also marked the beginning of a steep drop-off in public investment in domestic architecture. Housing developments increasingly depended on public–private partnerships. These developments were often more humanely designed than their predecessors from the 1960s and 1970s, but there were fewer of them and their impact was consequently diminished. This opened a space for a new form of quarantine. Three forms of housing, accessible only to the rich, became increasingly popular: the villa, gated community, and *cité* (the term *cité* is used for upscale, homogeneous communities like the *Cité florale* described below. This can be confusing, as it is also used for housing projects like the *grands ensembles*). Today, Paris is peppered with villas, especially in the wealthy west, that offer small-scale, upper-class oases. Michel Pinçon and Monique Pinçon-Charlot analyze the villa in their sociological study *Paris Mosaïque*. The villa in their assessment evokes an anti-urban vision of neighborhood: "The image of the village, which people like to use, captures the exceptional sociability of villas and *cités* in an urban environment where anonymity reigns."[66]

But if the villa embraces internal community, it takes hostility toward the external urban fabric to a new level. *Paris Mosaïque* euphemistically calls the villas "so many islands in the heart of the big city,"[67] whose borders are marked by gates and walls. Some inhabitants employ their own security forces to go along with internal governance boards with the power to approve or decline new neighbors. Private parking means that despite being in the heart of the city, the resident of the villa does not need to use pedestrian walkways, and one of the residents interviewed in the book expresses fear at the thought of his children playing in the street outside the community's gate. Le Corbusier's description of the street as a place where death always lurks returns. This is a defensive architecture.

Éric Hazan sees the phenomenon of gated communities as part of a wider militarization of domestic space in which residents increasingly doubt the benignity of the people with whom they share the city. With some hyperbole, he describes the Paris that has resulted as a city under apartheid:

> The line that marks the boundary of the apartheid is sometimes very sharp, like the boulevard de Rochechouart between the very bourgeois 9th arrondissement [. . .] and the turbulent 18th. Sometimes it's blurrier, as in the 10th, in the area around the Gare du Nord and the Gare de l'Est, where the Sri Lankan and Pakistani neighborhood that follows the rue du Faubourg Saint-Denis gradually tails off, if I can put it that way, where it meets the peaceful and residential area around the Saint-Denis hospital: mixed zones, as you could still find on the outskirts of Harlem in the 1960s. Apartheid, then, more than swarms of gated communities, unless we acknowledge that because of their entry codes every Parisian apartment building is gated.[68]

This is the flipside of the vision of the city mobilized by the Fête des Voisins. The village atmosphere that this movement dreams of re-creating inside individual apartment buildings reveals its dark qualities. While the fêtes are social occasions, the fact that they imagine neighborhood extending only to the limits of the building is the culmination of over a century of antisocial urban planning theory. It is part and parcel of a frightened and defensive domestic architecture that tolerates social encounter only under the tightest choreography, that limits the chaos of public life to a carnival day and invites only those who have already been screened by the landlord.[69] Anti-parasitic discourses that tie privacy to the prevention of noise and disease continue to structure this fearful and defensive thinking of domestic space—see the framing of noise pollution as a public health crisis by Anne Hidalgo's administration, discussed in the Introduction, or Jacques Chirac's notorious "le bruit et l'odeur" speech of 1991, in which the then-mayor of Paris declared that the "problem" with Muslim and black immigrants was that their noises and smells did not stay within their own apartments. However, the very fact that anti-parasitic architecture is still an ongoing project means that it has failed to accomplish its goals. This suggests some weaknesses that allow parasites to continue creeping back into the home.

Media as Wall in Michael Haneke's *Caché*

Domestic architecture as anti-parasitic fortification is the central theme of Michael Haneke's 2005 film *Caché*, which tells the story of a bourgeois couple in Paris, Georges and Anne Laurent (Daniel Auteuil and Juliette Binoche), who live in a villa in the 13th arrondissement. The film begins with an overlong, static shot of the family's house, a disorienting opening. The viewer eventually learns that this footage is actually from a tape that has been left anonymously on the family's front stoop, but as the shot drags on beyond the already lengthy opening credits, the viewer begins to worry that he or she is missing something. The composition of the shot is flat, and without any narrative context it is difficult to know where to look. Consequently, the viewer begins to look everywhere, scrutinizing details in search of some kind of meaning. One looks at windows, the street signs, the cars, the lamp. Everything that is normally background comes to the fore as a potential source of action. Finally an explanation is given, but in the form of a doubling of the spectator's bewilderment: Anne and Georges are heard offscreen studying the same footage, themselves confused about what they're watching.[70] An artificial rewind effect then distorts the screen, revealing that we have been watching not the film's present as recorded by Haneke's camera, but a past scene displayed on an intradiegetic screen.

The tape turns out to be the first in a series. Over time the tapes lead Georges to an apartment block in the *Youri Gagarine grand ensemble* in the suburb of Romainville. There Georges comes face to face with Majid, an Algerian man who had been adopted by Georges's family as a child following the disappearance of his parents in the infamous Parisian pro-FLN demonstration of October 1961, during which police massacred demonstrators. Many were pushed off the Pont Saint-Michel and drowned in the Seine. In the scenes of the film set in his childhood, Georges lies to his parents about Majid's role in the death of one of the family's chickens, leading the parents to send the child away to an orphanage.

Figure 2.2
The opening shot of *Caché* showing the façade of the Laurent family home. *Caché* (2005), dir. Michael Haneke, prod. Andrew Colton and Veit Heiduschka

These two men are brought together again by images of their homes. The buildings they inhabit are closely intertwined with their identities. The man responsible for the massacre that killed Majid's parents was police chief Maurice Papon. Prior to his appointment in Paris, Papon was the prefect of the Constantine region in Algeria, where he was famous for a draconian attitude to dissent. His promotion to Paris coincided with a new, softer approach to quelling unrest in the Constantine region, led by Paul Delouvrier. Delouvrier supervised the Constantine Plan: an effort to pacify Algeria through the construction of 200,000 new units of housing. These apartments were consistent with the contemporaneous vogue for *grands ensembles*, and Delouvrier's work earned him a transfer to Paris in 1961. There he would become known as the Haussmann of De Gaulle, supervising major new housing developments. Among these was the *quartier Youri Gagarine.* Majid, whose childhood is scarred by Papon's police violence, ends up in a housing unit built under the regime of Delouvrier. His living space, like the loss of his parents, is a Parisian continuation of colonial violence.

Georges tracks down Majid's apartment from a frame-by-frame analysis of one of the tapes left on his doorstep. Figuring out Georges's address is both easier and harder. From the first shot of the film the viewer knows that he lives at the end of the rue des Iris. From that it is easy to track down the address: 49 rue Brillat-Savarin in the 13th arrondissement. But, as Roland-François Lack points out, in the film's DVD extras one can see that the street sign next to the house has been changed to rue Vulpian.[71] This "*petit fait faux*" perhaps signals that the Laurent family lives in a semifictitious space, or that the camera does not perfectly translate reality—the house is, notably, framed by the rue des Iris, street of the lens of the camera and of the eye of the spectator.

"Iris" is also the name of a flower. The street is part of the *Cité florale*, a posh community of brownstones with private gardens whose flora have given their names to the streets that mark its borders. There are several of these little semi-gated communities in the south of Paris, little enclaves of the bourgeois intelligentsia sprinkled around Chinatown and the old working-class neighborhoods of Paris's industrial periphery. Georges, who hosts a televised literary debate program, and Anne, who works in publishing, fit in well with the cultured neighbors across the street. At first glance, an urbanist might wonder how these pockets have been allowed to persist amid the high-rises that tower all around them. In reality, they almost certainly would have been demolished, had it not been for a hidden ecological feature of the neighborhood: the Bièvre, Paris's second river, runs beneath them. It was covered in 1912 as a response to toxic fumes and unbearable odors produced by centuries of residents of the neighborhood casting their garbage and waste into the water. This is the dirty side of hygienic urbanism. Unhygienic waste is thrown into the water with the expectation that the current will take it out of the city, but instead the waste stagnates. And so the waste has to be swept under the rug again, paved over with a road. It is partly because of the presence of this river and the unstable construction base it offers that so many bijou neighborhoods can be found in this part of Paris. An aerial view of the area shows in stark relief the effects of the Bièvre, as a major depression in the elevation of the built environment tracks it through the left bank (see figure 2.3). The fact that private houses exist in this part of Paris is a direct consequence of the toxic effect humans have had on the environment. The luxurious Laurent family home is built on ecological violence.

The forgotten and polluted Bièvre also, in the context of the film, pointedly references the act of violence that killed Majid's parents, who were

Figure 2.3
Rue Brillat-Savarin viewed through Google Maps 3D view

likely among the dozens of Algerian demonstrators pushed into the Seine by French police in October 1961. The massacre was similarly swept under the rug—*caché,* per the title of the film—by French authorities who failed to recognize or memorialize it for decades after the fact. If the pollution of the Bièvre bespeaks the hygienic, biological side of anti-parasitism, the massacre is an example of the social side. In this massacre the unwelcome others of the social body—people who, through colonialism, had been made unwelcome in their own homes—were violently expelled from the social body in the same manner used to expel biological waste.

If violence mars the history of the Laurents' house, hostility is inextricable from its present. The home incorporates many of the antisocial features of villa architecture. It is triple-barred, with an external gate, a main door leading to a mud room, and then a secondary door. The house is set back from the street, creating a buffer between public and private space. Haneke seems to have wanted to further insist on this point as he covered the garage door with a white wall, removing any permeable membrane directly abutting the street. When Georges leaves his house he almost always does so in a car, a mobile barrier between him and public space. He drives to work, to the police station, and to his son's school, insulated from the outside world.[72] Stepping outside his car is harrowing for him. In one scene he is almost hit by a cyclist while crossing the street. The cyclist's height, black skin, and cornrows bring out the racial subtext of Georges's distaste for public spaces. Georges's fear of the street reaches its climax when his son goes missing while walking home from a friend's house. Anne worries that he's been hit by a car; Georges assumes that he's been kidnapped by Majid. In between the hermetic bourgeois households is a dangerous zone, populated by the other, where safety is guaranteed only behind the airbag-insulated walls of a car.

The film thus highlights the ways in which the interiorization of nineteenth-century domestic space has transitioned into securitization, and brings out the racist and classist ideologies and fears underpinning that transition. But what makes this film an interesting case study for this discussion of anti-parasitic architecture is how prominent media are in the securitized home. The walls of the Laurent home are covered in media. Bookcases fill the background of most rooms, interrupted here and there by shelves of DVDs or by the television. Le Corbusier believed domestic architecture could protect the autonomy of the individual if it embraced media technologies and its own media status. In *Caché*, media literally constitute the walls of the private space, protecting the Laurent family from what lies beyond their door.

The protection of the resident's autonomy in this film plays out in an explicitly political context. Michael Cowan draws attention to a series of scenes in which a television showing the news can be seen in the background as exemplary of media's protective function. The five news reports all concern global politics. The first is about the quarantine in China of people infected with avian flu. The second, which briefly occupies the full frame, is about the Italian government's desire to be on equal footing with other coalition forces occupying Iraq during the American-led invasion. The third concerns torture in Abu Ghraib. The fourth depicts wounded crowds running through smoke following a helicopter bombardment by the Israeli government meant to destroy underground tunnels in the Gaza Strip. The fifth concerns the establishment of a new government in India led, for the first time, by a member of the Sikh minority, Manmohan Singh. Cowan notes that the Laurent family never pays attention to these reports, and argues that "television news in Haneke functions to domesticate the violence it shows into a general wash of the visible, reassuring spectators that there is nothing else to see or know."[73]

As a literary talk show host and a publisher, Georges and Anne both work in media. The set of Georges's talk show, mimicking his home, is lined with (images of) books. In a scene in which we watch him editing his program, we see his mastery of these technologies. And yet, what drives the action in this film is Georges and Anne's inability to stop media in the form of the tapes from entering their home. For all of their mastery and power, these two characters are ultimately not in control of media. The technologies they use to protect themselves turn out to be too ambivalent, too open to interference, too vulnerable to parasites.

The television news could, in this light, be read just the opposite way. While the characters ignore the reports, the viewer of the film can't help seeing them. The television is especially bright in Haneke's shots and it is positioned in the center of frame, directly between the characters. The reports, which all have to do with epidemics, Western military action in Arab lands, colonialism, religious violence, occupation, borders, and walls, offer mordant commentary on the family's private problems. Georges watches the tapes on this same television. These unwanted images appear flush with the books and videos; they invade the mediatic wall that was intended to keep them out. A breach is opened in the hermetic mediatic fortifications.

This opening in the walls is made literal during a scene in which the Laurents host a dinner party for their intellectual friends. The doorbell sounds. Georges's face is stricken with fear. He goes outside to investigate, but finds no one. He shouts into the empty street and then, relieved, begins latching his gates and doors. But one of the doors will not close. Another tape has appeared in the doorjamb. It is in the wall, just as its images will soon be. The tape is a foot in the door for the repressed memories of colonial oppression that will surface over the rest of the film. The walls, in their indifference to the messages they transmit, are perpetually susceptible to transmitting the wrong ones. Attempting to become hermetic, the house becomes hermeneutic.

Despite Georges's supposed mastery of media, his situation is ultimately similar to that of Majid, who tells Georges that he stumbled upon his talk show while channel-surfing and immediately felt nauseous. Television is the means by which Majid is forced to confront trauma in his own home.[74] It makes him feel sick. There is asymmetry between the two characters' relationships to television—Majid's traumatism by his television does not require outside intervention, like Georges's does, and the police do not come to Majid's aid, as they will for Georges—but ultimately both inhabit media spaces over which they lack control.

In the film, the media channels that pervade the home are revealed to be more open than a theorist like Le Corbusier assumed them to be; an important follow-up question is: does that unexpected openness lead to communication? I have referred to the unwanted messages passed through these channels as parasites, a term that is typically used for noise. This implies a breakdown in communication rather than new opportunities to communicate. When Georges and Majid, brought together by what they saw on their televisions, meet one-on-one at the film's climax, no conversation takes place. Georges starts by asking a question about speech and meaning, *Qu'est-ce que ça veut dire?* ("what does that mean?" or, literally, "what does it want to say?"), and Majid gives an answer about presence: "I wanted you to be present." He removes a straight razor from his pocket and slits his throat. He forces open the boundaries of his body. Blood sprays over the wall, and Majid collapses against his door. The sound of blood gurgling through his open throat signals that noise has gained the upper hand on speech. For Kevin Stoehr, the scene is the culmination of the film's "danger of nihilistic surrender," an indication that "the opportunity for a genuinely redeeming conversation has been forsaken."[75]

It is true that the film is skeptical of conversation, with the possible exception of the final shot in which the sons of the main characters have an inaudible conversation in that place where we almost never see their parents, the street. But it is not necessarily the case that by forsaking conversation, the characters give in to "nihilistic surrender." Majid's suicide produces an excess, a trace. Blood sprays onto his wall like paint from an aerosol can. This trace echoes a gruesome postcard Georges's son receives at school. It is also the image on the poster for the film, which gives it an extradiegetic significance and iconographic status. Majid's blood is a kind of writing on the wall, another example of the wall serving as medium.

Georges understands the blood as a message, and he reads it. He interprets it as "dark humor," a reference to the beheading of a chicken that precipitated Majid's removal from Georges's family. However, the implication

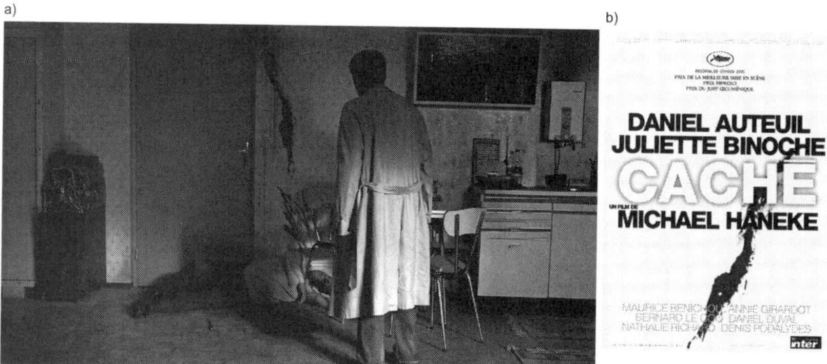

Figure 2.4
Majid's blood splattered onto the wall after his suicide and the poster of the film *Caché* (2005), dir. Michael Haneke, prod. Andrew Colton and Veit Heiduschka[76]

that this act of bloody writing has succeeded as an act of communication where the other messages received by Georges failed is undermined by the fact that the interpretation Georges gives of the blood is the same interpretation he has given to all of the other messages he has received.[77] The fact that Georges repeatedly dreams about the beheading of the chicken prior to Majid's death makes his reading all the more solipsistic: the suicide, like the image on the postcard received by Georges's son, seems to be drawn not from reality but from Georges's subconscious.

Majid's final trace fails to make Georges repent for his unjust behavior toward him. In that respect, it is another failed message. But Majid's act of wall-writing might have a different effect on the viewer. It might draw his or her attention to another form of wall-writing visible in the background of two shots: street art. The first of these is a Jérôme Mesnager on the exterior wall of Georges's next-door neighbor. The second is by Mosko et associés, visible through the car window when Georges picks his son up from school.[78] These works share a connection to the same festival, Lézarts de la Bièvre. Mesnager's painting was created as part of his residency in the second edition of the festival in 2002. The second work, if it was not created during the 2004 edition of the festival, replaced a work by Mesnager painted on that wall in 2002. The festival, as the name suggests, was created in honor of the Bièvre, the river that runs beneath the street in front of the Laurent home. Each year a street artist is selected to paint a series of

Figure 2.5
Jérôme Mesnager's "White Man" on the façade of a house neighboring the Laurent family's. *Caché* (2005), dir. Michael Haneke, prod. Andrew Colton and Veit Heiduschka

works along the path of the river. These paintings create guideposts for the river, making visible on the walls what is hidden underground. They draw attention to the forgotten river and the ecological violence behind its disappearance from the city.

The film's subtle quotation of the festival suggests a different interpretation of whether Majid's act of writing succeeded. While Majid never truly has a conversation with Georges, and while their fraternal relationship is never reestablished, they are brought into contact. Georges is forced to acknowledge Majid's existence, and to explain to his wife what he did. Memories of the violence in his past and the knowledge of his failure to live up to his ethical duties to another dominate his consciousness throughout the film. Communication repeatedly fails, but the repressed and hidden is still brought to the surface. Majid and his son never physically enter Georges's home, but Georges is forced to recognize their existence and their connection to his life, and he is forced to do it by the very media-architectural apparatuses that had promised to protect him from unwanted interpellations. Thinking again about the relationship between Georges's house and the Bièvre, we could say that, given its placement, the Bièvre could almost have seemed a moat for the Laurents' fortified domestic space; instead it turns out to be a channel.

This film thus gets to the fundamental paradox of anti-parasitic architecture: to create a wall is also to create a writing surface. This is a danger of which Le Corbusier was clearly aware, but it is one he thought that he could manage. The architect's task is to "breathe life" into walls, but the right kind of life. There is always a danger that these living membranes "will become parasites that consume the volume and absorb it to their profit."[79] In *Caché*, mediatic architecture, no matter how hermetic its intent, is always open to noise. It always lets in more than it is supposed to. By the end of the film, the walls are riddled with parasites. Blood, spray paint, images of war, memories of violence. Voice and dialogue may have been sacrificed (at least between Georges and Majid), but noise carries on.

This film shows how the mediaticity of domestic architecture, which for much of the twentieth century was theorized as a weapon against parasites in all their forms, in fact provides conditions enabling parasitism to take place. The other, noise, disease, reappear through the channel that had been deployed to keep them out. It also underlines the racial and economic politics of the mediatic home. Majid, an immigrant of lower economic status than Georges, does not enjoy the latter's systems of domestic fortification. He is buffeted by the television that for Georges is a means of exerting his dominance in cultural politics. Georges forcefully enters his home, as do the police; Majid is not allowed to reciprocate. He lives in a high-rise constructed by administrators who ran colonial policy in his parents' native country, the same people responsible for his parents' deaths. He lives in a shared space, while Georges's home is freestanding and gated. These asymmetries are explicitly tied in the film to the ethnic difference between Georges and Majid, and the colonial violence that ruptured their fraternity.

If *Caché* lays bare these political stakes and the inequality that characterizes the way different groups relate to domestic space and to the media technologies that have become part of it, it also shows that there are ways of resisting these power dynamics. The domination the host exerts over the parasite is unstable. In the film we see mediatic parasites entering the home despite all efforts to keep them out. Deprived of speech, Majid makes noise. He writes on the wall, making it possible to see how architecture functions mediatically, and making it impossible to ignore the violence inherent in his exclusion from the channel—and the violence and injustice of his exclusion from the status of *hôte*, Georges's equal, his welcome guest and his host in turn. The film poses the question of whether the desire to keep out parasites is always doomed to failure: if the parasites will always come back, if they are part of the home itself.

3 Wall

In *The Parasite*, Michel Serres writes: "Someone once compared the undertaking of Descartes to the action of a man who sets his house on fire in order to hear the noise the rats make in the attic at night." He imagines what it would take to build a house without rats, to get a good night's sleep, uninterrupted by scurrying feet overhead. A skilled and attentive mason might be able to pull it off if he worked uninterrupted and never took his eye off the foundations. When the house is finished, he can lie down to relax. While his eyes are closed, though, the predictable happens: "Well, the rats came back. They are, as the saying goes, always already there. Part of the building. Mistakes, wavy lines, confusion, obscurity are part of knowledge; noise is part of communication, part of the house. But is it the house itself?"[1] In this short passage Serres summarizes the dilemma of Le Corbusier's domestic architecture. The Corbusian home, with its insistence on cleanliness and hermeticism, is a house built to keep out rats. It is carefully machined with industrial techniques to exclude the mistakes and wavy lines of clumsy handwork. Just as Descartes's metaphorical architecture locked out the body in order to provide a stable space for the mind,[2] Le Corbusier's apartments try to provide privacy and security for the self by regulating views and managing sounds, reducing the outside world to an archive of carefully framed images and high-fidelity recordings. The body of the resident is stripped down to its sensory functions, serving as a cog in an apparatus of information processing and documentation. But as we saw in chapter 2, Le Corbusier's isolationism is ultimately futile. Unauthorized information sneaks in. No amount of care can banish the crackle from the recordings, or stop a smudge on the glass from bending the light, or stop the resident from making a mess. The rats find their way in. Noise makes it through the walls and into the house.

But is it the house itself? Is noise something that comes late to the party, creeping into systems of knowledge, disturbing otherwise stable signifiers, an accident that we can prevent with enough care? Or is it always there from the beginning: "the radical origin of things," in Serres's words? Serres argues the latter, since we know of no system that functions without loss. Against Descartes, he contends that error is the condition of possibility for knowledge, and noise is the same for communication. All systems, all exchanges, are conditioned by parasites, whether the system in question is "the telephone, the telegraph, television, the highway system, maritime pathways and shipping lanes, the orbits of satellites, the circulation of messages and of raw materials, of language and foodstuffs, money and philosophical theory."[3] One cannot eradicate loss, noise, parasites from any of these systems without, as the architectural metaphor puts it, burning them to the ground. Noise may interfere with a system, even cause it to break down, but it is also what makes a system possible.

The scope of Serres's rethinking of the parasite is, as his litany of networks shows, vast. The house to which Descartes metaphorically sets fire with his desire for rationalism stands in for a whole host of things, and in this book I will eventually examine the broader philosophical stakes of Serres's argument. For the time being, however, I want to take the architectural metaphor literally. Is noise the house itself? Throughout *The Parasite*, buildings occupy a privileged metaphorical space. The parasite needs a host. It's a trespasser in the home, an exploiter of hospitality. Architecture is a convenient way to visualize the parasite's transgression of boundaries and property. In chapter 2, I discussed hygienic attitudes to domestic architecture, and how the walls of buildings have been—unsuccessfully—deployed to keep parasites out of private space. In *Caché* we see a home invaded through the very mediatized walls designed to keep it safe and clean. The messiness of the outside world sneaks in through tapes, television, post. But while the focus in that chapter is on how the wall mediates between inside and out, there are also examples in *Caché* of walls mediating between emitters and receivers, of the material boundary of the house serving as a medium. Majid's suicide splatters blood on the wall of his home, turning the clean, white plaster into a writing surface. I suggested that this, too, is parasitic, a form of visual noise that Majid uses when communication has failed. Rephrasing Serres's question: is this parasitism something exogenous, a contingent disturbance of the otherwise stable wall, or is parasitism always latent in the very surfaces used to construct the home?

The wall stained by Majid's blood is an interior one. It is still part of the domestic space. The glimpses of street art in the background of the film are examples of this kind of interference taking place on the outsides of buildings. In recent decades street art has exploded into a major artistic movement, and Paris is one of its global centers. One of the first street artists in Paris was Xavier Prou, aka Blek le Rat. Inspired by a trip to Manhattan in the 1970s, he began tagging the walls of his neighborhood with spray-painted black rats. He explained the choice of his signature and alias in a 2008 interview: "rats are kind of like wild rebels, they scare people and they bring plague to the people. They are a pathogen element and they spread the plague everywhere, just like street art."[4] Blek le Rat presents his art as a form of parasitism, as a disease outbreak spreading through the walls of the city's buildings. Through street art the rats come back. Are they always already there? Moving one increment away from the private, from the interior to the external boundary, my focus in this chapter will be on the mediaticity of the façade. What can we say about parasites that aren't trying to get into the house, but instead remain at its surface? I am especially interested in the kinds of writing possible on the wall, the traces it can bear, and what constitutes noise on it. What parasites plague these channels, and what can we do with them?

Immediacy and Invisibility in Parisian Architecture

In 1934 the photographer Brassaï published "From the Cave Wall to the Factory Wall" in the surrealist magazine *Minotaure*. It was his first essay on graffiti. He had become obsessed with these engravings, which he attributed to schoolchildren. He saw in them an example of the "primitive" art then in vogue among painters like Picasso. For the rest of his career he would photograph them, often returning to a wall year after year to document its evolution. He collected his pictures and a series of essays in an anthology, *Graffiti*, published in 1960. In it, he makes a curious declaration. He writes that in the twenty-six years between his first essay on the subject and the publication of the book, "an historical event every bit as important as Cubism has taken place: the discovery of the wall by modern artists."[5] Now, looking around Paris today, one would be hard-pressed not to see something prophetic in that statement. Graffiti and street art are ubiquitous. But if the core of Brassaï's assertion has been proven true over these last sixty years, its provocative premise demands further scrutiny. By saying that the walls of the city were "discovered" in the 1940s or 1950s, Brassaï implies that they had, prior to that, been invisible: that artists had somehow failed to perceive them as media. How could such blindness be possible? And what makes the discovery of walls such a seminal historical event?

One explanation for the need to discover the media status of the wall can be found in one of the first texts in France to take a media-theoretical approach to architecture: the famous chapter "Ceci tuera cela," or "This will kill that," added by Victor Hugo to the second edition of *Notre-Dame de Paris* in 1832. Hugo argues that up until the fifteenth century, architecture was the primary form of mass media. With its ornate reliefs and painted windows, it was a way of transmitting stories to the masses, "the great book of mankind." Gutenberg's invention of the printing press put a stop to that. Architecture was rendered obsolete by a new, more flexible technology. "Beginning with the discovery of printing, architecture withers away little by little, becomes lifeless and bare." Narrative elements are replaced by geometric features. Proportion takes precedence over ornament. "The plain window replaced stained glass. The stonemason succeeded the sculptor."[6] Architecture's mediaticity was quickly forgotten.

This appears to give us a straightforward explanation for why Brassaï's contemporaries needed to rediscover the wall. They had to bring attention back to a capacity to transmit messages that had lain dormant in architecture since 1420. But this explanation has holes. The first is that, by writing this chapter, Hugo seemingly demonstrates that he was already aware of the mediaticity of architecture in 1832. And presumably all of his readers who paid attention to this chapter were as well. So why didn't the artistic revolution Brassaï describes take place a hundred years earlier? The second issue is that while architectural styles evolved in the fifteenth century, Gothic buildings were and still are present in Paris. Whatever messages they had been communicating in the medieval period were still being communicated in the centuries following, even if Parisians no longer relied on those buildings to know what the Bible said. While new buildings were perhaps less communicative, why should people suddenly have become ignorant of the communication taking place in the older buildings they still frequented?

Thirdly, while the church may have shifted its public relations from stone to parchment in the fifteenth century, the state and advertisers did not forsake walls so quickly. Posters were ubiquitous in Hugo's time. It is hard to believe that anyone could have been ignorant of the wall's capacity to carry messages in the aftermath of the 1848 Revolution, for instance, when thousands of posters appeared all across Paris, a mediatic efflorescence documented by Alfred Delvau in *Les Murailles révolutionnaires*.

Hugo's argument that a singular technological revolution precipitated the loss of architecture's mediaticity and Brassaï's argument that a singular aesthetic revolution led to its rediscovery both crumble under the weight of these questions. In my view, it is more plausible that consciousness of the media status of walls is something that oscillates with the ebb and flow of historical pressures: that Hugo and Brassaï were participating in a long-term battle over the visibility of the wall. In this section, I will discuss what I see as the two most important forces opposing them: (1) the difficulty of perceiving and locating mediation, even when one is looking for it; and (2) an ideology of immediacy that discourages awareness of the mediaticity of walls. Marshall McLuhan identified the first of these as one of the key challenges facing media theorists. He called the electric light "an invaluable instance of how people fail to study media at all. For it is not till the electric light is used to spell out some brand name that it is noticed as a medium. Then it is not the light but the 'content' (or what is really another medium) that is noticed."[7] Just because communication is taking place does not mean we perceive that mediation is taking place, or where and how it is taking place. Hugo himself falls into this trap. The medieval architect was a great artist, he says, because "all other arts obeyed, and placed themselves under the discipline of architecture,"[8] but Hugo does not actually devote a single word to architecture itself: the elevations, the materials, the volumes. He fixates on other media like sculpture, painting, and music that are contained by the architectural medium, and is blind to what the walls of the building do. The mediation possible in uncarved stone is totally invisible to him.

A similar kind of blindness characterized the reception of one of the French architects most influenced by Hugo: Henri Labrouste. Labrouste was born in 1801; in 1824 he won the Prix de Rome, which allowed him to spend five years in Italy. He returned to Paris in 1830, only one year before the publication of Hugo's novel. The connections between Hugo's book and

Labrouste's work were explored in the 1970s by Neil Levine, specifically the way Labrouste responded to Hugo in his design for the Bibliothèque Sainte-Geneviève.[9] Levine argues that the library, constructed between 1843 and 1851, incorporated Hugo's theory of literary architecture in order to make it not just a space for reading, but a space to be read. In a 2005 article, Martin Bressani and Marc Grignon build on Levine's text by performing such a reading. Of the façade, which is decorated with rows of authors' names and stone garland motifs, they provide two interpretations. The first, originally put forth by Levine, is that the carved list of names is an allusion to the library catalogue or bookshelf: "not only does this list allow users to 'read' the authors of the books preserved in the building, but it also signals the actual position of the books in the reading room."[10] The second interpretation, inspired by a description of the library by Anatole France, is that the austere façade inscribed with names is a kind of mausoleum: "The book, like the tomb, conceals a world separate from that of the living. With its simple volumetric character, its garland wrapping, and the names carved on the pieces of wall framed by the arches, Labrouste's building is unmistakably funerary." The latter interpretation echoes Labrouste's own writings about mausoleums, and it suggests a romantic, symbolic side to the architect's imagination that, according to Bressani and Grignon, invites the "reader" of the building to treat it like a work of literature. "The unsettling simplicity of the library's external form is only a preliminary impression that allows the viewer, thus liberated from conventional expectations, to move towards other, more poetic associations with sarcophagi, mausoleums, or Etruscan funerary stone chests."[11]

In the interior of the building, the symbolism of the exterior begins to take narrative form. The walls of the vestibule are decorated with *trompe-l'œil* frescoes of lush vegetation. Death gives way to life, and the painted leaves of the trees seem to spring out of the library walls. It is as though visitors are stepping out of the city and into Arcadia. From there a staircase carries readers up past a copy of Raphael's fresco *The School of Athens*, carefully situated to once again give a *trompe-l'œil* impression of depth and realism. The walls continue the play on the animate and inanimate, the real and its representation, begun by the façade. This discordant symbolism is resolved (and further complicated) by the main reading room. "The user of the library is [. . .] led to interpret entrance into the reading room as a departure from the world of (conventional) images and trompe l'œil,

Figure 3.1
Façade of the Bibliothèque Sainte-Geneviève in Paris. Cristian Bortes from Cluj-Napoca, Romania / CC BY (https://creativecommons.org/licenses/by/2.0)

in order to make contact with 'the real,' that is, with the books and their authors."[12] The reading room was technologically modern and utilitarian—gas lighting and heating were used for the first time to allow the library to stay open at night, while iron vaults maximized space and lighting in the day—but within this functional space, Labrouste continues to play with paradox. The iconography juxtaposes night and day, enlightenment and darkness, clarity and obscurity. There are allusions to the alchemist monk, Frollo, of *Notre-Dame de Paris*.

Bressani and Grignon argue that "the meaning of the library is disclosed through the reading of discrete sets of markings collected through experience. But these inscriptions are not stable signs indicating the practical function of the building; they are instead cyphers that operate in a slippery manner, never allowing for simple, monolithic interpretations."[13] In other words, it "is not that Labrouste tried to create an architectural equivalent to a literary work, a building that could be experienced like a book; it is, rather, that Labrouste continued to conceive architecture on the general level of fiction, as in the classical tradition, yet with a specifically romantic ideal of

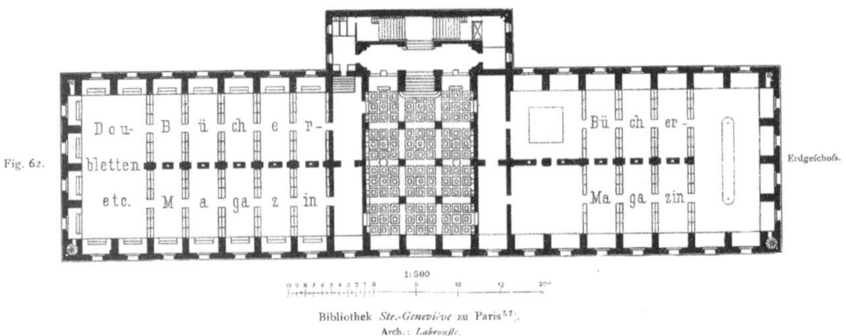

Figure 3.2
Floor plan of the Bibliothèque Sainte-Geneviève, originally published in *Handbuch der Architektur* (Durm et al.)

achieving a contact with 'the true and the real.'"[14] While Labrouste's work is decidedly not a novel, through its engagement with fiction it reactivates the complex narrative semiotics Hugo ascribes to medieval architecture. The vernacular has changed, but the walls of a building still convey messages.

However, most of Labrouste's contemporaries ignored all of this. Critics praised the building for its functional design and volumetric simplicity. Just as McLuhan's bad media critics don't see light, but only the words it spells out, Labrouste's contemporaries looked past the library's walls to the gas lighting inside. This failure to perceive the messages in the walls, and how they are constructed, also characterized the reaction to Haussmannization, which began the year after the Bibliothèque Sainte-Geneviève was completed. Haussmann's apartment buildings concretized a complex ideology with implications extending from the nature of private life to the image of the French state, an ideology in large part communicated through the façade.[15] Haussmann obeyed what he called "the doctrine of the straight line." Decorations like the balcony and the masonry strip drew the eye to the geometric purity of the long boulevards. They signaled the new roads as monumental and modern spaces. The homogeneity of the new buildings made each apartment into "a link in an unbroken chain."[16] To know one building was to know them all—and to know where in the hierarchy each resident stood. This expressed both the stability of the class structure and the hope of social mobility. Furthermore, by borrowing elements from

Figure 3.3
Jouannin and Singery's neo-Gothic façade at 61 rue Réaumur

Hardouin-Mansart's seventeenth-century buildings, Haussmann underlined the continuity between the Second Empire and the golden age of French power and culture under Louis XIV. All of this was being said, and yet contemporaneous critics routinely complained that the new buildings weren't saying anything at all. Louis-Charles Boileau, the architect of the Bon Marché, wrote at the time: "Creative artists and all men of taste were complaining about the lack of variety among the houses built on the new streets and their *lack of decorative significance*."[17] Critics looked for mediation in too narrow a spectrum and, failing to find things like sculpture and stained glass, they concluded that mediation was not taking place. They saw the façades as the unsignifying background of the city, not media in their own right.

Now, largely because of what Boileau describes, the period following Haussmann's ouster was marked by a new explosion of signification in the façade. As discussed in more detail in chapter 2, architects reacted

Figure 3.4
Guimard's signature on the façade of one of his buildings, the Agoudas Hakehilos Synagogue in rue Pavée, Paris

against their marginalization by Haussmann and opened up the building codes. The *concours de façades*—or façade competition—in 1897 turned the rue Réaumur into a showcase for new designs and new materials. Hugo's beloved medieval forms made a reappearance, as on the façade of Philippe Jouannin and Édouard Singery's decadent take on the neo-Gothic at no. 61. They were beaten out for first prize by Albert Walwein's carved *atalantes* at no. 116. When the competition was opened up to buildings anywhere in the city the next year, it was won by Hector Guimard's Castel Béranger, which twisted the façade into scandalous new shapes. This competition helped to promote the twin ideas of the architect as *auteur* (it was not long after architects began signing their buildings) and of the façade as their primary medium of expression.

It could be argued that there was a growing awareness of the media potential of the wall in this period. However, it would soon be counteracted by the second of the two factors driving the invisibility of the wall channel: an ideology of immediacy. Modernist architects in the twentieth century, led by Le Corbusier, established a new paradigm for thinking about the façade. While his predecessors can be accused of not perceiving walls as media, Le Corbusier was well aware of their media status. But he consciously sought to render it imperceptible. Le Corbusier, as discussed in chapter 2, believed that architecture should take the soap bubble as its ideal: its walls should be directly determined by the volume they contain, and only visible enough to render that volume perceptible. He suggests that façades adopt the form of the checkerboard or grid, which is to say that they should model themselves off the grid paper on which they are drawn. Like that paper, the façade should be the medium through which architecture is realized, but it should not be visible when one looks at the building.[18] Tellingly, Le Corbusier shared Hugo's admiration for Notre-Dame, but in his case it was based not on the church's narrative elements but on its simple geometry.[19] The front of the building was a Cartesian space on which abstract shapes could be drawn.

Le Corbusier promoted an ideology of immediacy when it came to walls. Jay David Bolter and Richard Grusin define immediacy as a logic wherein the medium aspires to transparency.[20] When one experiences immediacy, the medium disappears and one has the feeling of direct contact with the real. Bolter and Grusin argue that this logic has been dominant in Europe since the Renaissance, and give as examples Cartesian mathematics, Renaissance painting, and photography. When nineteenth-century critics wrote that in photography light itself was the brush acting on the photographic plate, and that photography was therefore not a medium at all but a way to access reality itself, they were invoking the central fantasy of the logic of immediacy. Le Corbusier—who often referenced photography in his buildings and theoretical texts—describes the same experience when he writes about the walls of his building disappearing so that we can be in direct contact with the volume. By comparing his walls to lenses or grid paper he acknowledges that they must mediate, but he demands that they do so in such a way that mediation disappears.

This ideological position was reinforced over time by technological breakthroughs. The invention of reinforced concrete removed the necessity for the building façade to serve a load-bearing function. Freed from this responsibility, the façade could shrink in depth and take virtually any form. The thick limestone of the nineteenth century gave way to thin curtain walls perforated by wide windows. Flat glass became increasingly prominent: first in temporary exhibition spaces, shopping areas, and industrial monuments like Les Halles, and then in domestic architecture. More and more walls became see-through.[21]

With these material developments came a rhetorical and ideological framework that identified transparency in architecture as a moral good. One of the founding texts of the modern style was Adolf Loos's "Ornament and Crime," which, as the title suggests, framed architectural immediacy as a moral imperative. According to twentieth-century theorists, transparent walls would improve health by allowing the free circulation of light and air. They would expose secrets (of individuals, of architects, of governments). They would bring the private into the public sphere for scrutiny. Transparency is quintessentially modern, undoing previous regimes of space and time by bringing everything simultaneously into view. André Breton fantasizes in *Nadja* about living in a glass house filled with glass furniture. Extending the modernist idea that glass architecture transcends space and time, Breton imagines that the law of gravity will be transcended by glass. His furniture will "hang in the air as though by magic." Glass architecture's power to render things transparent is so strong that it can even realize the surrealist dream of opening the subconscious to conscious analysis. "Before long who I am will appear to me engraved in diamond."[22] Walter Benjamin, a frequent guest at the Pierre Chareau-designed Maison de Verre (Glass House),[23] wrote: "To live in a glass house is a revolutionary virtue par excellence. It is also an intoxication, a moral exhibitionism, that we badly need."[24]

Curtain walls and glass architecture were slow to make their impression on Paris. It was really not until the second half of the twentieth century that the rhetoric of transparency would find full-throated expression in the built environment.[25] Glass-wrapped skyscrapers began to appear in the 1960s—after the discovery of the wall written about by Brassaï, another indication that Brassaï was taking part in an ongoing contestation, and that if walls had been discovered in his lifetime, the discovery could still be undone—and transparent surfaces were a centerpiece of the design aesthetic of François Mitterrand's *grands projets* of the 1980s. I. M. Pei promised that the walls of the Louvre Pyramid would use the most transparent glass ever made. Dominique Perrault wrapped his Bibliothèque Nationale de France (BNF) in flat glass, declaring at the time: "I don't like walls, I like transparencies."[26] Mitterrand's embrace of glass used the moralizing rhetoric around glass architecture to political ends. The transparency of these walls symbolized transparency of government and transparent access to knowledge.[27] It stood for the purity of French democracy (and offered a retort to contemporaneous accusations of secrecy and corruption in the awarding of commissions for the *grands projets*). The walls of these buildings argued, as Anthony Vidler puts it, "that light and enlightenment, transparency and openness, permeability and social democracy are not only symbolized but also effected by glass."[28] These walls weren't supposed to be seen, but they still spoke.

Perrault's BNF makes a neat point of comparison with the situation in the nineteenth century, as the national library that it replaced was designed by Labrouste. Labrouste, in his Bibliothèque Sainte-Geneviève, attempted to make a narrative building that could be read like literature. Perrault's library relates to literature symbolically instead: its four towers are in the shape of books. Labrouste experimented with an audaciously plain façade that alluded to the building's interior. Perrault substituted a transparent one. With Labrouste, the rhetoric of transparency masked the true symbolic breadth of the building. For Perrault, transparency is the message itself.

But what makes Perrault's building such a revealing case study is that the rhetoric of transparency deployed by the architect does not match up with reality. The BNF's glass walls turned out to be a liability when the decision was made for the library's four towers to contain physical books instead of a digital archive. The glass let in too much light to properly conserve the texts. As a result, the architect had to revise his plans and install slats of wood behind every pane of glass. The transparent building became opaque. As Vidler notes, this inversion is not specific to this one building. It is a problem that no glass building has yet managed to overcome: "Literal transparency is [. . .] notoriously difficult (as Pei himself admitted) to attain; it quickly turns into obscurity (its apparent opposite) and reflectivity (its reversal)."[29] Transparency for transparency's sake: the building foregrounds its own invisibility, and in the process renders invisible everything it contains. In so doing it belies what Annette Fierro calls the "fundamental supposition" underlying the enlightened rhetoric around glass: namely, that it allows equal amounts of visibility from within and from without.[30]

What buildings like the BNF and Louvre Pyramid allow us to see is the fundamental mendacity of the architectural ideology of immediacy, of the notion that walls need to disappear so that we can have direct, unadulterated

Figure 3.5
Façadisme in progress. A nineteenth-century apartment façade is left untouched as the interior is gutted for transformation into modern offices

access to the spaces, institutions, and resources of the city. Vidler asks why, given the failure of transparent materials to live up to the ideology they embody, did Mitterrand invest so heavily in glass monuments? He marvels that "we are presented with the apparently strange notion of a public monumentality that is more than reticent—indeed wants literally to disappear, be invisible—even as it represents the full weight of the French state."[31] We could extend this question to the corporate monuments, the glass skyscrapers huddled like awkward adolescents at their first school dance in the western suburb of La Défense.[32] Or of the complementary practice of *façadisme*, where nineteenth-century buildings are gutted and refurbished on the interior but left with their limestone façades so as not to disturb the continuity of the street. Why do these enterprises hide behind their façades? Why do they not want to be seen for what they are by passersby?

Pierre Pinon blames *façadisme* on the lack of creativity of contemporary architects.[33] Vidler suggests that transparent monuments are a capitulation

Figure 3.6
Headquarters of the NSA in Fort Meade, MD, USA

to the difficulty of constructing "a state identity of technological modernity against a city identity (Paris, Chirac) enmeshed in the tricky historicism of preservation."[34] Fierro reaches the same conclusion: that glass monuments express a new national modesty, "a beguiling desire to disappear, rather than to assert France's mythic presence."[35] Taken together, however, the desire for invisibility evinced by the enterprises that hide behind old façades and the monuments that erase both themselves and their content suggests not a capitulation but the culmination of the process by which façades in Paris have transformed from an interface between interior and exterior, between public and private, between state and individual, into a tool meant to interrupt those links. I think we should read these buildings not as architecture's failure to incarnate "the full weight of the French state," but rather as ways of concealing power in the places where it is concentrated. These buildings are little different from the American National Security Agency headquarters in Fort Meade, Maryland, which is built of glass yet nevertheless manages to make America's intelligence center into a black box as literal as it is metaphorical.

The spread of this invisible architecture, especially when it is commissioned by those in power, thus poses a problem, and not just to architecture critics. These buildings represent the culmination of Hugo's failure to spot the message in the architecture of his time. They exploit people's inability to perceive their surfaces as mediatic in two ways. First, the buildings are able to broadcast messages of openness, democracy, tradition, etc., to people who, failing to see how the message is constructed, are liable to perceive it as natural or intrinsic to the city. A kind of subliminal messaging. Second, they allow the areas in which state power is most concentrated to efface themselves from both the landscape and the public consciousness. Drawing attention to the façades of these buildings is thus a political act. It makes the wall's messages liminal, and reveals the mechanisms through which the contents of these buildings become hidden. The potential import of Brassaï's "discovery of the wall" is thus revealed. If graffiti, as he says, allows us to see the mediaticity of the wall instead of being blinded by the glare of mirror glass, by a misleading feeling of immediacy, then graffiti performs an important political function. But how does graffiti do what Brassaï says it does, and what are its limitations?

Parisian Street Art and the "Discovery of the Wall"

Brassaï describes his encounter with graffiti thus:

> Primed and given a coat of paint, at the outset a wall presents a smooth, uniform surface. But hardly have the workmen left it than it falls prey to all sorts of destructive forces and is subjected to constant alteration. Like new wine aging, like wood seasoning, and like the earth itself since it was born, a wall has to "set." The elements soon get to work, attacking the roughcast that shrinks in frost, expands in the heat, swells in the damp. Wind, fumes, gas, and rain deposit soot and dust. The surface begins to flake, layers of paint peel off. Humidity occasions patches of rot and sometimes sprouts a world of vegetation. These at first almost invisible alterations spread quickly. Accidental scratches, a child's doodle, scribbles, an overenergetic brushstroke or two, a few bits of print rubbed out or painted over, some torn scraps of poster, and the "picture" [*tableau*] is finished.[36]

The wall starts as a flat surface, a mute channel, but over time it transforms. Nature works on the wall. But that is not enough to capture our attention.

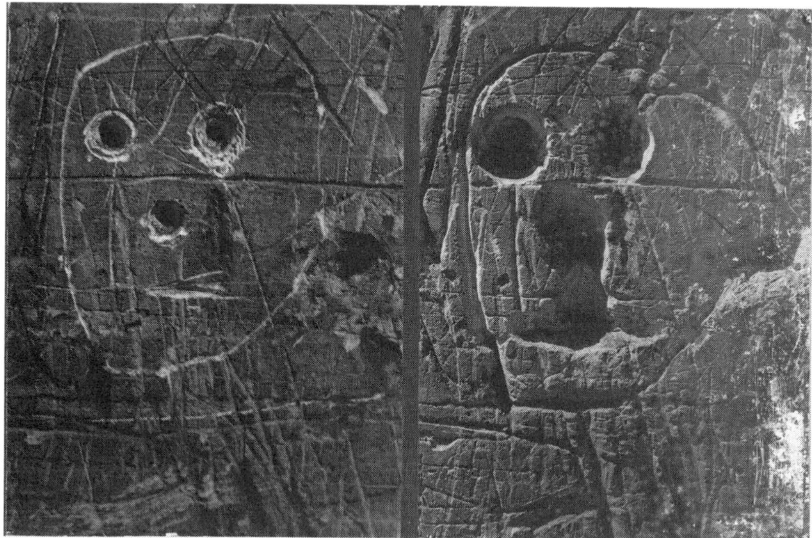

Figure 3.7
Montage of two faces. Graffiti, Brassaï, circa 1935–1950, Toulouse, Musée d'art moderne et contemporain, les Abattoirs, ©Estate Brassaï—RMN-Grand Palais

The wall becomes a tableau, an object for the eye, only when graffiti, posters, and other texts become superposed on it. In a discussion with Picasso, Brassaï will talk about the importance of photography in allowing one to see the wall.[37] Graffiti does not work its magic on its own; it works alongside other media to catch our eye, and then we suddenly see the cracks, the texture, the materiality of the wall. This is the reverse of what happens in Hugo's *Notre-Dame de Paris*, where the presence of other media causes the narrator to miss the wall itself.

One way to understand the process Brassaï describes is through Bolter and Grusin's notion of hypermediacy. Whereas in the logic of immediacy mediation effaces itself, so that we feel that we are in direct contact with the message, in hypermediacy multiple media clash and become layered. The result is "a heterogeneous space, in which representation is conceived of not as a window on to the world, but rather as 'windowed' itself." In such media environments, they argue, it is impossible to ignore the presence of the medium.[38] When a wall is covered with posters and painting and street signs and graffiti, it becomes impossible not to see that mediation is going on. Following this argument, what allows us to discover the wall as medium is not graffiti *per se*, but graffiti as one among many modes of mediation whose proliferation creates a hypermediatic space.

There are some elements of Brassaï's description, however, that do not match perfectly with Bolter and Grusin's description of hypermediacy. Why is Brassaï particularly interested in graffiti that lacks form? Why is he captivated by "accidental scratches" and "scribbles," in posters torn to shreds? Brassaï dedicates an entire section of his book to pieces where he can't tell if there is a message or not.[39] Hypermediacy is engendered by the nesting of multiple forms of mediation, but Brassaï seems to be more captivated by failed attempts at mediation. It's the loss of the signal that catches his attention. It's the noisiness of the wall that makes him notice this channel. It's the wall's parasites.

Figure 3.8
Illegible graffiti. Graffiti, Brassaï, circa 1935, Paris, Centre Pompidou, Musée national d'art moderne, Centre de création industrielle, ©Estate Brassaï—RMN-Grand Palais

Brassaï's description of his encounter with the wall comes closer to Serres's version of how immediacy is broken than to Bolter and Grusin's. Serres writes: "Given, two stations and a channel. They exchange messages. If the relation succeeds, if it is perfect, optimum, and immediate, it disappears as a relation. If it is there, if it exists, that means that it failed. It is only mediation. Relation is nonrelation. And that is what the parasite is."[40] When communication takes place without noise, the user experiences immediacy. The "relation" or medium disappears. But if parasites appear, if there is static in the channel, then the user's feeling of immediacy is broken and their attention is drawn to the medium. This is what happens to Brassaï. The breakdown of communication in the wall, the presence of torn posters and illegible signs, is what makes him alert to the channel itself.[41]

There is an echo here of Le Corbusier and his theorization of architectural immediacy. In *Toward an Architecture,* he writes: "it is the architect's task to bring the surfaces that envelop these volumes to life, without their becoming parasites that consume the volume and absorb it to their profit."[42] He returns to the word "parasite" later in the text, in his discussion of ornament. For Le Corbusier, the parasite is whatever in the wall detracts from the immediate experience of space and volume. Just as static on the phone reminds a listener that their interlocutor is not standing next to them, parasites in the wall break the illusion of immediacy and remind the viewer that they are not in direct contact with the volume of the building. Combining Brassaï's observation and Le Corbusier's warning, graffiti is a parasite that breaks the wall's illusion of immediacy and allows one to see how it mediates.

How do these dynamics play out in contemporary graffiti and in the vaguely defined movement of street art? Brassaï writes about graffiti in the literal sense: things engraved (*graffito*) in the wall. Commercial availability of aerosol paint in the 1960s transformed what most people thought of when they heard the word *graffiti.* When a Greek delivery boy in Manhattan began signing the alias Taki 183 (a reference to his address on 183rd Street) on buildings to which he had made deliveries, he set off a wave of spray-paint graffiti across New York. These tags evolved their own colorful and stylized alphabet, and graffiti became an important artistic subculture.

In the 1970s, spray-paint graffiti migrated to Paris, primarily thanks to young artists who had been inspired by visits to Manhattan. Blek le Rat was one such artist who blended serigraphic techniques he had learned

Figure 3.9
"Peek-a-boo," a characteristic work by Seth Globepainter. The painted boy looks into the wall. A young passerby is led by the work to look more closely at the wall with him

in art school with spray-paint writing. Other artists active in this period include Jef Aérosol, who was experimenting with the same methods as Blek in the city of Tours, and Jérôme Mesnager, who in 1982 co-founded Zig-Zag, a group of graffiti artists working in industrial zones on the outskirts of Paris. In 1983 Mesnager created "the white man," a design that has become an icon of Parisian street art. He has frequently collaborated with Némo, another Paris-based artist whose work began to appear in the mid-1980s and who has since become famous for a signature black-silhouetted figure. While Mesnager freehand-paints his work, Némo uses the stencil technique pioneered by Prou and Jef Aérosol. Speedy Graphito also came to prominence as a street artist in 1983, introducing a new language of advertising and pop-cultural imagery. 1985 marked the beginning of Miss.Tic's career. One of the few women street artists at the time, Miss.Tic became known for her use of wordplay to combat the objectification of women in the street.

In the decades since, spray-paint graffiti and street art have become ubiquitous in Paris, with new techniques introduced all the time: posters, mosaic, sculpture, bas-relief, pottery, photographs, augmented reality, origami, barcodes, poetry, glass, and object art.

The growth of street art poses questions about how to define it as a movement. While it is tempting to define street art as illegal, urban, and public, none of these terms is without exceptions. Artists are fined less today than they were in the 1980s, and many have done commissions for corporations and the municipal government, undermining the idea that street art has to be illegal. Projects like Djerbahood, a major street art exhibition in a village on the Tunisian island of Djerba, problematize the notion that this art has to be urban. And many street artists have done work indoors, in private areas, or in galleries. In my view these tensions and contradictions are what make the study of street art stimulating, and I am not especially interested in delineating between street art, mural art, land art, graffiti, etc. Street art is not a coherent movement with clear boundaries. With that said, too many exceptions risk making "street art" too vague a term to be useful, so I will offer the following working definition. I will use the term to refer to artistic and scriptorial interventions in Paris whose creators, at least sometimes, work in public and without official permission.

We come, then, to the key question: how does street art resist the transparency of the wall? If one prefers Bolter and Grusin's hypermediacy paradigm, there is much to work with. Whereas Brassaï describes the superposition of a fairly limited number of media (poster, engraving, paint), contemporary street art brings a much greater variety of media to bear on the wall. These multiply alongside one another, creating a hypermediatic experience that causes the viewer to look more closely at the wall, questioning how it mediates.

Or, using Serres's framework, we could think of street art as noise, as a contentless static that breaks the illusion of immediacy. JR's 2016 installation on the Louvre Pyramid is one example. By wrapping the pyramid in a poster bearing the image of the palace, JR carried out the disappearing act Pei promised when he declared his glass the most transparent ever. The artist has not added much to the channel—this is a view that is ostensibly always available. Instead, what JR has done is create a kind of glitch in the surface. He has frozen the view of the palace (made it static) and drained it of color. The pyramid disappears by becoming opaque. The black-and-white

Figure 3.10
Mosaic by Invader, woodcuts by GZUP, poster by Fred le Chevalier in the rue de Poitou

paper makes it stand out just as it is vanishing, and the vanishing itself is revealed to be a trick of perspective. JR shows that what we saw when we thought we were looking through the pyramid is actually a view generated by the surface of the pyramid. With this act of interference, he draws our attention to the ways in which transparency and opacity work alongside one another.

JR's intervention is somewhat exceptional, because it is on a monument and it was done with the museum's permission, but the same dynamic plays out in more quotidian ways all over the city. Glass walls are not the only ones aspiring to transparency. Mismatched party walls, noise barriers, temporary façades of buildings under construction, secluded alleyways: these are all walls we are not supposed to see. They try to disappear into the background. Party walls, though they are frequently long-tenured fixtures of a

Figure 3.11
2016 installation on the Louvre Pyramid from the front (above) and from an angle (below), by JR

street, are quintessentially transitional; they exist in anticipation of their erasure. The same is true of the plywood barriers placed around buildings under construction. In the Anglophone world, such walls are frequently marked with a sign saying "Watch this space," as though the sign is a mere film between the viewer and pure volume. It promises immediate access to space itself. Figure 3.12 shows a similar sign on a building under refurbishment next to the BHV (the Bazar de l'Hôtel de Ville) in Paris in 2017. The sign is a sloppy translation begotten by the French obsession with English marketing lingo, but it is also a pure expression of the logic of immediacy. What's coming is not just a concept store (what is a concept store anyway?) but a new concept. When this temporary barrier disappears, we will realize the dream of architectural immediacy: a city where we access concepts directly, never having to pass through mediation.

Walls like these that aspire to transparency are the ones where street art is most common. This is an ironic feature of their transparency. Graffiti's ability to survive and thrive on such surfaces is an example of how the police themselves are fooled by the lacunae produced by the hierarchies of visibility in the city. Considering one wall less significant than another, they are less attentive to these channels, and leave them open to be exploited by anyone. Some of the interventions have virtually no

Figure 3.12
Sign on a building being refurbished in the rue du Temple, photo by Ellen Iredale

content—one anonymous artist in Paris throws balloons filled with paint at walls—while others are more message-based. But as artists converge on a wall, tear down previous work, overwrite it, reinscribe it with their own, the wall gradually approaches what Brassaï describes: a pseudo-palimpsest of torn posters, illegible script, and obscure fragments. The encounter with this visual noisiness draws the pedestrian's attention to the channel, interrupting the transparency of the wall and making the viewer reckon with the mediaticity of the surfaces that surround him or her.

Theorists like Le Corbusier and Loos argued for a logic of immediacy in architecture, and warned against the parasites that would draw the viewer's eye to the wall. Street art operates as just such a parasite. Its chaotic proliferation on the walls in the city that most aspire to transparency creates a kind of visual static that allows the viewer to see the wall not as a container

Figure 3.13
A palimpsest of street art made of torn posters, illegible text, and paint

or support for other media, but as a medium in its own right. This parasitism can, as I suggested above, have political effects. It draws attention to invisible architecture, to power centers that use building façades as masks, and to the mechanisms by which these disappearing acts work. And it can also bring to the surface the subliminal messages that pass through these normally invisible channels of the city, opening up ideas like the moral purity of transparent buildings to contestation.

An extreme example of how relatively phatic street art can intervene politically in the city could be found in Cairo in 2012. A year earlier, on January 25, 2011, an estimated 50,000 protestors occupied Tahrir Square for the beginning of what would be known as the Egyptian Revolution. In the following months, protests continued to be held in the square. Images of those gatherings circulated internationally, becoming front-page news and spreading through social media. The enormous crowds became symbolic of the popular will, and precipitated the fall of President Hosni Mubarak. In March 2012, the military blockaded the square with imposing stone barricades to prevent large demonstrations and the startling images they produced. A group of artists responded. They painted the walls in a *trompe-l'œil* style to look like the streets they were blocking, an intervention that Mona Abaza compares to Banksy's use of *trompe l'œil* to "pierce" the West Bank barrier in 2005.[43] The street art gave Cairo's citizens the illusion that they could see through the walls, while reminding them that the walls were there and that access to Tahrir Square was being denied. Locked out of the media space of the square—with its promise of access to the front page of international newspapers—the artists fell back to the media space of the wall. Images of their work taken by Associated Press photographers were distributed to international news outlets. CBS ran one online alongside the headline: "Cairo artists sustain revolution with graffiti."

The Egyptian example is a hyperbolic version of the play between transparency and opacity that takes place throughout Paris and other cities on a regular basis. It speaks to a utopian side of street art and parasitism. It speaks to the potential of these noisy practices as ways of contesting urban space. Parasitism, of course, is not just a biological and mediatic term; there is always the social dimension, the question of who has a right to access a home, a meal, a property, a set of resources. The Cairo street art is one example of how graffiti and street art have been deployed within dissident movements around the world, and testifies to the wall's capacity to serve

Figure 3.14
"No Walls" street art outside Tahrir Square in Egypt, photo by Mosa'ab Elshamy

as a popular forum. Much of this political street art goes beyond the Cairo artists' clever play with transparency and opacity. It does more than break immediacy. It contains messages. It makes demands. Likewise, in Serres's media theory, drawing attention to channels is not the only function of parasites. In the next section I will examine the relationship between street art and the message.

Engaged Street Art in Paris

Not all of the walls in the city are transparent. Some walls make no secret of their capacity to transmit messages. Some messages, like advertisements and street signs, are officially permitted. More recently, architects have experimented with embedding LCD screens in the walls of buildings, digitizing the façade medium. The wall can transmit video. There is no need to draw attention to these channels, because the goal of these communication technologies is to assail the pedestrian's attention. But parasitism is not irrelevant here. If anything, its political utility is more obvious. Parasites don't just draw attention to mediation; they can also disrupt communication.

They can "prevent [a message] from being heard, and sometimes, from being sent," and they can "divert what is carried" so that what arrives at the receiver is not what was encoded by the emitter.[44] Street art can be parasitic by interfering with other messages carried by walls.

This dynamic is present in the work of Clet, a French artist who modifies street signs by overwriting them: for instance, turning the T of a dead-end street sign into the cross on which Jesus is crucified. Clet's work critiques the norms of "our 'common visual space'" and resists official signage's "highly invasive aesthetic." He states: "My adhesives are developed to add a further level of reading constructed on the base of [the sign's] original signification in order to maintain its utility but give it some intellectual, spiritual, or simply amusing interest."[45] The messages authorities mean to convey by these signs are transformed, and the sign ends up transmitting its own critique. ZEVS rose to prominence in the 1990s for his literal defacement of billboard advertisements, which involved blacking out models' eyes with spray paint. He coined the term "visual kidnapping" for his interventions: "If the brand on the billboard kidnaps the attention of the public with the purpose of consumer demand, I reverse the situation and I kidnap the model on the poster and I demand a ransom of 500,000€ from the brand. This sum represents the symbolic price of an advertising campaign for the brand."[46] It is common in Paris to find anticapitalist messages in marker or paint written on or next to advertisements in the street.

These interventions call to mind the famous law of July 29, 1881. Nominally, this law reestablished freedom of the press by annulling controversial censorship laws, but it also included provisions formalizing the government's power to police the walls of the city. Local mayors were allowed to designate walls for official proclamations and advertisements, and anyone found defacing such messages could be fined or imprisoned. The irony of this law is that the walls it protects are often designated as such with painted references to the law. Trying to prevent writing on the walls, they illustrate that such writing is possible. It is no surprise that walls bearing these signs attract street artists.

Street art can also undermine official messages in a more indirect way: by introducing so much noise to the channel that the signal becomes hard to discern. As texts and images multiply, the boundary between official and illicit blurs. Invader offers an instructive anecdote: once, while he was cementing one of his mosaics to a wall in Paris, he was yelled at by a police

Figure 3.15
A tag written over a No Posting sign, photo by Marc Olivier

officer. To avoid a fine, he pulled his mosaic down and tried to hide it. To his surprise, the officer called out: "Don't touch that mosaic, it's not yours, it's a municipal coat-of-arms!"[47] The officer stood by and watched while Invader cemented his street art to the wall. The authority charged with policing the wall, with ensuring that only state-approved messages appear on it, lost the signal amidst the noise.

Street art's flouting of restrictions on the wall and its ability to subvert official messages both speak to its potential as a dissident tool. Serres at times can be quite utopian about parasitism. Every channel, every system, is susceptible to parasitism. You can't keep it out. And you can't argue with parasites, because they use your own messages against you. Serres's reevaluation of the parasite engenders a revolution in which traditional power dynamics are thrown into chaos: "The parasite gets power less because he occupies the center than because he fills the environment."[48] This language is especially appealing in Paris, whose history has been dominated by a power imbalance between center and periphery. A whole host of oppressive hierarchies—center and *banlieue,* native and immigrant, enfranchised and disenfranchised—seem liable to unravel thanks to parasitism. But things are not so simple.

Serres opens *The Parasite* with Boursault's fable of the city rat and the country rat. The city rat invites his country bumpkin cousin over for dinner. Their feast will be the scraps left on the floor by the owner of the house, a tax collector. The rats are parasites of the man—another reminder that in ancient Greece a *parasitos* was a poor person allowed to eat at a rich man's feast. The man goes to bed, and the rats come out to play. The problem is that once they sit down to eat, they transform; they become *hôtes*, the French word meaning both host and guest. They themselves become liable to parasitism. Their mouths make a noise that wakens the man. He leaps out of bed and his feet thud on the floor, frightening the rats. He, too, is a noise-producing parasite (his day job as tax collector is also a kind of parasitism). What was initially a unidirectional relationship between one host and one parasite, between a man and a rat, becomes an intricately nested chain. A rat's nest of parasitic relations. The country rat parasites the city rat, the city rat parasites the man, the man spends his days working as a parasite for the king, and at night defends his home from the two rats by making noise (parasites). Whoever can stay parasite for longest will come out on top: "[The man] jumps behind those who were eating behind his back and chases them. The parasited one parasites the parasites. One of the first, he jumps to the last position. But the one in the last position wins the game."[49]

Parasitism is not a stable relationship but an open-ended chain. A parasite is always liable to become a host for someone else, and once it does it loses its advantage. The parasite must not speak on its own behalf. This is a problem for street art with a message. Around 2005, Blek le Rat took a break from stenciling rats to create life-size images of Paris's poor. Blek represents the homeless as stencils on the wall: they recede into the background, becoming part of the décor rather than participants in street life. As stencils, they are repeatable—almost literally stereotyped. The man in Figure 3.16 looks down, a hood veiling his face. At the same time, he is not a seated, passive beggar. He is upright, even leaning forward slightly, in a confrontational stance that demands attention. This image is less about making visible the wall as medium than making visible the city's homeless. Blek shifts from the mediatic meaning of parasitism to the social one, from making noise in the city to the question of who eats, who has a right to the

Figure 3.16
Stencil titled "the beggar" by Blek le Rat, photo by Lionel Belluteau, unoeilquitraine.fr

city's resources. However, while Blek may have gone from representing one kind of "parasite" to another, the artist's own status as parasite is lost. This piece has a message, challenging viewers to see the people in the streets from whom they normally avert their eyes, or whose presence in the street is criminalized. Blek is saying something; he is not just drawing attention to mediation anymore, or obfuscating someone else's message. He becomes an emitter, which makes him susceptible to parasitism. Other artists can overwrite his work and alter its message, preventing it from arriving at its destination in the form intended.

It is not just other artists who can interfere with the message of a work. As with Boursault's tax collector, the state can get in the game, too. Those who occupy centers of power can leave them and become parasites. Figure 3.17 shows a work by the artist SOBR, alongside an advertisement for Microsoft Surface. Microsoft has done multiple street-art-based advertising campaigns for the device, playing on the media-architectural metaphor

Figure 3.17
Microsoft Surface street-art-inspired advertisement alongside work by SOBR, rue des Francs-Bourgeois

that has been the company's signature since the release of Windows. In this image it is not clear which intervention is parasiting which. SOBR's images, created from photographs of young women dancing in nightclubs, are often accompanied by the declaration "It's time to dance!" Here that message has been reinscribed so that the woman appears to exclaim: "I love Surface." While it is not clear which of these two works came first, their juxtaposition undermines the carefree joy of SOBR's project by subordinating it to a corporate advertising campaign. The admittance of Microsoft into the discursive space of the wall, which is seemingly endorsed by the woman adopting Microsoft's slogan, confers a degree of countercultural cool on the company, potentially benefiting its public image and sales.

Earlier, I argued that street art can indirectly undermine official messages by masking the signal with noise and blurring the boundaries between official and illicit. This, too, can go both ways. The embrace of street art by the municipal government, which once sought to eradicate it, and its growing institutionalization and commercialization are further examples of this parasitic practice being parasited by the powerful. In 2015, when the *cadenas d'amour* or love locks were removed from the Pont des Arts, City Hall replaced them with murals by Jace, Brusk, El Seed, and Pantonio—four prominent street artists. El Seed also did a mural on the façade of the Institut du Monde Arabe. Artists like Jef Aérosol, Némo, Mosko et associés, and Jérôme Mesnager have done commissioned mural art. The government has endorsed exhibitions and major installations, like Tour 13, to promote Paris as a global destination for street art. It has given its permission for dedicated street art walls like the M.U.R. in the rue Oberkampf. Rather than trying to exterminate street art, the state hops to the end of the chain and uses it for its own ends.

At its heart, Serres's theory is agnostic about power. While one can find optimism in the idea that power is always circulating, that there is not a monodirectional relationship between an empowered and emplaced center and a disenfranchised periphery, Serres's work at times calls to mind biology's Red Queen Hypothesis, which summarizes the evolutionary relationship between host and parasite using the words Lewis Carroll's Red Queen says to Alice when she passes through the looking glass: "here [. . .] it takes all the running you can do, to keep in the same place."[50] Artists may identify as parasites, but being a parasite within a given communication framework requires constant adaptation. It means always being on the run. This is a problem for artists who set up shop, who assume a position of emission and populate the walls with their own messages, dissident though they might be. It ought also to serve as a warning for street artists who are no longer on the run from the police. French street art has from the beginning been more closely tied to traditional art institutions than the American graffiti that inspired it. Blek had formal training, as do many other street artists. An increasing number of galleries in Paris cater to street artists, and for many young artists, work in the street is a way to get publicity for more traditional gallery work. Invader states on his website that his work doesn't need to be "openly political," because it's *de facto* political by virtue of being illegal. That invites the question: what happens when it stops being illegal? What about the street artists who have literally set up shop by creating framed prints of their work and marketing it in galleries or displaying it in museums?

Following Serres, there is reason to be skeptical of both politically engaged street art and the growing institutionalization and commercialization of street art. However, that does not mean street art is purely entropic. I will now discuss a subset of Parisian street art which tries to avoid the trap of parasites that become hosts for other parasites.

Street Art as Quasi-Object

Toward the end of his text, Serres suggests that parasitism can be the basis for an alternate mode of subjectivity. He asks the reader to imagine a rondo, a circle of football players passing a ball. The ball, he says, is a quasi-object: object because it is acted on by the players, but quasi because possession of the ball confers subjectivity. This subjectivity comes with conditions. A player can experience it only by passing the ball, by surrendering the quasi-object. If someone were to hold the ball, to pick it up and go home, the game would be over and the power would lose its meaning. At no moment is the group in a state of perfect equality, but the power that comes with subjectivity is always in circulation. "Participation is the passing of the 'I' by passing. It is the abandon of my individuality or my being in a quasi-object that is there only to be circulated. It is rigorously the transubstantiation of being into relation. Being is abolished for the relation."[51] Serres says the best players of this game are the ones who defer to the ball, who use its momentum to send it on its way, not the ones who bring it to a stop and apply their own new impetus to it. The best players become relays, parasites who modulate the ball's movement, but don't control it.

We can observe something like this dynamic in the work of a group of French street artists who have tried to make their art into platforms for collective encounter and exchange. The first example is JR's Inside Out Project, which is funded by a $100,000 TED Grant. "A Group Action is when one or more people decide to create a project as a part of Inside Out. A Group Action uses 5 or more portraits (of different subjects) to convey a message of a cause that you are passionate about. The portraits will be printed as posters and displayed at a location of your choice."[52] Through logistical and financial support, the project reduces barriers to writing on the walls. JR himself does not produce messages, but instead creates a platform through which others are able to appropriate the wall. JR's infrastructure is a kind of quasi-object that a large number of players can seize and pass along. In 2011 JR set up photo booths in select cities to speed the process, allowing people to sit for a portrait and walk away with a poster a few minutes later.

A similar project is Julien de Casabianca's Outings Project. Rather than asking people to take a picture of themselves, Casabianca asks them to go into a local museum or art gallery and photograph one of the paintings. The painting must depict a nonfamous person. The participant then emails the photo to the artist with a fee, and receives a large-format poster with instructions for posting it. Again the goal is to reduce barriers to creating street art. In this case, the use of smartphones creates an experiential echo between street art and online visual media platforms.

The third example in this incomplete list of collective street art is "Umbrellas," organized by Le Mouvement. The artists stop random passersby and ask them to participate in a street art workshop. Those who are willing pose for a photograph, which the artists print at life-size on location. Le Mouvement then pairs participants and instructs them how to cut their silhouette out. Each person poses their image alongside their partner's to create an encounter. On their Facebook page they state: "It's important for us to bring people face to face with their own image and to democratize access to art. We work directly with Parisians." The artists try to involve people from different backgrounds, and during the creative process they push participants to discuss political questions.

These artists try not to position themselves as emitters with something to say. They try to create quasi-objects. They try to spark encounter via the wall, and allow people to partake in a subjectivity that is constantly circulating. The artists do not necessarily attain these goals. They all impose tight constraints on participants. Because of their position in the supply chain, they exert a degree of editorial oversight that means they never really lose control of the message. All three are guilty of problematically assimilating participants' contributions to simplistic metadiscourses about the importance of dialogue or representation in democracy (e.g., JR: "[Art is] a neutral place for exchanges and discussions and [that] enables it to change the world").[53] This devalues what participants do with the quasi-object, and allows the artist to sneak back into the position of emission. A truly parasitic street art platform would anonymize the artist even more, and allow for more transgressive and surprising ways of playing the quasi-object.

Nevertheless, it is important to acknowledge that projects like these open up access to the wall channel to new people. They might presage less strictly regimented platforms, or they might have some effervescent aftereffect. Perhaps participants are more likely to write on walls on their own after getting a taste for it in these structured settings.

Indeed, this possibility is something about which Brassaï himself fantasized. He believed that walls call out for collective appropriation: "A high wall throws down a challenge. Protecting property, defending order, it is a target for protest and insult, as well as for demands of every sexual, political, or social persuasion."[54] Walls dare you to write on them. He refers to the *emprise* of the wall, the hold it has on anyone who stands before it. *Emprise* is a loaded word. In French it describes a dark, almost supernatural influence, a spell cast over the mind. But it also has a bureaucratic meaning: it refers to the public expropriation of private space, and to the land on which transportation networks are built. Taking these together, it is as if the wall impels one to seize it as public property, to make it into the means by which the collective is held together. Not to *ap*-propriate it as a channel for personal expression, but to *ex*-propriate it as a popular forum.

This desire I am reading into Brassaï's phrasing, which is explicitly invoked by JR, has a long history. Alfred Delvau, who collected the thousands of political posters that appeared in Paris following the 1848 collapse of the French monarchy, described the walls of the city as "a collective work whose author is *Monseigneur tout le monde*," the everyman. (He also used parasitic language, calling the urge to write on the walls "a contagious disease.")[55] During the protests of May 1968, painted graffiti appeared all over the Left Bank. Many of the slogans called on the masses to start writing on the walls: "First, disobey; then write on the walls (Law of 10 May 1968)."[56] The mass expropriation of the wall was conceptualized not as a starting point for political speech but as a revolutionary act in its own right.

However, while many have fantasized about a popular coming-together in and through the wall, street art currently falls short of that universalist fantasy. This is not only because most people don't write on the walls, but because those who do don't represent everyone. Most street artists are men. There are exceptions. Miss.Tic, mentioned above, juxtaposes feminist wordplay with sexualized female bodies. Kashink creates gender-ambiguous faces with distorted features. Wild Wonder Woman's posters and stickers emphasize the breasts, genitalia, hair, and bodily functions of female bodies. Mars.L creates posters of the clitoris layered with classic works of art by men, most but not all of which represent the female body. Intra Larue attaches clay sculptures of her breasts to the walls. With the explicitly feminist themes of their work, these artists critique the violence and objectification many women experience in the streets of Paris, and the complicity of advertisers and the art world in that objectification. They also draw attention to the ways in which the absence of women from the city's streets as artists is linked to the hostility of the streets to women in general. Many of these women find their work is even more ephemeral than street art by men, more often torn down or written over. Intra Larue noticed that many of her pieces were disappearing, and was uncomfortable with the idea of people stealing casts of her breasts. She decided to use more fragile materials that shatter on contact.[57] The artistic proxy of the artist's body acts out the violence done to feminist art and the violence done to women's physical bodies in the street. Fear of the latter is often cited as a reason for the gender disparity in this discipline that traditionally requires artists to venture into dark corners of the city alone.[58]

One of the underlying principles of Serres's parasitic collective is that anyone can take part by making him- or herself available to the quasi-object. But just as in the sport of football, which he uses to illustrate his point, who gets to play is more complicated than that. The poor representation of women in street art belies the universalism Serres ascribes to his groups, and it is a reminder that the everyday politics of the street still matter in transgressive uses of it. It also offers a different perspective on street art's parasitism. The use of metaphors like plague and viral outbreak by street artists is an expression of the idea that the media politics of the wall is also a biopolitics. When street artists describe their work as parasitic, they situate themselves as antagonists to a certain thinking of the city as body politic. They resist a way of conceptualizing the city that marries hygiene and informatics, bodily purity and immediacy. But parasitism is not a stable identity. It is a fractal chain, where every parasite is in turn a host for something else. The gender bias in street art is one way in which this dynamic plays out. Within street art as a practice, another layer of hosting and parasitism takes place. Some bodies occupy the center, while others live at the margins.

Viral Media: Invader's Digital Street Art

There is one more dimension to the parasitism of walls that I would like to discuss: the growing virtualization of urban walls and their imbrication with digital technologies. In his conversation with Picasso, Brassaï declares that graffiti is more dependent on photography "than any other form of artistic endeavor." Picasso responds, "Without photos, graffiti exist, but it is as if they didn't exist."[59] These statements are too categorical, but there is some truth to them. Graffiti and street art have two primary limitations: they are ephemeral and immobile. Photography is a natural complement to them, bestowing a long life on the work and allowing it to circulate. The development in the past two decades of online image- sharing platforms like Flickr, Facebook/Instagram, and Urbacolors (the latter explicitly focused on street art) has reinforced and expanded photography's role in street art creation. Many artists have their own accounts on these sites, where they share their work. In a variety of ways, both subtle and obvious, their work is shaped by the hope that it will eventually circulate on these platforms. Some artists sign their work with hashtags, URLs, or Instagram screen names so viewers have an easier time finding the artist online, ensuring that they can connect any pictures they take to the right virtual communities. Others exploit technologies by which mobile phones interact with the physical world, like Quick Response (QR) codes and Augmented Reality (AR), to append hyperlinks to their work, taking the viewer directly to the artist's online profile (or online store). Artists try to entice pedestrians to take pictures by giving their images the ineffable quality of being "Instagrammable," for instance by making them fit comfortably within the platform's square aspect ratio. These techniques allow artists working in an intrinsically local medium to build global audiences, and they are another dimension of the mediaticity of the wall.[60] One French artist whose work engages in a critical way with the virtualization of urban walls is Invader, and he does so using a parasitic vocabulary. In this final section, I would like to examine how Invader's work exploits and problematizes the superposition of virtual and real that is occurring on the walls of contemporary Paris.

Invader is world-famous for his mosaics depicting characters from the 1970s arcade game *Space Invaders*. The mosaics range from the size of a human hand to big enough to be visible from a satellite. He has cemented them to walls in roughly eighty cities. One of the core concerns of Invader's work has always been the virtualization of the wall. In a 2011 interview he stated: "In this project there's the idea that we're bringing the virtual into reality."[61] But the superposition of real and virtual has never been a neutral or innocuous phenomenon for him. He has consistently framed his work as a virus.[62] The growing permeability of the barrier between real and virtual space allows for new forms of contagion.

Given the artist's video game imagery, it is fair to assume that Invader's virus is a computer virus—although, as Jussi Parikka argues, the "computer virus" is one example among many of a biological and epidemic lexicon being applied to the malfunctions of digital technologies, and a clear expression of Serres's central premise: that the parasite traverses the biological and the mediatic.[63] What is it about viruses that appeals to Invader? A biological virus is a strand of genetic material (a nucleic acid) surrounded by a protective sheath of protein. It propagates by infiltrating another cell and co-opting that cell's replicative system, either by inserting itself into the DNA of the host cell or by using the cell's protein transcription systems. It allows itself to be read, exploiting the universality of the genetic code. The cell makes copies of the virus until it breaks down, at which point the many copies are released into the environment to look for new hosts. A computer virus behaves similarly. It, too, is a bit of code that allows itself to be read by a host computer. In that act of being read, it can reproduce itself by commanding the computer to forward copies to new hosts, it can jam the system and cause it to break down, or it can give a third party illicit access to the host machine.

By calling his work a virus, Invader implies that it relates to the city in this way. His mosaics hijack the city, granting third parties illicit access to it. They glitch the city. Such effects are not unique to Invader. I have described numerous examples of street art glitching the wall medium or opening up that medium to new users. What makes Invader different is, first, his attention to the digital and to the virtualization of the wall, and second, his emphasis on the act of reading. Viruses, unlike other parasites, act on the host by allowing themselves to be read. Invader's work incorporates this dimension in creative ways and, in the process, critiques the viewer's role in street art.

Invader's work engages with the permeability of the barrier between virtual and real in several ways. He represents virtual characters using concrete materials like tile and cement. Figures familiar from a digital world appear in the real one. He plays on the visual similarity between the mosaic form and pixelization, using solid materials to reproduce the visual signature of electronic displays. But Invader's blending of real and virtual is not simply symbolic or representational. His mosaics are interfaces between digital technologies and the concrete. In 2008 Invader created a series of works based around QR codes—square matrix barcodes that can be read by cameras on mobile phones. The image stores text data that is outputted when it is scanned by a camera. The device will display a message, activate a hyperlink opening a website, or compose an email, depending on what information the code has been programmed with. These codes are a way to store digital information in a two-dimensional image. The form of these codes—black squares distributed on a white grid—is little different from the pixelated graphics of classic video games, and is just as easily reproduced using mosaic. Invader inscribed one of his Space Invader characters in the code grid as a signature. The result was a tile work that, when scanned by a smartphone, would reveal a digital message: for example, "this is an invasion," "nice art," "I love you," or "not for sale."

QR Code art was Invader's first step toward incorporating the reading of his work by hosts into the work itself. He took another with the release of his mobile app, Flash Invaders. The artist assigned point values from 10 to 50 to each of his works. These values and the location of each work are recorded in a database. When a user opens the app, the phone's camera is activated and a crosshair is overlaid on the screen. This simulates the reticule of a first-person shooter. The user is encouraged to use their camera to shoot the Space Invaders in the streets. Pressing the fire button takes a picture. The device's location is compared to the database, and if the photograph contains a Space Invader, the user is awarded the point value assigned to that work. Their total score is recorded in a global leader board, and their photograph is automatically uploaded to a digital gallery. The images uploaded to the gallery are displayed in a grid, another nod to the mosaic form. Players of Invader's game thus collectively produce a virtual metamosaic through their participation in the game. They become Invader's curators. More than that, they participate in the spread of the virus. They read the work using their devices, and in so doing they create copies that spread to other devices, other hosts, allowing the work to rapidly spread across the globe.

Invader's reinscription of photography and virtual sharing as the vector of his work's viral spread is also a commentary on the phrase *going viral*. Viruses are a popular contemporary metaphor for how texts spread through digital media. Jeff Hemsley and Robert Mason define virality as "a word-of-mouth-like cascade diffusion process wherein a message is actively forwarded from one person to others, within and between multiple weakly linked personal networks, resulting in a rapid geometric increase in the number of people who are exposed to the message."[64] The viewer or reader of a text is moved to share it with their circle, who read and share it in turn, allowing it to spread rapidly to large audiences. Many street artists hope their work will go viral by being shared on platforms like Instagram and Flickr. They hope the image of their work will trigger one of these cascades of sharing, allowing them to reach a large audience. Invader's game is a *mise en abîme* of the competition street artists constantly engage in for the attention of cameras and digital likes and shares.

The metaphorization of image-sharing as a virus implies a loss of agency for the viewer, who shares not as a rational choice but as a reflexive response, like sneezing. While one might aspire for one's text to go viral (and while marketing firms have done a great deal of research to find out how to ensure their texts go viral), the term usually implies a degree of randomness, as if the network determines what goes viral, not the author or readers. This terminology reflects the long-standing anxiety (see Derrida's essay on Plato's *pharmakon*)[65] that media are disease agents, that they infect their users and diminish their autonomy, that author and reader do not master the message but are instead manipulated by it. Invader's interrogation of virality puts a digital spin on the questions of agency and collectivism identified above with regard to Serres's quasi-object. The spreaders of viral media are, like the players in Serres's ball game, less subjects than relays for a text that circulates among them. (Invader has also, like JR, Julien de Casabianca, and Le Mouvement, encouraged his fans to create their own Space Invaders, and at one point he sold "invasion kits" containing everything needed to do so.) The players of Invader's game experience this liminal state between subjectivity and objectivity. They point the camera, but when they press "fire" their device is co-opted for the artist's purposes.

By foregrounding the issues with agency that emerge in the viral spread of street art, Invader draws attention to the mutually parasitic relationship between street artists and their audience. He also (more inadvertently) draws attention to another problematic loss of agency that both artists and their audiences experience: that effected by surveillance. When users of Invader's app take a picture of one of his mosaics, their device transmits their GPS coordinates to the artist. That data can be used to create maps. Early in his career, Invader published invasion maps in book or paper form, guiding his fans to his work.[66] In Montpellier he positioned his mosaics in the streets in such a way that when viewed on a map they would produce a dotted outline of a Space Invader. The paper maps played with the relationship between the city as it is experienced on foot and the city as it is represented and mediatized. But these were created using data the artist collected himself by hand. The spread of computerized tools for mapping has allowed the artist to digitize his maps (another form of virtualization), but in turning to these tools Invader has opened his work up to appropriation by surveillant corporations. To the extent that they rely on platforms like Facebook/Instagram to spread their work, this is something all street artists are forced to grapple with.

Invader's website, which has an old-school appearance evoking the graphics of the games he references and the halcyon days of GeoCities,[67] has a page entitled "World Invasion." Here we find a global map. Each city the artist has tagged is represented with a red Space Invader. Clicking on one brings up photographs of selected works in that city and statistics about the total number of pieces the artist has done there. In the bottom corner we read that the map is produced using a Google platform. The icons resemble those used by Google to identify points of interest on its mapping service. Invader wipes all of the icons for businesses and restaurants off the earth and replaces them with his own icons. He invades the map, just as he has invaded cities. Invader's installation at the offices of the newspaper *Libération* adds another dimension to this invasion of cartography. The offices are housed in the upper floors of a repurposed parking garage. The building's opaque concrete-and-glass façade betrays its previous purpose and makes it stand out in the rue Béranger, though its roof line matches

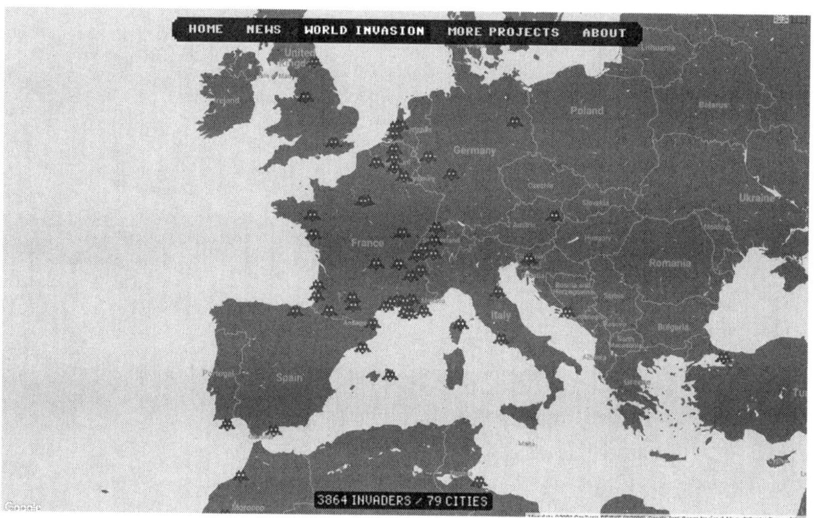

Figure 3.18
Invader's "World Invasion" map, https://www.space-invaders.com/world

the Haussmannian façades on either side, evincing a desire to blend into the surroundings. It is a strange example of *façadisme*. Invader plays on the disconnect between the frontage of a parking lot and the interior of a media empire with a work invisible from the street. His mosaic covers the roof and is large enough to be seen by satellite. The only way for most people to see it is by using a medium like the satellite view on Google Maps. (Invader also sent a mosaic to the International Space Station, a literalization of the Space Invader name and a symbolic invasion of the extraterrestrial satellites this installation relies on.) At a certain level of zoom, the bright red-and-white mosaic functions like the red icons on the artist's world map or Google's multicolored balloons that mark businesses and restaurants. The artist invades Google's map again, but this time by using analogue means to imitate a digital icon.

In some respects, Invader is parasiting Google, but as is the case with Microsoft's street art advertisements, the relationship is not a stable one. Using a Google map platform to track his work means sharing his location data with the corporation. They in turn parasite him. Search for Invader on Google Maps and several red balloons tagging the artist's work as tourist attractions appear, the same icons whose bias toward the commercial the

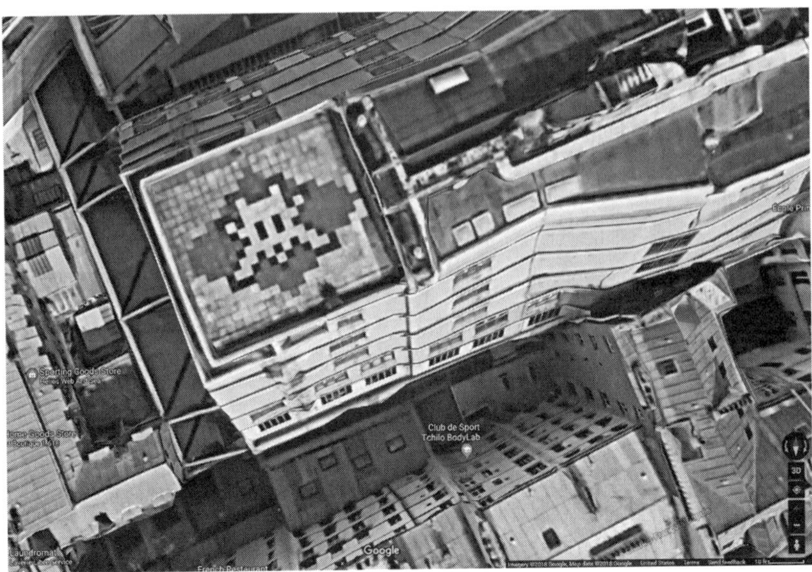

Figure 3.19
Roof of *Libération* by Invader, rue Béranger, viewed in Google Maps

artist undermined with his rewritten map. The corporate advertising platform is able to assimilate Invader's work into its economic vision of the city.

Invader's dependence on Google and his exploitation by them is no different from street artists' broader dependence on corporate image-sharing platforms. Artists rely on multinational corporations for the documentation and dissemination of their work. Each image uploaded carries with it data about the artist's movements and those of his or her audience. Street art as a whole is forced by its reliance on these platforms to participate in a global data economy that monetizes attention and movement: what Shoshana Zuboff terms "behavioral surplus." Street art becomes, like the other imageable parts of the city, part of "a living tourist brochure, surveillance target, and strip mine, an object for universal inspection and commercial expropriation."[68] Street art's institutionalization and commercialization is thus not only effected by galleries, auction houses, and corporate sponsorships; it also takes place in invisible ways through the digital platforms that allow this art to circulate.

Invader's attentiveness to the effects of these technologies and the corporations that oversee them raises more questions about street art's limitations as a dissident or even resistant artform. It also gives us cause to examine the relationship between parasitism and mapping in greater depth. Panoptic mapping technologies are data-driven. They transform information and mediate the city. They are therefore presumably susceptible to parasitism. In chapter 4 I will ask what role noise can play in disrupting surveillant technologies. To what extent can a body's movement through the city be a form of parasitism, and what other parasites take advantage of those bodies in turn?

4 Street

In his memoirs, published around the time of his death in 1891, Haussmann recounts an origin myth for his project to reconstruct Paris. Eighteen months after the coup of 1851, he was invited to a meeting with Napoleon III. "The Emperor," he says, "was in a hurry to show me a map of Paris on which he had himself traced in blue, red, yellow, and green, according to their level of urgency, lines representing the new streets he wanted to create."[1] This map would be the prefect's guide for the next eighteen years. Haussmann's story carries a lot of ideological subtext. The fact that this is a single map of Paris rather than several maps of its neighborhoods foreshadows the prefect's holistic approach to the city. The color-coding says that this was a long-term project with a clear plan. The authority he ascribes to the map as document foreshadows the bureaucratic approach he would take to urban renewal. It also signals the priority he would give to geometric regularity, to his doctrine of the straight line; any edifice touched by one of the lines on this map would have to come down, regardless of how that affected the people living in and around it. Lastly, with the detail that the Emperor has drawn the lines in his own hand, Haussmann implies that this was neither his own vanity project nor the product of an indifferent bureaucracy. He gives a personal touch to Haussmannization while shifting responsibility from the prefect—who had been criticized for overstepping his authority—to the leader of the country.

This story communicates a lot about how Haussmann wanted his work to be perceived. But it also tells us more than that, because in order for this anecdote to make sense, certain ideas about mapping and government authority had to be already in place. These ideas began to be formulated at the end of the eighteenth century, and were developed and codified into law in the decades preceding Haussmann's rise to power. As Min Kyung Lee describes, it was in 1783 that the French government established that a line drawn by a government official on the map of the city could carry legal authority, articulating for the first time a relationship between urban planning and cartography. In 1807, the Paris building council resolved to create a map of road alignments, setting up the map as the key "mediator between public and private interests when it came to the management and construction of space." Three years later this mediating function was expanded in the law establishing eminent domain, as the government promised to publish a map whenever it seized private property. In 1815 it put into writing a standardized visual vocabulary for maps, with a clear system of color-coding. An 1837 law required buildings to match their plans. The map went from being descriptive to prescriptive; the city had to match it instead of the reverse.[2]

These laws are the back story to Haussmann's mythic master map, drawn in the head-of-state's own hand, which he as prefect would have to obey and to which the city would be forced to conform. The laws testify not only to the growing reliance by the state on cartography, but also to the growing power of a certain kind of cartographic thinking. Gilles Palsky has argued that maps in this period shifted from ways of documenting a view—the *carte spectacle*—to tools for navigating and managing space.[3] The adoption of orthographic perspectives and the standardization of cartography's visual vocabulary indicate that these maps were being drawn not for the pleasure of an individual but instead for the use of the bureaucracy. City maps no longer attempted to simulate a human gaze.[4] They became diagrammatic. In Lee's terms, this reflected "a growing culture of diagrams and an appreciation of quantitative representations and methodologies." The evolution of cartography was closely intertwined with the emergence of the science of statistics. Governance increasingly depended on data collection and processing, and maps became tools for condensing and visualizing data about the city. They were both "products and productive of urban knowledge for the administration."[5]

This knowledge was not just about the landscape or the built environment. It also concerned people. These maps had a surveillant function. Alongside initiatives like the numbering of buildings (ordered by Napoleon I in 1805) and the division of the country into cadasters,[6] cartography provided the state with knowledge about the location, identities, and movements of its citizens, and allowed the state to interpellate them individually if necessary (e.g., for policing or taxation). Maps brought both the city and its people into view.

If Haussmann's master map was a tool for the exercise of state power, it was also the expression of an ideal. If the city could be made to correspond to the map, then it would take in all of the latter's virtues: abstract purity, rationalism, cleanliness. A city that could be fully visualized would be whole in a way it had never been before. A map could give Paris clear boundaries and a clear identity. Mapping was thus not just a statement of what the city was or what it would be; it was a statement of what it should be. And yet, as Lee argues, the very proliferation of maps in this period goes against this cartographic idealism. The need to constantly produce maps implies that each map was deficient in some way, that no single map was capable of fully representing the city. Each new map was proof that there was some knowledge about the city that the state had yet to acquire. The fact that the Paris building council frequently requested in-person site visits to settle disputes over maps suggests that there was some knowledge about the city that maps could never provide.[7] There was a persistent gap between the city as it was mediated through these technologies and the city as it was experienced "on the ground."

In "On Rigor in Science," Borges describes a map that reproduces a country at 1:1 scale. Never unfurled, because to do so would block out the sun and plunge the land into obscurity, this map is the exception that proves the rule: a map is never equivalent to the territory it represents.[8] It is interesting in this regard to compare Haussmann's master map, in which Paris is rendered as lines, to a map Invader included in the second volume of his *Invasion Guide to Paris*. He calls it the "Minimal Map of the Invasion." On it, in red and green color-coded icons, are depicted the locations of the first thousand mosaics he affixed to the walls of the city. Missing from this map are all of the lines that appear on Haussmann's. There are a few monuments, yes—difficult to identify from their simple outlines—but there are no roads, no transportation networks. No lines, only dots. The city fades away, like the atmosphere at night, to reveal the immense constellation of Space Invaders. The streets have been devoured by parasites.

Invader's map provides the location of each one of his works in Paris. But, omitting the streets, it does not show how to get to them. Location without direction, visibility without accessibility. Ordered and abstracted,

Figure 4.1
Detail from Invader's "Minimal Map of the Invasion"

the Paris shown in this map is nevertheless difficult to navigate. For Invader, the confusion produced by this illegible map is part of the work. It is only by walking the streets that the icons on the map can be inscribed into a network. In his invasion of San Diego, part of the Viva la Revolución exhibit organized by the San Diego Museum of Contemporary Art in 2010, Invader complemented his mosaics with GPS-based directions for a walking tour whose course traced a Space Invader on the grid of the city streets. The pedestrian becomes a stylus inscribing a new, ephemeral work on the map. In Montpellier, Invader placed mosaics in the city so that they traced

Figure 4.2
Aerial View of San Diego Walking Tour by Invader

the dotted outline of a Space Invader on the map. The artwork emerges in the tension between global and local, cartographic and pedestrian, virtual and real.

Invader is by no means alone in his interest in this tension. The uneasy relationship between cartography and the city has been a major point of interrogation for artists and writers in Paris since the end of the Second World War. Artists have resisted cartography's deployment as a tool for surveillance, and questioned what biases underlie the gap between what maps make visible and what they don't. They have proposed other ways of mediating the city streets. Battle lines have been drawn—or rather, the right to draw lines has become a battle. In this chapter I will approach the question of the gap between cartography and the city through the lens of parasitism. The fact that maps mediate the city in imperfect ways is not surprising, given my discussion of the relationship between noise and media. But noisiness is not the only way in which the discourse of parasitism concerns cartography. Many of the artistic practices I have alluded to place the body at the center of their interrogation of cartography, inviting a deeper reflection on the relationship between the media that visualize urban space and the biopolitics of the streets.

What the Map Doesn't Show: Postwar Challenges to Cartography

Paul-Henry Chombart de Lauwe was a great admirer of aerial photography. His first book was a guide to the practice, and he was deeply moved by the new perspective it offered on the ground below. The title of his book, *La Découverte aérienne du monde*, echoes the "découverte du mur" or discovery of the wall attributed by Brassaï to graffiti artists. For Chombart de Lauwe, to see the world from above was to see it for the first time. He was also a sociologist. When France began to come to terms with its housing shortage in the aftermath of the Second World War, Chombart de Lauwe applied his techniques to the problem of urbanism. This led to his second book, *Paris et l'agglomération parisienne* (1952), the work for which he is best known. His application of aerial photography to urban planning had its roots in Le Corbusier, who had already used aerial photos in his documentation supporting the Plan Voisin and the Ville Radieuse.[9] "For Le Corbusier," Anthony Vidler writes, "only an aerial photograph reveals the whole truth, shows what is invisible from ground level."[10] Chombart de Lauwe complemented his pictures with maps and statistics, creating a mathematical view of the city and its citizenry. He mapped the distribution of Renault factory workers and the voting patterns of the city's districts. Most famous of all was a map the author attributes to a Monsieur Alibert tracing the movements through Paris of a young girl over the course of one year.

Chombart de Lauwe gives little background on his researcher, Alibert, or the methodology behind the map. It is not clear how the girl was tracked. She is not identified, except through what we would now call her metadata. Chombart de Lauwe identifies the three nodes on the map where she spends the most time: the École des Sciences Politiques in the 7th arrondissement, where she is a student (roughly the center of figure 4.3), the home of her piano teacher in the 8th arrondissement (the top of the triangle), and her own residence in the 16th arrondissement. The author tells us that the map epitomizes what the view from above can reveal that the view from the ground cannot. It sadly shows "the narrowness of the Paris in which each individual actually lives."[11] The narrowness to which Chombart de Lauwe refers is not just a spatial narrowness. It is also economic and experiential.

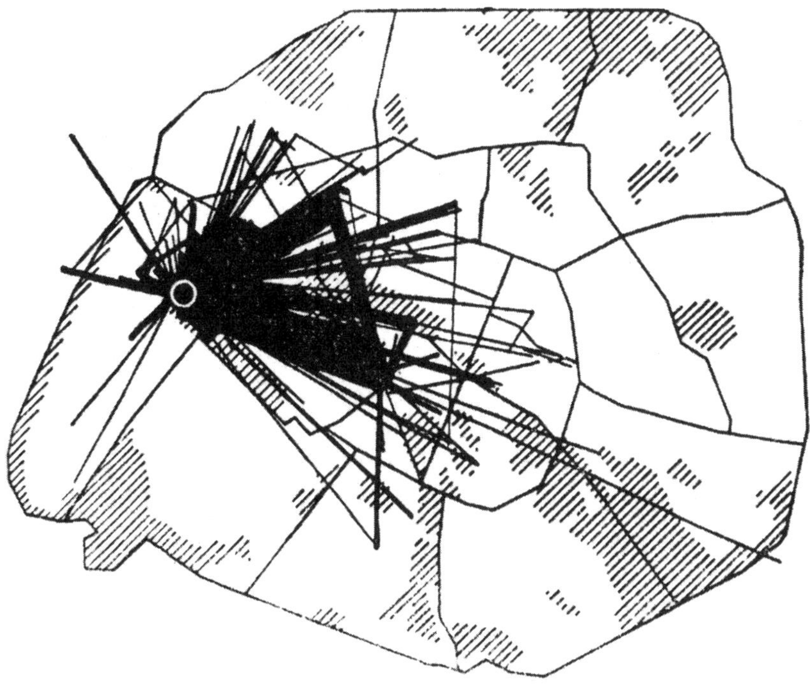

Figure 4.3
Map from *Paris et l'agglomération parisienne* (PUF, 1952) showing a young woman's movements in Paris over one year

The 16th arrondissement is one of Paris's richest, most aristocratic, and most conservative. This map comes only a few pages after one depicting the concentration of the working class in the east of Paris. The reader is thus encouraged to take this young girl as emblematic of the failure of different classes to mix in the city. This is an example of what Éric Hazan has called Paris's "invisible apartheid," which I discussed in chapter 2.[12]

An anonymous person's movements are plotted on a map of the city. The sites most frequented are identified, and a persona is extrapolated from them. It is notable that Chombart de Lauwe specifies that the subject is a young girl. The Parisian city walker is, by tradition, a male figure, from Rétif de la Bretonne in the eighteenth century to Charles Baudelaire and the nineteenth-century *flâneur* to Louis Aragon and the surrealists in the twentieth. Women who walk the streets have historically been less subject than object, submitted to a variety of male gazes—the catcaller, the stalker, the artistic genius (Breton's *Nadja*). This girl is not the author of this map; it is produced by a (named) man who watches her, records her movements, and submits them to public judgment. This is precisely the dynamic parodied and inverted by Sophie Calle in works like *Suite vénitienne* and *L'Ombre*. The gendering of urban space is a question that came up at the end of chapter 3, and it will recur throughout this one. Already this is an example of how the body enters into cartographic mediations of the city.

The gender politics of the map did not cross Chombart de Lauwe's mind. Nor are they discussed by Guy Debord, who referenced the map in his essay establishing the principles of the *dérive*. Debord was the leader of Letterist International, an offshoot of the surrealist circle, and its successor group, Situationist International (SI). Debord's group formed in 1957. It brought together writers, philosophers, and urbanists critical of what they perceived as the growing commodification and atomization of urban life. Debord was "indignant" that anyone could live like the young woman in Chombart de Lauwe's map. He believed that her claustration was being fostered by postwar urban planning policy. He and his group proposed *la dérive* (the "drift") as a response. The *dérive*, partly inspired by the surrealists' random walks and by *flânerie*, was conceived of as a mode of research into the urban subconscious. After placing themselves in a state of heightened suggestibility (often with alcohol), the situationist researchers would roam the city, allowing themselves to be moved by its subliminal attractions and repulsions. By noting the trajectories that resulted, they would be able to identify Paris's hidden frontiers. They could measure "the distances that actually separate two areas of a city, and which are nothing like what the approximative perspective of a map would have you believe."[13]

SI had a visceral hatred for Le Corbusier, and Debord opposes the Corbusian valorization of the top–down view when he attributes to it only an "approximate perspective." However, cartography and aerial views were not really anathema to SI. They complemented the *dérive*. "One can, with the aid of old maps, aerial photographs, and experimental *dérives*, create a cartography of influences that has so far been lacking." The final product of the *dérive* was the psychogeographic map, a collage of maps where the city was blown apart and reconstituted. Arrows of greater or lesser size represented the gaps in the urban tissue and the tenuous processes by which they could be crossed. The hope of SI was that these maps would do the opposite of what a map normally does. Rather than establish frontiers within space so that it could be understood, the psychogeographic map would be the battle map for a concerted assault on the city's subconscious boundaries, ultimately leading to a city that could be experienced in a permanent state of aimlessness, a muddled space apprehended affectively.[14]

However, the *dérive* had its problems. The first of these was that a psychogeographic map necessitated multiple points of view—otherwise it would not be possible to say whether an individual was producing a map of his or her own psychological limits or those of the city. SI tried to combat this danger by performing *dérives* in groups, but the groups were logistically limited: "Above four or five participants the *dérive* starts to lose its special character, and in any case it's impossible to go beyond about ten people without the *dérive* splitting into multiple simultaneous *dérives*."[15] Mapping on the scale the situationists imagined, a map capable of transforming the city, would require many independent practitioners. SI called this "unitary urbanism," a movement in which everyone would become an urbanist.

SI believed that play could encourage unitary urbanism. They argued for play—not as a synonym for leisure, restricted to certain moments of the day and encroached upon ever more by the imperative to work, but as the dominant mode of life. The labyrinth became a recurring architectural motif in their writing, and Ivan Chtcheglov (writing under the pseudonym Gilles Ivain) reinforced the connection between architecture and games when he wrote: "This need for *absolute* creation has always been closely linked to the need to *play* with architecture, time, and space."[16] In texts like "Projets d'embelissements rationnels de la ville de Paris," SI made urban planning into a parlor game. The text records the group's half-serious ideas for urban renewal, including: all museums should be destroyed, and their artworks redistributed to bars; prisons should offer a lottery to win a month-long sentence (a game they hoped might appeal to spelunkers and other people who take unnecessary risks); and underground areas should be opened to exploration.[17]

Despite these efforts, the *dérive* failed to achieve the potential dreamed of by SI. There are a few obvious reasons why this happened. The first is the contradiction between the need for new practitioners and the authoritarian dominance exerted by Debord over his group. Debord was famously fickle; SI experienced a number of ideological purges and acrid public excommunications of sympathizers like Henri Lefebvre. This was problematic not only because it reduced the number of proponents of SI's ideas; it also reflected and reinforced Debord's insistence on a top–down, centralized form of community. Debord's exertion of ideological control inhibited the spread of his group's game by restricting how other players were able to personalize and adapt its rules. This resistance to reappropriation and evolution—ironic given the group's advocacy elsewhere of *détournement*, or the modification of an existing text in order to critique the message the text was originally meant to communicate—ultimately resulted in the *dérive* struggling to attract practitioners not already affiliated with the group. It never achieved the universality key to unitary urbanism.

The project to psychogeographically map Paris, whose purpose was to transcend social boundaries within the city, itself remained within a small group of like-minded thinkers. It was a victim of the boundaries it sought to overcome. The project nevertheless showed a willingness to confront a problem intrinsic to mapping that cartography had historically elided. Chombart de Lauwe's aerial images present the cartographer as a figure detached from the city, hovering in midair. They argue that cartography involves taking up a position outside the city—and, by extension, outside the group of people who inhabit it—in order to obtain a totalizing view. SI places the cartographer at the heart of the space and community he or she hopes to represent. The mapper is not exempt from the psychological and social limits of the city. In its essence, SI's argument is that any attempt to represent the city must first come to terms with these limits. Failing to do so leads to maps whose borders are, in some way, already predefined. The dream of unitary urbanism is a kind of limit toward which cartography ought to tend: a total map of the city demands that every person in it enter into the cartographic community.

SI's implicit argument is that the practice of representing the city is inextricable from the constitution of a collective within it. The relation between these two elements has been taken up in recent years by a number of authors and artists. Their works are distinguished from SI's in two ways: first, rather than attempting to walk at random, allowing subconscious forces to dictate their trajectory, these projects adopt a mathematical imperative that they use to structure movement through the city. One of the first to articulate this new method was, unsurprisingly, an Oulipian: Jacques Roubaud.[18] He writes: "I have an acute taste for *obligatory routes* whose itinerary is unpredictable insofar as I've never travelled it, but which becomes nevertheless necessary as soon as I've selected the rule or rules that will guide my steps. These rules can be very constraining, absurd, bizarre; limiting myself to the city, I can decide to move forward only along streets with place-names, for example."[19] Joshua Armstrong calls these "empiritexts" to capture the methodical and observational rigor their authors bring to urban writing.[20] Second, these projects all involve supplementing or opposing the map with other media—writing, photography, and video, among others. But like SI, these projects seek to reveal the hidden barriers of the city, and to test their durability.

Jacques Réda and the Imprecision of the Map

As an explorer of Paris, Jacques Réda normally has little in common with Roubaud. Réda expresses skepticism in *La Liberté des rues* about the mathematical mode of urban exploration promoted by his contemporary. "Many people lock themselves into the small magic of algorithmic or stochastic walks which give them nothing more than the illusion of control or of knowledge of their situation."[21] Réda aligns himself with the *flâneur*, the nineteenth-century figure of curious and desultory urban wandering. The *flâneur* was declared one of the icons of Parisian modernity by Charles Baudelaire—a position later echoed by Walter Benjamin. *Flâneurs*, who moved through the city at the pace of a tortoise,[22] were the best-placed observers of modern life owing to their ability to be simultaneously part of the crowd and at a remove from it, within the whirlpool of the boulevard but too deliberate to be swept up by it. From this position they could study the new aesthetic paradigms being put in place by mass urbanization, commercialization, and modernization.

Réda is an inheritor of the *flâneur*'s legacy. The larger part of his *œuvre* is devoted to descriptions of his explorations of Paris. Like the *flâneur*, he presents himself as an outsider detached from the crowd, able to observe it in a pseudo-empirical manner. He describes Paris as a text that can be understood through poetic rewritings, echoing the importance Baudelaire accords to poetry in the *flâneur*'s practice. Réda's most explicit invocation of Baudelaire's legacy is his adoption of the prose poem in his book *Les Ruines de Paris*. This same form was pioneered by Baudelaire as a way of capturing Parisian street life. As Federico Castigliano and Filippo Zanghi have both noted, the fact that Réda writes almost exclusively about Paris and its suburbs when he writes about the city is its own form of allusion to Paris's status as the "capital of the nineteenth century," the incubator of *flânerie*.[23]

Réda is one of the closest modern analogues to the unconstrained strollers who let their whims lead them through Baudelaire's Paris. In 1997, however, he dabbled with another approach. He assigned himself a constraint, setting out to follow the Paris Meridian from the north of the city to the south. His project was similar to the urban walks organized by the art group Ici-même in the early 1990s, where participants followed a straight line across the city as closely as possible, but whereas Ici-même's were drawn arbitrarily, Réda chose one with historical significance.[24] The Paris meridian was created in the seventeenth century and defined to pass through the Paris Observatory (completed in 1671). It was the reference point that made possible the Cassini family's map of France, commissioned by Louis XIV in 1679, an immense project that would be revisited by generations of family members until 1815.[25] The establishment of the meridian, which at the time was internationally recognized as the prime meridian, made Paris the mathematical center of the world. Réda attempts to follow this invisible line, relying on its unexpectedly material traces: a series of bronze plaques embedded in the pavement along the meridian's path, an art installation created by Jan Dibbets in 1994 as a tribute to the astronomer François Arago. Réda documented his experience in a book, *Le Méridien de Paris*.

The Paris meridian both expressed and enabled abstract, geometric thinking about space, and it was a precursor to the rationalization urban cartography would undergo in France in the nineteenth century. The mapping projects that took it as their reference point over time became increasingly mathematical in their approach. During the French Revolution, for example, Abbé Sieyès proposed redrawing the borders of the country's districts by tracing a geometric tessellation on one of the Cassini maps.[26] Rationalism took precedence over geography or local identity. Now, while he is interested in this geometric spirit, Réda's attempt to reproduce the meridian by following it "on-the-ground" puts it to the test, because it is precisely this subjective and embodied knowledge of space that the abstract approach to mapping denies.

Despite possessing a map of the plaques and a detailed guide to finding them, Réda repeatedly gets lost. He learns that regardless of the quality of the map, one only ever finds what one is looking for by accident. The documents he uses demonstrate their own disquieting lack of precision.

His guide lists the total number of plaques as 122 in one place and 135 in another, but it gives instructions for finding only 121. Réda himself finds between 75 and 80, and he can never get the same number when he tallies them up. In various ways the day-to-day life of the city prevents him from putting his map to use. In some places where the sidewalk has been repaved, Réda notes that a plaque has been replaced in the wrong orientation, such that the north–south line engraved on it no longer points in the right direction. He suspects that some of the plaques removed for road work were never replaced at all. Weather is another complication, as snow and ice make some plaques almost invisible. Traffic prevents him from accessing other plaques. As Jean-François Rémy Duclos puts it, "we find ourselves in a situation familiar to anyone who has tried to find their way with a map: getting lost because the 'text' and our reading of it are never exactly the same."[27]

For Duclos, the problem is a fundamental one, intrinsic to the meridian itself. The meridian is an artifice constructed to render space geometrical, but by this same token it is alien to the earth whose surface it purports to traverse. The meridian does not and cannot exist in the real world, any more than a perfect sphere or a line without width could. And yet its utility relies on its inscription in real space by land surveyors (whose work, Réda points out, is similar to his own project).[28] Duclos reads Dibbets's installation as enacting this paradoxical quality by inverting the relation between cartographic artifice and terrain: "lines that are supposed to be used for the abstract calculation of positions appear on the ground [and that] upsets the relationship between map and terrain."[29] By embedding the meridian in the ground, Dibbets makes the meridian "real," but strips it of its practical utility. There is no point of view from which one could view the plaques all at once, or even see more than one at a time. The meridian appears to the viewer of Dibbets's work not as a line but as a set of isolated points. The map breaks down on contact with the space it represents.

The gap between the map and the city inspires Réda. He says his goal is to occupy that gap in order to create an opportunity for the unexpected, to discover "what vivid surprises emerge when you make contact with a strict mathematical rule."[30] The result is that Réda makes uncertainty and imprecision appear within the meridian itself. He takes a mathematical concept, and time after time makes it return contrary, unpredictable, unusual numbers. It is not that with his body he adds noise to the system (though he does that by constantly getting distracted); he finds noise that was already lurking in it. Attempting to explain the difference between his final tally for the plaques and the contradictory numbers in his guide, Réda concludes that the responsibility lies not with him but with the system: "In my opinion we will never know exactly how many medallions there are along the path of the meridian through direct observation. Even if a hundred people could agree on a number, we would never know for certain that they arrived at that number via the same math."

Réda calls this "la revanche du flou," which we could translate as the revenge of fuzziness or blurriness.[31] Or, more liberally, the revenge of information loss or the parasite. Such turnabouts are recurrent in Réda's work. The author, who worked for years as a jazz journalist and is famed for his use of the vernacular *vers mâché* (chewed-up verse) in his poetry, also punned the title of a collection of poetry on the metric system.[32] The Paris Observatory is where the official measures used for the meter and kilogram were once stored. Réda is fascinated by the idea that abstract mathematical concepts are defined according to real physical objects and places, with all the material imprecision that entails. If Réda, a poet famous for wandering, is drawn to the mathematical rigor of these scientific tools, it is because at the heart of his work is a desire to unearth the imprecision of the meter that, whether he wants it to or not, measures out both his walking and his verse. In other words, just as Réda introduces swing rhythms into the classic *alexandrin* through the manipulation of the silent e, he reveals the straightness of the meridian to be an illusion.[33]

The imprecision he locates in the meridian is more than just a mathematical or poetic observation. The meridian, after all, is not just a technology for mapping; it is a technology for mapping in the service of the exercise of state power. Réda alludes to this obliquely when he notices that the meridian passes through a post office. He fantasizes about an employee stamping letters right on its path.[34] The postal system, as noted above, developed alongside cartography to allow the state to interpellate citizens.

The social and political side of cartography is invoked more directly when Réda's walk along the meridian is impeded by physical barriers and warning signs that stop him from entering certain spaces. He hits a series of fences and walls before he arrives at the second plaque.[35] He is livid when he discovers that the seventh plaque is in a private courtyard, and rails against the notion that "the *mire du sud* and even a portion of the meridian could be privatized." These moments echo the critique proffered by SI, but with the difference that a walker on a *dérive* follows the city's internal boundaries so that they can be mapped and later destabilized, whereas Réda reveals that the lines are already unstable, and thus permeable. By giving his constraint priority over the conscious and unconscious rules of the city, he forces himself to go into areas he otherwise would not enter. That poses an immediate challenge to the social order of the city. When he sneaks into a private courtyard to find plaques 14 and 15, he meets a stranger who turns out to be an amateur of "Paris's little eccentricities."[36] The two briefly work together to find plaque 15. Transgressing the city's boundaries opens the door to a new relationship.

However, Réda does not seem entirely convinced of the benefits of these encounters. While he parts from his comrade on good terms, his narrative adopts a passive-aggressive tone that suggests the author was happy to be on his own again. He describes the man's stories about his favorite spots in Paris as "an instructive, but fairly fastidious, technical lecture," and sounds fatigued by the "interminable demonstrations of mutual affection" that are exchanged by way of goodbye. Only moments later, a second attempt at conversation with a stranger ends in failure: Réda asks a kiosk attendant if she is aware that her stand straddles the meridian, and she acknowledges this fact with a "a blasé and possibly even resentful look" which suggests that Réda is one of "dozens of idiots" to pose that question.[37] Elsewhere in the text, the author is more than happy to be left alone. In the first chapter he is accosted by someone he describes as a personal enemy; he lies and says he is presenting a paper on Joyce at the nearby library as an excuse to get away. Most tantalizingly, he is at one point obliged to ask for help from young men whose accents indicate that they come from the "so-called disadvantaged suburbs." They ignore his questions, and Réda concludes that the socioeconomic differences between them are too great for the two parties to even be mutually perceptible.[38] He ultimately settles into an antisocial mode of urban exploration that betrays the hope for unexpected contact that motivated the exploration in the first place.

This gives a much more urgently disappointing inflection to Réda's recurring complaint: that nothing happens. Not only does he not experience the emotional transcendence he hoped for while traversing the city; he also ends up just as isolated as he was at the start, having failed to alter Paris's social politics. While one could ascribe this failure to Réda's defensive attitude, the fact that the problems he encounters can equally be found in the practices of *flânerie* and the *dérive* suggests that they are more structural. This hypothesis is supported by comparison with another work with much the same inspiration: Philippe Vasset's *Un livre blanc*, published a decade after *Le Méridien de Paris*.

Carte Blanche: Selective Visibility as a Political Problem in *Un livre blanc*

Vasset's book shares many of the same concerns as Réda's. Like Réda, Vasset hopes that by confronting a map of the city with an on-foot exploration of it, he will produce the unexpected. In his case, he assigns himself the task of visiting every one of the blank spaces in the official map of Paris published by the National Geographic Institute. Doing so will reveal what the map fails to represent, and force Vasset to come into contact with (and, in his words, take a machete to) barriers that normally pass unnoticed in the city.[39] Like Réda, he will find people on the other side of these boundaries, people with whom he would normally never enter into contact. In his case, they are predominantly houseless people and undocumented migrants. But unlike Réda, who shies away from these encounters, Vasset is transformed by them. He writes: "suddenly unveiled, this invisible misery filled my field of vision and changed my point of view on the city."[40] Even the so-called beautiful neighborhoods reveal themselves to be filled with migrant caravans, and the author reorients his project around making these people visible to the rest of the city's residents as well.

Whereas Réda seeks a kind of personal transcendence through communion with the meridian, Vasset remains attentive to politics throughout his book.[41] At one point, a friend insists that the blank areas on the map are military sites that have been masked by the generals.[42] In practice the friend is wrong (as discussed in chapter 3, when power hides its buildings it does so in plain view), but the friend is right to bear in mind that the map is the product of official decisions about what merits visibility. Where the friend expected the erasure of power, the author finds the erasure of the powerless—instead of power waiting to be deployed, power in action.

Vasset's understanding of the map as an articulation of who and what is visible to the state, and his understanding of his own task as the expansion of that sphere of visibility, aligns him closely with the political theorist Jacques Rancière. Rancière defines democracy as a system of government where power is not distributed according to any intrinsic traits of the citizens. That does not mean that democracy produces or is founded on a homogeneous space. On the contrary, Rancière pushes back against the notion that democracy is government of the people and for the people. The democratic community is broken by two divisions. The first of these is structural: while leadership is distributed arbitrarily, there is an oligarchy that manages the state. The community relates to this oligarchy through demands and grievances it lodges for the oligarchy to resolve. The second division is a division in the ways the community is counted. The first way of counting includes only "citizens"—that is to say, members of groups recognized by the state. Rancière calls this mode of counting and the power structures that protect its limits the police. The second count brings in a supplement to the first count. This supplement is drawn from what Rancière calls the *demos*. The *demos* is "a class without a class"—it is not equivalent to the proletariat or any other defined subset of the population. Rather, it designates the part of the population that is excluded from modes of categorization that would make it incorporable into the police division of society. By virtue of its exclusion from the police count of society the *demos* is, Rancière argues, invisible, and its demands are inaudible. He calls the second count, the count that incorporates some portion of this invisible population, politics.

"Politics is above all an intervention in the visible and the speakable."[43] A population that structurally cannot be heard fights to makes its demands heard by the state. Key to this conflict is the *partage du sensible*. This is the universe of shared visibility maintained by the police. Citizenship is the condition of having a share (*partage*) in the universe of official perceptibility. Politics is a contestation of the limits of that universe. It is the means by which some portion of the *demos* asserts its right to be heard by the state, to be counted, to receive the rights of citizens, and to have its demands answered. Politics is necessarily paradoxical: what is defined as inaudible demands to be heard and is heard.[44] Rancière resolves this contradiction through a process he calls dissensus. Dissensus begins with a flattening, an appeal to the basic equality of the community. Atop this rhetorical *tabula rasa* a portion of the *demos* attempts to construct a new *partage du sensible* in which it has a share. In the climactic phase, this alternate universe is inscribed in the public space governed by the police, creating a conflict. Two worlds are made to coexist. Their reconciliation effects a displacement of the democratic community's frontiers of perceptibility. A successful act of dissensus exploits a gap in the state's mode of counting to produce a contradiction it then forces the state to confront.[45]

This corresponds to how Vasset sees his project. The ING map represents the *partage du sensible*. The homeless populations Vasset discovers in the areas "judged too vague or too complex to be represented on a map"[46] are the *demos*. His observation that this map is the map used by the police accords with Rancière's argument that the police maintain the *partage du sensible* and the disenfranchisement of the *demos*. The signs and fences Vasset encounters around the Roma shantytowns are paradigmatic of this police function.[47] In opposition, Vasset strives to say: "Look, this is how people live in your city, and you don't see any of it; even worse, you do everything you can to hide them."[48] He attempts to produce dissensus.

To this end, Vasset makes recourse to a wide variety of media. However, he struggles with which medium is most effective. In his conversations with the houseless he ignores personal details, thus missing an opportunity for a platform of self-representation. He is more concerned with how these spaces are being appropriated by developers than how they have been appropriated by the houseless themselves, diminishing the agency of the people he encounters. He nominates himself to speak on behalf of these people in order to rectify their plight, echoing Marx's epigraph to Edward Said's *Orientalism*: "They cannot represent themselves; they must be represented." He imagines himself literally speaking for them, even quoting himself in direct discourse. To make their plight legible he collects details of their living quarters and consults data, which he plans to publish as a white paper (or *livre blanc*). But, "when I tried to synthesize all the information I'd collected, my sentences just wouldn't coalesce into arguments."[49]

Abandoning the idea of intervening directly in the political sphere through a policy paper, Vasset goes on to try an almost parodic number of forms for his dissensual act. He traces the limits of the blank zones in spray paint on the ground. He undertakes an art project installing furniture in abandoned areas to make them perceptible as homes to passersby, but the installations are quickly dismantled. He takes photographs of the sites he visits, but the pictures are not compelling. He leaves poems on some of the sites, but returns to find that no one has picked them up. He imagines setting up a transmitter to send an SMS to anyone who passes nearby, but the technology proves too costly. When he asks a friend to come with him, the friend laughs and turns him down. With the help of other friends, he sets up a website to provide a crowdsourced, illustrated map of the changing blank zones of the city; the address is no longer active.[50] The book gradually begins to be more about the failure of representation than about the people and places it wants to represent. Vasset laments that he begins to slip into an Orientalizing mode that cements, rather than undermines, the unintelligibility of the disenfranchised populations he encounters: "My texts explained nothing and told no stories, and they even at times hinted at a fascination with these existences pushed to the extremes of publicness that made me uncomfortable."[51]

Vasset's final idea is to set in motion something like unitary urbanism. He turns to the game, imagining a collective mode of urban exploration that could mobilize the masses. He writes:

> My collective fantasy was never realized in the end, but the desire remains, implicit, present in this text, and it's the reason for its open form. As I was writing I gradually started to feel that art in general and literature in particular would be better off if they invented practices and were explicitly programmatic, instead of making finished products and begging people to come admire them. You could even imagine a new artistic discipline made of statements and formulas: put the onus on the amateurs, if they so desire, to carry out the projects described, knowing that the majority won't do anything, preferring to imagine what might happen based on the instructions. The work itself would be that oscillation, the precarious equilibrium at the threshold of expression.[52]

Rather than describing what he has seen, Vasset imagines providing a set of instructions and a platform permitting potential practitioners to contribute their own walking experiences to an evolving mosaic of urban exploration. Réda reaches the same conclusion, suggesting that he could open his text up to "les hasards du jeu," the randomness of play, and thereby bypass the limitations of his single perspective.[53]

But neither Vasset nor Réda follows up on the idea. Vasset ultimately abandons the mediatic variety he discusses over the course of his work, and retreats to the comfort of relatively conventional literature. His writing is essayistic, and it resists some of the clichés of writing about the urban periphery, but he talks about exploding the boundaries of his medium more than he does it. More problematic than Vasset's style—since literature can, as I will argue in chapter 6, play a part in the transformation of urbanism—is his decision to disseminate his experience in a printed, single-authored narrative that does little to challenge the authority of the author, or to incorporate multiple perspectives. Whereas some of the digital media the author toyed with deploying might have allowed *Un livre blanc* to evolve over time in response to the constant changes of the urban environment, as a printed book *Un livre blanc* is, as Vasset acknowledged in his next book, *La Conjuration*, out of date as soon as it's published. And even if a reader takes the hint and heads out to the blank areas of the city, there is no way for that participant to inscribe whatever experience they might have in Vasset's text for other readers to encounter. Vasset, like Debord, always maintains a position of dominance over the practice he theorizes.

Un livre blanc actually contains a scene that anticipates the author's failure to enlist multiple participants in his practice. Vasset's narrator finds some young people challenging each other to climb dilapidated edifices in one of the blank spaces he travels to. He invites them to join him for a guided tour of vacant lots the next day. He maintains a haughty distance *vis-à-vis* their "much less contemplative practice," in which, "like graffiti artists," they dare each other to reach inaccessible and dangerous areas.[54] He ignores (with a measure of ironic self-awareness) the fact that what the kids are doing is much more fun than what he proposes. He sets himself up as a potential leader and pedagogue who will explain to them how to explore the city. Unsurprisingly, no one shows up to his proposed rendezvous. The author is left alone while the real game of urban exploration takes place elsewhere. While Vasset does not provide much detail on what his interlocutors are doing, on the basis of his description we can assume that they are participating in one of several recreational activities that have become popular in Paris in recent years. A closer look at these practices provides an example of an alternate way of conceptualizing the collective's relationship to mediation. This alternate approach avoids the didacticism of which Vasset is guilty, and comes closer to sparking unitary urbanism. Part of its success, I will argue, is owed to its adoption of Serres's model of parasitic relationality.

Paris Sportif: The Contagious Attraction of Parkour

The description the teenagers give of their practice fits a number of subcultures. Urbex, or urban exploration, involves seeking out hidden, barred, or neglected areas of the city. These targets are prized both for the thrill of surmounting legal or physical barriers to get to them and for the unique views they offer, views that are often captured and exchanged photographically. In a fortuitous wink to SI's imagined prison lottery, Urbex is sometimes called "urban spelunking." The catacombs, sewers, and abandoned metro stations are particularly popular sites to break into. A similar practice is rooftopping, in which people photograph themselves in precarious positions atop skyscrapers. Rooftopping is often conflated with skywalking, which involves free-climbing industrial structures, often in rural areas, and documenting the results with video or photography. But all of these practices share an ancestor with origins in the Parisian *banlieue*: parkour.

Parkour was invented in Lisses in the 1980s. As has now been well documented, it emerged as a modification of *Hébertisme*, a method of obstacle course training first introduced to the French Navy in 1910 by Georges Hébert. David Belle learned the principles of *Hébertisme* from his father, Raymond, who had become enamored of the method when he was exposed to it at a military school in Vietnam. David, along with a friend, Sébastien Foucan, then adapted those principles, originally conceived for natural environments, to the suburban architecture of their surroundings. Over time, parkour has also incorporated techniques from tumbling, gymnastics, and capoeira, resulting in a striking blend of military power and balletic artistry. Parkour, like the other practices discussed so far, involves confronting an urban map with an embodied experience of urban space. Parkour is often defined as "moving from A to B in the most efficient way possible," and traceurs (parkour practitioners) often depict themselves as trailblazers identifying routes through the city that cartography does not capture. Traceurs sometimes evoke the fantasy of tracing a straight line on the map and finding a way to turn it into a path. This is what Réda does with the meridian, but whereas he goes around the walls he encounters, traceurs climb over. In this respect a traceur is akin to Haussmann, who razed any structure that stood in the way of his straight lines on the map. (And yet, in an inversion with echoes throughout this chapter, contrary to parkour's rhetoric of the line, it often takes place at a single point on the map—a park, a rooftop, an esplanade—and a traceur often ends a session back where he or she started.)

Parkour's engagement with cartography gives it much in common with the modes of urban exploration developed by SI, Réda, and Vasset, but it distinguishes itself from those practices through its use of media. The place of media in parkour is a subject of debate within the practice. In the early 2000s, Foucan broke away from Belle to pioneer his own version of the training system. His appearance in the 2003 documentary *Jump London* cemented "freerunning" as the name for this alternate practice, which put a greater emphasis on stylized movements. Foucan would go on to play a terrorist bomb-maker in Martin Campbell's *Casino Royale*, leaping from cranes with Daniel Craig's James Bond in pursuit. Some parkour purists see this as a degradation of the utilitarian roots of their training, and insist instead on a physio-spiritual discourse of communion with the environment, mastery of fear, and humility. They reject freerunning as a brash corruption of Hébert's principles. Jeffrey Kidder notes in his interviews with traceurs in Chicago that they dismiss participants who lack interest in serious rituals like safety, humility, and personal growth. They react negatively to media coverage that highlights parkour's danger or assimilates it into adolescent rebellions like skateboarding, drug use, or loitering. In my own email interview with the leaders of Parkour Paris, the official parkour organization of Paris and a recent partner of the Mairie in public health initiatives, the same will to blame media is evident: "Parkour has been mediatized in 'connotated' films. The traceurs depicted in those fictions were friendly delinquents a bit like Robin Hood. Friendly, yes, but for the immense majority of people they were still delinquents from the banlieue. It's been very hard to shake that image."

There are echoes here of Guy Debord's rejection of visual media, which he classed among the atomizing forces of the modern city. Although visual media address many spectators at once, they prevent each from entering into any kind of direct relation with the others: "the spectacle reunites the separate, but reunites it as separate."[55] The spectacle also interposes itself between the spectator and things, replacing tangible reality with its representation. For Debord, the concern is primarily economic: the commodity disappears behind advertisement and behind the image of the lifestyle it represents. But a more literal reading accords perfectly with the skepticism of mediatization evinced by parkour purists: the image is a rift opened between the subject and the environment. Parkour purists reject the idea that all knowledge of the city is mediated, and hope that by distancing their practice from visual media they can achieve direct knowledge of urban space through movement and touch.

I will return to this supposed distinction between antispectacular parkour and frivolous freerunning later in this section, but for now I will set it aside, because it does not match up with how parkour is practiced and perceived by the majority of people. In Kidder's studies of Chicago traceurs, there are just as many participants there to make videos as there are to tell them that's not what parkour is about. Parkour Paris may feel that films have given people the wrong ideas about parkour, but the films they are alluding to include several starring David Belle, the figure who, in the schism with Foucan, supposedly represents traditional parkour. Parkour Paris has posted dozens of videos of their members performing tightly choreographed, dangerous parkour runs on YouTube. Ultimately, if some traceurs bristle at their practice's association with certain films or videos, and feel they have to police their colleagues' practice, that is because of the close association between parkour and video in the minds of the broader public. Visual media—digital media in particular—are integral to parkour's identity, and the distinction purists make between parkour and its supposed corruptions is more prescriptive than descriptive.

Traceurs engage with digital media in two primary ways. First, they use digital maps to organize parkour sessions. Second, they create digital videos that are shared on online platforms like YouTube, Facebook, and Instagram. These videos collectively constitute parkour as a meme. Limor Shifman defines memes with reference to viral media. The latter, as discussed in chapter 3, are individual texts that reach a large audience through word-of-mouth sharing. A meme, by contrast, is not a single text. It is a framework upon which users improvise and iterate, resulting in a large number of distinct texts that are nevertheless recognizable as part of a single discursive field.[56] Whereas the viral moves its viewer to share it, the meme invites the viewer first to rewrite it and then to share it. Most memes are still images, but, as in the case of parkour, they can take the form of videos. Video memes like parkour present viewers with a framework into which they can inscribe their bodies to produce a new iteration.

Shifman describes the meme and the viral as two poles: a video or an image can start as a meme and a single iteration of it can go viral, or a viral text might inspire a meme. There are some parkour videos that come closer to Shifman's definition of the viral—high-quality productions with millions of views characterized by celebrity participation (Belle or Foucan) or brand partnerships (French Freerun Family's advertisement for the *Assassin's Creed* video game franchise)—while others are more memetic. For Shifman, more memetic means more incomplete.[57] While a viral stands alone, a meme is somehow not self-sufficient. It adds something to a discourse while simultaneously opening a gap that demands to be filled by more texts. In parkour, incompleteness can take the form of a move that is not executed properly, production values that are too low, or a feeling that a given traceur is not spatially transgressive or dangerous enough. Many of the most popular parkour videos are of "parkour fails": compilations of failed stunts. The popularity of such videos is a kind of *mise en abîme* of the fact that every contribution to a meme is deficient. To put it another way: on some level, all parkour is a parkour fail. The inexorably unsatisfying videos push viewers to respond by supplementing the lack with more videos of their own. Memes are also fueled by the social and economic incentive of likes, views, and shares, which bring status within the ephemeral community of the meme. This further incentivizes upping the stakes of existing videos by playing in spaces that are more restricted, more dangerous, and more spectacular. The group Hit the Road has made a name for itself by doing illegal parkour in symbolically weighty targets, like the Eiffel Tower or the restricted area of Chernobyl.

Vasset compares the traceurs he sees to graffiti artists who tag the city, and there are strong similarities between the way parkour engages with digital media and the way graffiti and street art do. In chapter 3 I argued that street art, especially when it encourages viewers to become artists, is an example of Serres's parasitic mode of relational subjectivity, and that is even more true for parkour. Serres's parasitic collectives are held together by the circulation of a quasi-object, which allows subjectivity to constantly move through the group. In the case of parkour, the quasi-object is the digital video platform. A player takes possession of it by producing a video and uploading it with the right tags and title for it to reach other traceurs. Anyone can add a video with almost any content to the network—it does not have to meet any established idea of what parkour is. A search for "parkour" thus returns pastiches of parkour videos, misunderstandings of parkour, the aforementioned parkour fails, and total *non sequiturs*. As shown by the purists described above, there can be a strong urge by one player to police how other participants play the quasi-object, but the structure of Serres's game is such that no single player determines how or by whom the quasi-object is played. A video that calls itself parkour is parkour, regardless of how poorly it corresponds to other iterations on the meme. This fundamental openness to "bad" play was parodied in an episode of the American version of the sitcom *The Office* in which characters who have watched a parkour video climb and tumble their way through the office, knocking things down as they go. They yell out "parkour" again and again. With these exclamations they tag their practice and inscribe it in the discursive space of the meme. As Jim Halpert says, that is all it takes for a text to be part of a meme: "the goal is to get from point A to point B as creatively as possible, so technically they are doing parkour as long as point A is delusion and point B is the hospital."[58]

One of the questions I raised in chapter 3 regarding Serres's parasitic game concerned the loss of agency experienced by the players. Serres encourages players to defer to the ball, becoming relays along its path rather than masters of it. These same questions are raised by parkour in particular and by memes in general. The word "meme" was coined by Richard Dawkins in *The Selfish Gene*. Dawkins proposes a Darwinian explanation for the spread of culture, and offers the meme as a hypothetical analogue to the gene. Just as the gene is the basic informational unit of biology, the meme would be the informational unit of culture, the building block out of which concepts are built. The central argument of *The Selfish Gene* is that natural selection does not act on organisms, but on genes. Dawkins anthropomorphizes genes, ascribing selfishness to them. This rhetoric implies a displacement of agency from the organism to genes. Organisms are vehicles, Dawkins says; genes are the drivers. An organism is sometimes discarded, sometimes allowed to die, if it is in the interests of the gene. The same principles apply to Dawkins's hypothesized memes. These units of information spread through minds, replicating themselves as best they can. The human is not the agent of culture. The mind is the host or ecosystem in which units of culture battle for supremacy. Dawkins uses "viral" in this context for parasitic memes that do not act in the best interests of the minds they inhabit. Viral media are true parasites in the biological sense, exogenous pathogens that take up malignant residence in a host organism. Dawkins's theory of memes has little currency in biological circles, and his definitions of meme and viral do not correspond to how the terms are used online today, but his notions of selfish memes, conceptual parasites, and of the mind as host rather than agent of culture remain relevant. They tie into ongoing anxieties about agency and digital culture. These anxieties are often expressed using the language of disease—for instance, the sociological terminology of "affective contagion," which Tony Sampson applies to viral media.[59]

Parkour is a particularly fruitful area in which to examine these dimensions of the meme, because it directly implicates the bodily health of the participant. Traceurs are exposed to real physical danger when they hang off the sides of buildings and leap onto concrete structures. Dawkins discusses the extreme case of an organism that is allowed to die so that its genes can better spread; in parkour, there is a real chance of the organism dying in the interests of the meme. This direct threat to the body actualizes the contagious rhetoric around memes. Doctors have warned parents against the dangers of letting their children be exposed to parkour videos online. Dr. Kenneth Frumkin, in a letter to *Annals of Emergency Medicine*, uses an invasive vocabulary to describe parkour: "this activity started in France and remains largely outside the United States," but risks becoming "(very) dangerously cool" if the medical profession does not intervene.[60] In his interviews with traceurs, Kidder finds that many of them took up the practice because of this kind of exposure. He quotes one whose explanation is emblematic of the idea that participation in the meme is reflexive rather than conscious: "I watched it online, and I was like, 'Cool, I'll do it.'"[61] Some parkour clubs have responded to the fear of their practice's contagious spread with pseudo-medical warnings *à la* cigarette packaging on their websites, and Parkour Paris includes footage of failed stunts in their videos as a way of underscoring the danger.[62]

Fears of contagion are ubiquitous in representations of parkour as well. Many video games that reference parkour, or in which the player character's movement through the world is inspired by parkour, tie the player's parkour abilities to some kind of bodily infection. In *Infamous*, the protagonist, who can do parkour, is trapped in a dystopian city by a viral outbreak. The protagonists of the *Assassin's Creed* games get their parkour abilities by plugging into a computer program, but doing so leads to brain disease. The main character of the zombie game *Dying Light* is an undercover soldier sent into a blockaded city to recover a stolen file. His parkour abilities, the player is told, give him superiority over the undead who cannot climb. In the game's opening sequence, however, the player is bitten, and over the course of the game he slowly succumbs to the virus. He becomes the disease parkour was supposed to exempt him from. In an alternate mode, the player can reverse roles, playing as a zombie instead of a survivor. The traceur is coded as a contagious figure who, though liberated by his athletic abilities, represents an ongoing threat of infection to the wider network.

Parkour, in sum, is intersected by a variety of biological, infectious discourses. It encourages players to adopt a relational mode of subjectivity based on the circulation of a quasi-object—what Serres calls the parasitic collective. This parasitic way of relating to mediation turns parkour practice into a meme, itself a genetic metaphor for the transmission of ideas which implies that culture is a form of parasitism. New players are drawn in, and alter their relationship to the city through the contagious transmission of affects. The definition of parkour that emerges is a noisy one, riddled with internal contradictions engendered by the free circulation of the quasi-object. Parkour is frequently represented, by both artists and doctors, as an epidemic threat to the social body and to the city. These medical discourses are not entirely hollow, either, because people have died from parkour. People jump off buildings to get views on YouTube.

In these ways, parkour is starkly different from what on the surface are similar modes of urban exploration like Réda's and Vasset's. Those practices, though they might open the door to the game, or fantasize about the participation of the masses, fundamentally inhibit the epidemic spread that characterizes parkour. They do this by failing to deprioritize the position of emission. Vasset fantasizes about a work in a "precarious equilibrium at the threshold of expression," but he and Réda both ultimately settle for expression *tout court*. They publish their projects as single-authored books, sharing a view of the world rather than creating a platform for others to do so. Both authors implicitly ask readers to listen rather than participate, just as Vasset asked the traceurs he met to follow him on a guided tour. Even if a reader were to accept these authors' invitations to reproduce their methodologies, the authors' media-technical choices would inhibit the kind of mass participation we see with parkour. Memes rely on a low technical bar for entry. It is relatively quick and easy to produce a video and upload it to an online platform. That is key to how parkour spreads. Réda and Vasset, by contrast, opt for printed literature as their mode of mediation. That is a much harder quasi-object to take possession of, as a reader wanting to play along would have to write, edit, and find a publisher willing to market another book about exploring the vacant lots of Paris or following the meridian.

In juxtaposition to the lonely explorations described by SI, Réda, and Vasset, parkour presents an epidemic attractiveness. It has seduced thousands of new practitioners into its ludic form of urban movement. Its appeal is sufficient to overcome not only the normal rules of urban life, but also practitioners' instinct for self-preservation. Parkour offers a flat, parasitic playing space whose rules are articulated through the constant circulation of a virtual quasi-object. However, while Vasset struggles to instantiate a collective, his work directly engages with the politics of the city. It seeks to make visible, and thus to incorporate into a *partage du sensible*, populations that are marginalized and effaced. Likewise, for SI, moving through the city in new ways was valuable only to the extent that it provoked a challenge to social, political, and economic barriers. If parkour succeeds in constituting a group driven to move in a new way, does it also change regimes of urban visibility? Does it have any political effect?

PK Vision: The Limitations of Community-Building through Contagion

Traceurs describe a variety of mental changes that come with training in their discipline. Giving a figurative inflection to the dictum that parkour is going from one point to another in the most direct way possible, they claim to become better at decision-making. They develop a new, positive relationship to fear. They become better acquainted with the physical limits of their bodies, and describe entering a state of spiritual communion with their environment.[63] These changes are connected to what practitioners call PK Vision. PK Vision is when elements of the urban environment that previously faded into the background become visible as potential components in a parkour run.[64] New paths through space open up, giving the experienced traceur a markedly different psychogeographic map than the ordinary pedestrian's.

Some theorists of parkour see in this perceptual transformation the roots of a utopian and revolutionary praxis. Michael Atkinson calls parkour a form of "anarcho-environmentalism" that "destabilizes and disrupts technocapitalist meanings of a city's physical and social landscape."[65] Matthew Lamb, adopting a Foucauldian perspective on architecture, sees parkour as a way "to imagine alternative possibilities in challenging disciplinary and constraining regulatory norms."[66] Such readings draw inspiration from Henri Lefebvre's concept of the socially constructed city and Michel de

Certeau's theory of everyday resistance. In a famous essay, de Certeau looks down from atop the World Trade Center at the ordered grid system of the Manhattan streets. In the heart of the regimented, Cartesian city, he sees people jaywalking and discerns in their movement tiny acts of resistance against the imposed logic of the city planners. Parkour, which reappropriates railings as vaults and walls as climbing surfaces, is a similar form of resistance to the rationalizing ideologies of the urbanists.

This reading of parkour is common in films and video games that depict it. In the *Banlieue 13* films, starring David Belle, the Parisian *banlieue* has been physically walled off from the city center. Belle's character, who inhabits one of the ghettos, uses parkour to traverse the boundaries excluding him from the city center, and is eventually able to make himself indispensable to the government. In the first film he prevents a nuclear explosion that would destroy the *banlieue*. In the sequel he exposes a corrupt government official who plans to redevelop the area into luxury apartment blocks once he has succeeded in tricking the French president into authorizing air strikes on it. (In a sublime testament to the script's ambition and subtlety, the development contractor is called Harriburton.) By the end of the films, Belle and his multiethnic team are smoking cigars with the president. The same dynamic plays out in video games like *Mirror's Edge*, *Watch Dogs*, *Vector*, and *Brink*, whose traceur protagonists are trapped in dystopian societies. Parkour allows them to elude the surveillance state, and ultimately overthrow it. In all of these texts political freedom is figured by freedom of movement, liberty from oppression by physical liberty, social mobility by real mobility.

However, there are a number of issues with the idea of parkour as a politically revolutionary practice. First, if we look more closely at PK Vision, we find that traceurs describe the perceptual changes they undergo through parkour training purely in terms of urban furniture. They feel excitement in the presence of railings, staircases, and climbable walls. The visual transformation Vasset experiences in *Un livre blanc* opens his eyes to large numbers of marginalized people, but with PK Vision people never enter into the discussion. Online parkour videos reflect this, with traceurs typically working in empty spaces. Indeed, if there is an urban space most associated with parkour, it is not the street but the roof. The roof is where the risks and rewards of parkour are at their greatest. But the roof is a space that offers virtually no chance of an unexpected encounter. The rooftop traceur is an isolated figure, raised up above the city, closer to Chombart de Lauwe's aerial photographer than to the young girl on the ground.

Now, one could argue that unexpected physical encounters are less important for parkour than they are for Vasset, because of traceurs' membership in an immense virtual community. Here, too, however, there are problems that echo those of street art, the other practice I have identified as an example of Serres's parasitic collective. In the second *Banlieue 13* film, *Ultimatum*, parkour is practiced by a diverse team made up of a black man, an Arab man, an Asian woman, a Roma man, and—so no one is left out—a skinhead, but in reality the vast majority of traceurs are young white men in their athletic prime. There are few women, few minorities, few elderly people, and few people with disabilities. In chapter 3, I pointed to the everyday gender politics of urban space as a possible explanation for street art's gender imbalance. That explanation is relevant here as well. As feminist geographers like Doreen Massey and Linda McDowell have argued, space is not experienced in the same way by all bodies. City streets are the locus for a spectrum of gender-based forms of violence. In Paris these range from the symbolic (in 2015 less than 3 percent of streets were named after women) to the verbal to the physical. As Lauren Elkin writes in *Flâneuse*, her book of essays on the absence of women from the cultural imaginary of Parisian walking, "a woman still can't walk in the city the way a man can."[67] Because parkour normally necessitates the movement of the participant's body in public space, it is affected by the inequalities present in that space. One can make a similar argument for the paucity of traceurs from other marginalized groups.

But not all of parkour's demographic homogeneity can be attributed to everyday inequality. Parkour produces a number of discourses about the body that contribute to its demographic issues and raise questions about its status as a dissident, antihegemonic practice. I have argued that, as an example of a parasitic collective, parkour lacks a univocal ideology and is riddled with contradictions. Well, one of those contradictions is that the contagious discourse of parkour, which portrays it as an epidemic threat to young people and to order, coexists with intensely hygienic, even eugenic, discourses. These discourses give a problematically fascist color to parkour's rhetoric of actualizing the power of the body and finding political liberation through physical fitness.

David Belle, as I said above, adapted parkour from the principles of Georges Hébert's "Natural Method," developed for the French Navy, to which his father had been exposed in Vietnam. Inspired by the physical fitness of French colonial subjects in Martinique, where he had been stationed, Hébert advocated a goal-oriented approach to training that would take place in the natural environment, not in the gym. While Hébert did promote women's fitness and opened a gym for women in Normandy, his method was developed for male soldiers, and he idealized the male musculature. He encouraged soldiers to train topless as a way of activating their natural virility. Hébert used a primitivist discourse, pitting a flaccid and sedentary civilized French male against a powerful and uncultured other. This discourse obviously had strong racial undertones, and it appealed to French eugenicists in the 1920s, 1930s, and 1940s. The undertones were barely undertones for figures like Thevenet, the chief instructor of the Société de préparation et d'éducation sportive (SPES), a physical fitness research institute run by France's far-right Croix de Feu party. He wrote, in a paean to *Hébertiste* methods, "Negroes don't need physical culture to run or jump, but we, we are organic degenerates." SPES's director of physical education was Gaëtan Maire, a dues-paying member of the Groupement Hébertiste, a society for the appreciation of Hébert's teachings. He saw the Natural Method as a necessary tool to reverse the decline of the French race.[68] During the Second World War, *Hébertisme* would be researched and promoted by the Fondation Alexis Carrel, Vichy France's official eugenics institute, and the Vichy government would formally adopt *Hébertisme,* rebranded as "The French Method," as the national physical fitness program.[69] In 1942, Hébert himself wrote admiringly of the fitness programs of Nazi Germany.[70]

While contemporary traceurs do not explicitly reference the far-right connections of *Hébertisme,* it is difficult to separate parkour's discourse of perfecting the body and its attractiveness to white men from the racist, eugenic, and fascist ideologies of the practice of which it calls itself the inheritor. Modern parkour continues to mobilize the militaristic, masculinist rhetoric of its forebear. The name *parkour* is a modification of the *Hébertiste* term *parcours du combattant,* or path of the soldier.[71] Kidder sees the performance of masculinity as central to parkour practice, calling it a way of "spatializing gender" for the "accomplishment of masculinity."[72]

Parkour's status as an antihegemonic practice that opens up the city to the disenfranchised is further undermined by its practitioners' friendly relationship with authorities. Parkour's origins in the Paris *banlieue* have conferred on it a certain amount of countercultural credibility. The *Banlieue 13* films are built around that association. They draw heavily on the symbolism of a form of expressive movement being invented in an area that many French people associate with the burning car, one of the most lasting images of the 2005 *banlieue* riots and a symbol of supreme immobility. But Lisses, where David Belle and his friends created parkour, is a middle-class suburb, miles from the impoverished suburbs hyperbolically rendered in the films, and Belle's first parkour video to go viral was filmed in the local park, not in a dilapidated high-rise. Above, I quoted the members of Parkour Paris, who were keen to distance themselves from "delinquent" practices. The group's website lists over thirty government and corporate partners,[73] and traceurs have been featured in advertising campaigns for Nike and Adidas. The Paris mayor's office expressed its support for parkour—as well as its desire to confine it to preapproved spaces—by including a sizable parkour gym in the canopy of the high-profile redesign of Les Halles in the historic center of the city. A practice that was initially illicit, outdoor, and peripheral becomes approved, indoor, and central. Hard concrete is replaced by padded walls, and the threats posed by parkour to both the individual body and the body politic are neutralized. Other, smaller parkour practice areas have been approved in other parts of the city and around France. Looking one last time at *Banlieue 13*, we can see that parkour does grant David Belle's character a level of personal social mobility, but in the film he works with an undercover police officer and becomes a partner of the government, preempting explosions that would reset (albeit catastrophically) Paris's political and social power structures.

Politically, parkour thus brings us to an impasse. On the one hand, it demonstrates a remarkable ability to spread. It demonstrates the power of virtual communities, armed with their own incentive structures, to alter the behavior of individuals in real space. Embracing Michel Serres's parasitic group dynamic gives it a flat internal power structure, where anyone can articulate his or her own vision of the group's orientation. On the other hand, parkour falls short of its utopian rhetoric in its failure to move beyond a masculine and strength-oriented notion of freedom. While on the surface it seems to accomplish the dream set forward by previous theorizations of politically oriented urban exploration, like the *dérive*, in its obsession with the potential uses of the environment it loses sight of the social stakes that pushed groups like SI to study that environment in the first place. As a result, it reproduces power dynamics and patterns of exclusion that might have seemed incompatible with its structural egalitarianism.

Another issue with the notion that parkour is a fundamentally transgressive and antihegemonic practice concerns its relationship to digital media. As noted above, traceurs use digital maps to organize practice sessions. Filming, often with phones, is integral to the activity. They share videos of their exploits on digital networks with global reach. This is key to parkour's large number of participants, and allows the practice to exhibit the features of Serres's parasitic collectives. But the networks on which parkour relies are not public utilities. As discussed at the end of chapter 3, they are owned by private corporations whose immense revenue streams are built on skimming behavioral surplus off users. Traceurs' reliance on these networks allows their practice to be assimilated by the economy of surveillance capitalism. It allows both for the monetization of the traceur's movements and for the tracking of his body.

Cartography returns. By blazing new paths through the city, traceurs claim to transcend the map's knowledge of space; by recording and sharing their movements, however, they ultimately enable the reinscription of their bodies on a map—this time one belonging to a corporation. The traceur ends up in a position like that of the anonymous young girl whose movements through Paris were meticulously tracked by Monsieur Alibert and published in Chombart de Lauwe's book.

In this respect, parkour is little different from mobile games like Niantic's *Ingress*, *Pokémon Go*, and *Harry Potter: Wizards Unite*. In parkour, as in these games, participants are encouraged to transgress urban norms by the incentives of a virtual community, but any transgression that takes place is counterbalanced by the fact that participants' bodies are tracked and monetized throughout. These games are, moreover, a reminder that while SI may have advocated play as a way to resist the utilitarianism of modern urban life, not all forms of play are transgressive. Play can be recuperated by capitalism and by the state. Niantic is a particularly insidious example. The company began as an internal startup at Google with the goal of monetizing the vast amounts of location data the company was collecting through its cellphone-tracking and mapping programs. The company's first creation was *Ingress*. Players' phones show them an alternate reality map of their actual location upon which a virtual turf war is taking place. Players select one of two factions, the Enlightened or Resistance, and cooperate to stop the spread of an alien substance called "Exotic Matter." They "[act] as coordinated human antibodies that work to exploit the invasive matter while also regulating its presence."[74] Players purchase computer viruses in-game to unleash on their opponents. Figures of parasitism—biological, mediatic, and social—pervade the game world. *Ingress* presents a city besieged by infection and faceless foreign invaders. The other is necessarily disease-bearing, and sanitation is vital to secure the borders of the city.

But what takes place on top of this virtual biological warfare is the extraction of surplus-value, by Google, through data-mining and advertisement. The game's programmers channel players to real-world sites by creating in-game rewards. They then auction that influence to private companies. On its website, Niantic claims that in 2019, real-world events connected to its games generated $249 million in tourism revenue. The data gathered from players is turned into user profiles that enable targeted advertising. Nathan Hulsey and Joshua Reeves use Roberto Esposito's theorization of the *munus* to describe the relationship between Google and the players of these games. The *munus* means both a gift and a set of duties, and its exchange is what defines membership in a community. The *munus* represents each member's exposure to the others; in a community no one is independent, because some part of each member is always exposed to, shared with, given to, the other. Esposito contrasts community with immunity, a state of exemption from the bonds of reciprocity. The immune subject can enjoy the benefits of community, but doesn't have to give anything and isn't exposed. Esposito traces how this political status was medicalized and naturalized through the theory of the immune system—a topic that will be discussed further in chapter 5. In a game like *Ingress*, players form a community through their teamwork. They rely on other players and are exposed to them in ways that are, consistent with Esposito's observation about the medicalization of the *munus*, metaphorized as contagion. In this universe of unstable borders and weaponized viruses, Google enjoys immune status. Google takes what players give—their time, their data, and the movement of their bodies—and reciprocates nothing. "Google is empowered with the exceptional privilege to extract players' communal contributions from the cycle of reciprocal exchange. Once released from this system of communal reciprocity, the *Ingress* community's gifts are monetized, generating capital that becomes the exclusive purview of Google."[75]

The mix of contagious imagery and hygienics, transgression and institutionalism, that we find with parkour is not as cynical as what we see with companies like Niantic, but the similarities between these two forms of playful urban exploration are significant. Parkour's exploitation of digital maps, image technologies, and media platforms implicates it in a broader surveillant apparatus, inhibiting its participants' ability to truly transgress urban boundaries and norms of movement. Traceurs go to places the map can't see, and move in ways the map can't predict, but with their tracked bodies they extend the visibility of the map, and help to gradually fill in its blind spots.

Similar problems emerge in Vasset's practice, despite his preference for analogue technologies. Vasset, as I suggested above, has a Rancièrian understanding of the relationship between cartography and urban space. Those who have a share in the *partage du sensible*, who are visible to the state, can expect to have their petitions answered by the government, whereas those who are invisible are disenfranchised. In Rancière's framework, every gesture that extends the sphere of visibility is a progressive one, endowing more and more people with access to the state's resources and respect. When Vasset discovers a gap between the map and the city, when he finds invisible populations living in the empty spaces of the map, he dedicates himself to making them visible. He strives to correct the map by filling in its blank spaces. But extending the map until every person and place is represented on it, including all people in the police's sphere of visibility, is precisely the goal of the surveillance state. Do the houseless people the author encounters desire that kind of visibility?

At the core of Vasset's project, SI's psychogeography, and parkour is a desire to correct the map. All three approaches to urban exploration start from the observation that some elements of the city are not represented on maps, whether they be the blank areas populated by houseless people, subconscious barriers between one area and another, or paths that require physical strength to travel. All three attempt to render those elements visible by rewriting maps or by supplementing them with other visual media.

Looking beyond Paris, there are numerous contemporary artists whose work engages with cartography. Jeremy Wood, Teri Rueb, and Esther Polak have all used GPS tracking to record the movements of bodies through urban space, producing maps that are high-fidelity versions of Monsieur Alibert's. George Legrady's installations often involve the mapping of data collected from visitors, who either give it freely or have it taken by surveillance equipment. Michelle Teran's walking tours, called *Life: A User's Manual* in tribute to Georges Perec, involve a portable television and a radio scanner that together allow participants to tap security cameras and watch what they see live. These projects share the interest in cartography and urban movement of SI, Réda, Vasset, and parkour, but they are much more attentive to surveillance. And yet, while these artists foreground surveillance in various ways, they do not really undermine it. Their goal—borrowing the title from one of Legrady's installations—is making visible the invisible. They allow the public to take part in surveillance as a voyeuristic pleasure. They turn data-mining into an aesthetic object. They test cartography's aptitude to capture emotions or identity. But just like SI, Vasset, and parkour, they seek to extend, correct, or supplement what the map can see, not to obscure it.

Out of the projects discussed in this chapter, only Réda's takes the opposite approach. Réda's purpose is not to fix maps. Instead, he revels in their failure to master the city. He casts doubt over cartography's capacity ever to overcome its lacunae. Réda's narrator repeatedly complains that nothing happens during his walk through the city, and it is true that little has changed by the end of the book. But, read in the context of ubiquitous surveillance and data monetization, Réda's theoretical critique of cartography offers more direct opposition to the exercise of power in the city than the more openly *engagé* writings of Debord or Vasset. Réda's argument against the fidelity of maps is an argument against the omniscience of the surveillance state and Big Data. From this can be extrapolated that the exercises of power founded on those regimes of visibility will always be limited in some respect.

Réda's critique of cartography intersects with recent work by Luciana Parisi. In *Contagious Architecture* she takes issue with the conventional axiomatic view of algorithms that sees them as rational tools capable of translating reality into a finite set of probabilities and calculations. She argues that such a conception is flawed by its failure to account for how finite algorithms process infinite data. For Parisi, algorithms are inexorably marked by their encounter with what cannot be numerically processed. "The programming of generative algorithms [. . .] does not simply lead to new orders of complexity [. . .] but instead encounters a wall of data that cannot be synthesized in smaller quantities. This wall of incompressible data instead overruns the program, and thus neutralizes or reveals the incompleteness of the axioms on which the program was based in the first place."[76] Algorithms do not take the chaos of reality and remove randomness and contingency from it, offering us mathematical determinism in their place. Forced to confront infinite amounts of data that necessarily can never be fully processed, algorithms output contingent results. "Randomness has become the condition of programming culture."[77]

Warnings around surveillance and data collection often center on a fear that they will result in panoptic visibility, and that this will bring with it total control over individuals' economic and political behavior. Opposition to surveillance and data collection has many justifications, but Parisi's argument goes against the notion that perfect visibility is attainable, or that such visibility could be translated into a deterministic understanding of behavior. Parisi insists on the fundamental inability of these technologies to ever eliminate noise. Tools for mediating the *polis* and the populace cannot eradicate their parasites.

Parisi uses a variety of biological terms in her argument. The immanence of randomness in programming is a "contagion"; algorithms are "infected with" infinite quantities of data, and experience "outbreak[s] of randomness." Like Serres, she argues that the parasites of programming are not contingent errors to be overcome with greater refinement. They are integral to what algorithms are and do. Taking a stand against the rhetoric of "data pollution" and its epidemic undertones, she advocates the embrace of contingency in computation.[78] She speaks of an aesthetics of algorithms, where noise is not controlled or excluded but interpreted and appreciated. This attitude toward noise will come up again in the final chapter of this book.

Serres does not address cartography directly in *The Parasite*. Instead he talks about the harpedonaptae, the ancient Egyptian surveyors who used geometry to divide the land into agricultural plots. These proto-cartographers rationalized space, turned it into property, and created the conditions for economic value to be extracted from it. They were called in as judges when boundaries were disputed, when a sneaky neighbor crossed a line. As he does throughout his text *Le Mal propre*, Serres plays on the double meaning of *propriété*: property and cleanliness. Harpedonaptae abstracted space by cleaning it, by expelling the life, complexity, and mess from it. Their work, however—like that of the Cartesian architect of chapter 3—is never complete. Parasites always linger at the edges of the field. They sneak in at the corners. Once a parasite gets into abstract space, "it immediately opens a gap, a disequilibrium. The system all of a sudden changes. It drifts [*Il dérive*]."[79] The rationalization of space is always incomplete, always temporary. There are no stable equilibria. Parasites maintain a gap between abstraction and the real. Geometry, cartography, surveillance, algorithms never fully succeed at visualizing space, at imposing their logics upon it. The city is always in some way beyond what they can see.

Charlie Hebdo and Parasitism

In conclusion, I want to consider an example of the breakdown of the tools used to visualize urban space, and anticipate and control the behavior of the bodies within it. On January 7, 2015, Paris was the site of a major terrorist attack targeting the offices of the satirical magazine *Charlie Hebdo*. In a related attack the following day, hostages were taken and four of them murdered at a kosher supermarket. Both attacks also involved the killing of a police officer. Shortly thereafter, the French government called for a demonstration to show unity in the face of what was perceived as an attack on the core national values of press freedom and religious liberty. A *marche républicaine* took place on January 11.

These events brought together several of the themes discussed already in this book. The attack on the magazine's offices was parasitic in the sense that it was an attack on a media channel, an attempt to disrupt mediation. The attacks were also parasitic—with emphasis on *para*, adjacent or nearby—in their curious tendency to miss their mark, to show up next door or in liminal spaces, to involve the neighbors. *Charlie Hebdo*'s unmarked office was at 10 rue Nicolas-Appert. Chérif and Saïd Kouachi initially showed up at number 6, two doors down. After realizing their mistake, they accosted a postwoman and demanded the correct address. Then they went to the wrong floor, misled by the artist Coco, whom they took hostage on the staircase. Likewise, before taking hostages at the Hypercacher market in Porte de Vincennes (the frontier of the city), Amedy Coulibaly attempted to attack a Jewish school in Montrouge. Following his death, police found a map in his car marked with the locations of Jewish schools. His attack missed its target, and landed somewhere else in the neighborhood.

The *marche républicaine* and the associated demonstrations that took place following the attack made ample use of street art and graffiti as well as viral media and memes. The hashtag "Je Suis Charlie" was tweeted 3.4 million times by the end of January 8. The total number would reach almost 14 million. A hashtag is an example of a quasi-object. Users append a message to it, and circulate the subjectivity it confers. Within hours, this quasi-object migrated to the walls of the city: the street artist Jef Aérosol produced a stencil reading "Je Suis Charlie," and disseminated it through social media. The Morice Brothers' monument to the Republic in the center of the Place de la République became a quasi-object as well. Over the course of January 11, hundreds of demonstrators seized the monument, hanging banners and posters from it and writing on it with spray paint.[80] The monument conferred subjectivity on those who climbed upon it, and that subjectivity circulated over the course of the day. Messages piled on top of one another, producing a noisy palimpsest. The rain that would fall on January 13 would make the posters sag and the ink run, rendering the text visually noisy in addition to being semiotically so.

We can also find examples of the limits of cartography and related technologies in these attacks and the demonstration they triggered. The day before the *marche républicaine*, the Paris police released a map whose purpose was to predict and prescribe the limits of the demonstration. A blue-green geometric shape represented the zone demonstrators would occupy, while blue and red color-coded lines marked the paths the march would follow (see figure 4.4). There are obvious echoes of the color-coded lines drawn by Napoleon III on the map of Paris in 1853; indeed, the three streets designated—Boulevard Voltaire, Avenue de la République, and Avenue Philippe-Auguste—were created by Haussmann. They were, we can assume, among the lines drawn by the emperor. The map issued by police came with a press release that prescribed the type of speech (or lack thereof) that would be exercised in the state-sanctioned *manifestation*. This was to be "a silent republican march." The police hoped to preempt both the litigious, discursive mode of collective politics described by Rancière and the noisiness of the parasitic collective. The crowd would possess clear borders, and it would not speak.

However, as the day went on, new marchers arrived at the Place de la République at a rate much greater than the one at which they were dispersing from the Place de la Nation, the square the police had designated as

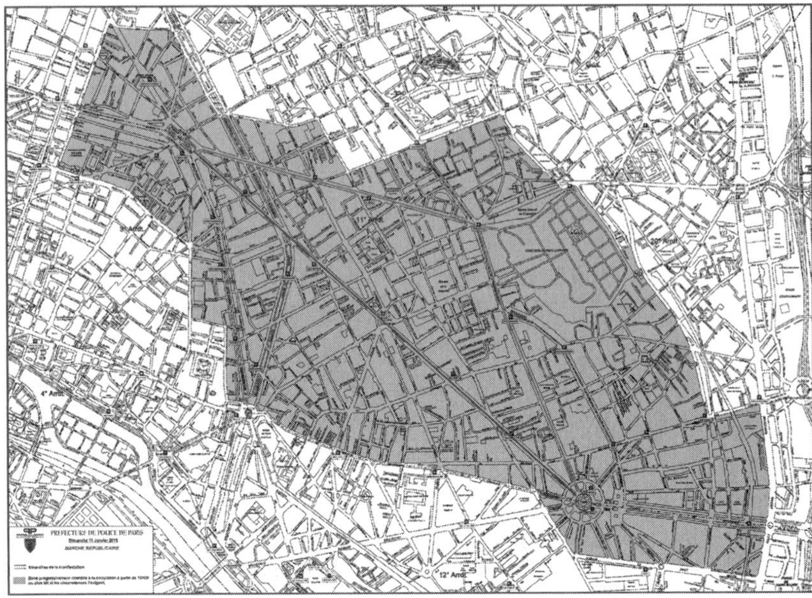

Figure 4.4

Map released by the Préfecture de Police de Paris. Lines mark the approved paths of the march; the shaded region represents the zone that would be closed to traffic

the end point of the procession. This produced blockages. The boulevards filled up, and the march came to a standstill. In response, people began to branch into side streets and adopt new destinations. The crowd advanced past the borders of the area highlighted on the police map. It lasted long after the projected dispersal time of 6 p.m. It was not silent. It went beyond the spatial, temporal, and rhetorical limits the police had attempted to impose. The march spread out of control. The Interior Ministry responded by deploying another cartographic technology: aerial photography. Video taken from a helicopter could provide a live, bird's-eye view of the march. The images that the Ministry published, however, did the opposite. The demonstration was so large that in order to bring its full extent into view, the camera had to be elevated to an altitude that made bodies impossible to see (figure 4.5). The crowd vanished into the streets. Police attempts to visualize the collective showed nothing at all. The Ministry would later state that counting people in a march of that size was "impossible."[81]

Figure 4.5
Still from French Ministère de l'Intérieur's helicopter video of the march, taken from a video report by VTM News

The metro map broke down as well. Before the march, police closed ten metro stations and recommended that marchers arrive by the stations at Châtelet, Strasbourg-Saint Denis, and the Gares du Nord and de l'Est. As the crowd began to overflow initial projections, an additional dozen stations were closed, including two of those recommended by the police. The network entered a state of arteriosclerosis. The interactive RATP map filled up with traffic cone icons warning of new closures all over the city. It served the opposite of its intended function: no longer a guide of how to get to the march but how not to. A map that normally renders the city as lines that transport people from place to place instead became a map of points representing the places one could not go.

It became, in the end, like Invader's Minimal Invasion Map of Paris referenced at the beginning of this chapter. Invader's map shows neither streets nor borders, only the shapes of a few monuments and one thousand icons. Those icons represent an itinerary: the places a player would have to visit to play Invader's game. The exact direction of that itinerary, the streets

Figure 4.6

RATP interactive map of the Paris metro at the height of station closures[82]

to be used, the detours to take, are left obscure. Position is given without direction, location without any suggestion of how to arrive there. So too do the lines of movement on the RATP map transform into points of stasis. These points tell the reader where the march is, but not how to get there. Participation in the demonstration will require going on foot, retracing the lines between these points with the movement of the body, *à la* Invader's installation in San Diego.

These two maps and the Interior Ministry's aerial photographs are all examples of the limits of the cartographic gaze. In these maps we see the desire to rationalize urban space through its geometrization, and the desire for an objective point of view. And we also see the imprecision Réda locates in cartography, the gap between cartography and the real, the parasites that always threaten to interfere with and interrupt mediation. The breakdown of these maps is also the breakdown of a surveillant gaze. The Interior Ministry's helicopter view was surveillant both in the literal sense of watching over from above and in the conventional sense. It was an attempt to gain control over the crowd by establishing a panoptic perspective. The police's recognition that the images it produced did not allow it to count the crowd indicates that if the cartographic gaze is limited by its imprecision, so too is the surveillant gaze.

Of course, one could just as easily find evidence for that in the actions that precipitated the march. One of the primary criticisms directed at the French police following the *Charlie Hebdo* attack was that they had carried out direct surveillance of the Kouachi brothers, yet had failed to thwart them. How could the government have looked directly at these men and not anticipated the violence they were to commit? The government's response was to pass the *Loi Renseignement*, expanding the police's powers to monitor French citizens and eliciting new fears from the public of the end of privacy. Such fears are legitimate and, as I said above, the fact that surveillance is imperfect does not mean it is benign. But the example of the Kouachi brothers is a reminder that mapping is not the same as seeing. Having the brothers on the grid did not, in the end, result in their actions being predicted. Expecting it to ignores the gap between citizens and the state's technologies for localizing them. It ignores the noise that is intrinsic to any technique of representation. This is a challenge that is not alleviated through increased data collection; if anything, it is rendered all the more intractable. The United States NSA documents leaked by Edward Snowden in 2013, for example, though they revealed a panoptic intelligence apparatus far more extensive than was publicly understood at the time, included "not a single instance where analysis of social media predicted a social uprising or political movement."[83]

The difficulty French intelligence faced in translating looking into seeing and seeing into controlling testifies to the noisiness of cartography and to the inevitability, paraphrasing Réda, that surprises will emerge when the city is subjected to an abstracting, rationalizing gaze. Another noisiness has also permeated this chapter and the previous one: that of parasitic collectives where subjectivity circulates constantly. The discourse of a practice like parkour is rife with contradictions. Depending on how you look at it, parkour is either a dangerous epidemic driving people to tear up their bodies so that they can go viral, or it's the hip-hop Hitler Youth, the means by which body and spirit can be purged to unlock new forms of holistic health. It is either a means of tearing down walls, or a practice that could not exist without them. It is either the supreme expression of the potential of a multicultural, decentralized France, or a continuation of long-standing top–down efforts to use public health as a tool for constructing an idealized French race. Contradictions and confusion also characterize the discourses that emerged from the circulation of quasi-objects during the *marche républicaine*. The slogan "Je Suis Charlie" appears to symbolize unity. It enacts the consolidation of the collective within a single subject position (not *nous* but *je*) and its adoption of a shared identity. In practice, though, this quasi-object was appended to a variety of contradictory discourses. The hashtag could be used with praise of Allah and calls for secularism. It could be used to get attention for statements with no connection to the terror attack. Over time, the phrase itself was problematized, and appended to critiques of *Charlie* and of the call for unity. Some argued, for instance, that while the press freedom *Charlie Hebdo* symbolized was an important shared value, the magazine's editorial positions, particularly its provocative criticism of religion, should not be assimilated into French republicanism. While in some cases that opposition was disseminated with alternative hashtags, like "Je Suis Ahmed,"[84] a reference to a Muslim police officer killed during the attack, in other cases it spread using the very hashtag it critiqued. Those uncomfortable with the magazine's content reframed "Je Suis Charlie" as a way of saying one supported *Charlie Hebdo*'s right to exist, but not its particular beliefs. The logic was supported with a quote that has long been erroneously attributed to Voltaire: "I don't agree with what you say, but I will defend to the death your right to say it." To say "I am Charlie" is in this gloss a way of saying "I am my own right to difference from you." The fact that the phrase did not actually come from one of the founding fathers of French republicanism only engendered more confusion and contradiction, parodied in a cartoon by Patrick Chappatte (see figure 4.7). In the end, the discourse produced by the circulation of this hashtag, a phrase that promises unification of the collective around a shared voice, was cacophonous and self-contradictory.[85]

In this chapter I have made repeated references to Rancière's political theory, both because of its direct relevance to the cartographic texts I have been exploring and because I see it as emblematic of a reigning tendency in contemporary politics to valorize the voice and communication. For Rancière, a key stage in a group's transition from *demos* to citizenry is subjectivation, which he describes as an emergence from noise. In *On the Shores of Politics* he writes that dissensus is an act by which an argument is "torn from the sub-world of obscure noises and inserted by contingent force in

Figure 4.7
Cartoon by Patrick Chappatte depicting a nonplussed Voltaire asking the *Charlie Hebdo* cartoonists how to interpret the quote misattributed to him by protestors, © Chappatte, *Le Temps*, Switzerland, www.chappatte.com

the world of meaning and visibility."[86] Noise is opposed to meaning and visibility. Noise is where the *demos* lives. Noise is tantamount to silence. To achieve rights and state recognition, a group must eliminate noise from its speech; it must create the conditions for communication to take place. For Rancière, politics begins with the voice. If you can't speak clearly, you have no hope of being heard. A group that contradicts itself, that lacks an identity, that cannot master the cacophony of its members is, in the end, no group at all, and has no hope of intervening in the space of democracy.[87]

The idea that a group has to speak with one voice in order to engage in politics appears to be contradicted by the *marche républicaine*, which was cacophonous but nevertheless an important political event. Writers like Moisés Naím and Clay Shirky have argued that disorganized movements mediated by digital networks have revolutionary potential, and augur the "end of power."[88] However, in the years since the *marche républicaine* many critics have questioned whether it actually produced any political effect.

One year after the attacks, a number of French journalists were already asking if anything remained of the "esprit Charlie." Similar questions have been asked of other mass protest events that relied on digital quasi-objects like the hashtag: Occupy Wall Street and the so-called Twitter Revolutions in Moldova, Iran, Tunisia, Egypt, and Ukraine. The research team of Manuel Cebrian, Iyad Rahwan, and Sandy Pentland has pessimistically observed that "most of these events burst upon the scene, occupy our attention for a few days, and then fade into oblivion with nothing substantial having been accomplished."[89] Looking specifically at the social interactions among Occupy Wall Street participants, a separate group of researchers found that few, if any, social connections were formed that lasted beyond the end of the movement.[90] As I will discuss further in chapter 5, Rancière's theories accurately describe the dismissiveness that often greets protest movements that fail to make clear demands.

Perhaps, then, Rancière is right, and collectives founded on the circulation of a quasi-object are politically inert because they are noisy. Serres himself equivocates when it comes to the political utility of parasitism. He writes: "far from transforming a system [. . .] the parasite makes it change states differentially. It inclines it. [. . .] Often this inclination has no effect, but it can produce gigantic ones by chain reactions or reproduction. Immunity or epidemic crisis." Parasitism can be conservative or revolutionary; he does not take sides. Elsewhere he notes that biological parasites must keep their host alive or risk their own death, a fact that leads him to suggest a reading of the parasite as that which "gives the host the means to be safe from the parasite."[91]

Serres's parasitic collectivism may be politically sterile. However, if it is, the blame does not lie exclusively with those producing the noise. It also lies with those listening. Cebrian et al. may have found no long-term effects of Occupy and the Twitter Revolutions, but their methodology is graph theory, a particularly cartographic paradigm for interpreting collective behavior. Perhaps they would reach a different conclusion if they did not try to put these movements on a map. In the same way that they lament that current methods cannot identify, and therefore cannot account for, online behaviors that do not successfully percolate into protests in the real world, the effects of these movements might occur precisely within that portion of the community that is not visible to a graph. A version of this argument is made by Zeynep Tufekci: "the future trajectory or potential impacts of networked movements cannot be fully understood by using only the conceptual models, indicators and benchmarks that we have gathered from the histories of earlier movements."[92] While it is possible that parasitic collectivism is as conservative as Serres at times implies, it is also possible that, just as Parisi calls for a new aesthetic to engage with messy and contingent algorithms, a new hermeneutic is necessary to a proper engagement with the political effects of urban activities that neither achieve nor seek univocity. In chapter 5 I will examine different ways of conceptualizing the relationship between the collective, the voice, and noise, and between the body politic, the bodies that make it up, and parasites.

5 Bodies

Does a collective need to have a voice to be politically effective? What kind of body is necessary to produce a voice? What is the relationship between the individual body and the collective body? How do you distinguish between the two?

In chapter 4, I briefly discussed Roberto Esposito's work on immunity and community. These two terms merit a fuller explanation. The words share the root, *munus*, which in ancient Rome meant both gift and duty. Politically speaking, the *munus* was a set of duties required of each Roman citizen. To be part of the com-*mun*-ity, a citizen had to do certain things for the collective. They had to have some skin in the game. Esposito writes that being duty-bound in this way made each member of the community fundamentally open. They relied on the other members, which meant they were exposed to them. Immunity was a special political status. As the name suggests, the immune were exempted from the duties other citizens were expected to contribute to the community, but they still enjoyed all the rights of full citizens. An immune subject got the benefits of being part of the community, while avoiding the openness and vulnerability that were supposedly their price.

Esposito's central argument is that Enlightenment political philosophy enacted the immunization of the collective. In Hobbes, Locke, Descartes, Rousseau, and Kant he identifies a consistent desire to insulate the individual from the other members of the community. Hobbes, for instance, seeks to protect humans from the violent encounter with one another (the vulnerability of community) by replacing the myriad horizontal relationships between them with a single vertical relationship between each individual and Leviathan. The members of the community are no longer exposed to one another. They have been immunized.

Now, for most of the nineteenth century, the political ideology of immunity coexisted uneasily with biological science. With the advent of hygienics and the concept of public health, states began to understand their citizens as sharing health, as forming a collective body whose health could be acted on at a macrosocial level. A city could have health, and its health could directly influence the health of its residents; hence the Haussmannian corporealization of Paris, with its belly, lungs, innards, and veins. The miasma theory of disease held that disease filled the environment and that the body, through its metabolic functions, was always open to disease. The body was a permeable membrane. The medieval metaphor of the body politic, in which each member of the community formed one part of a massive collective body (visualized in the frontispiece of Hobbes's *Leviathan*), remained in use. The king and his two bodies were put to death in the French Revolution, but they would return over the course of the nineteenth century, as would other corporeal figurations of the state, like the female and maternal body of the Republic.[1] The idea that each person is part of a larger organism, the idea that the health of each individual depends on the health of the collective, the idea that disease is always passing through the body, all go against immunization of the subject, which tries to isolate each individual from the others, and to grant them autonomy. How can one be autonomous and part of a vast, interconnected body at the same time?

A solution came in the form of a reconceptualization of the biological limits and openness of the body. The theory of biological immunity offered a biological analogue for political immunity, allowing the Enlightenment idea of the autonomous self to be grounded in scientific observation. The theory stated that the body was not a permeable membrane; the skin was its boundary, and it destroyed any invader that crossed it. The body was not open to the environment and to the community, but instead naturally fought to preserve its independence from them. "Instead of evoking the organism's essential connection *to* the world in which it lives," Ed Cohen writes, "immunity refigures medicine as a powerful weapon in the body's necessary struggle to defend itself *from* its life-threatening context." Cohen argues that the biological theory of immunity enabled the emergence of a new concept of the body, "the modern body." This is an atomized and autonomous body. The individual human is defined as coextensive with his or her skin. The limits of biological immunity are made to match up with the limits of political immunity. "The modern body proffers a proper body, a proprietary body, a body whose well-bounded property grounds the legal and political rights of what C. B. Macpherson famously named 'possessive individualism.'"[2]

The concept of the modern body emerged at roughly the same time as the science of parasitology. This is no coincidence, according to Cohen. Up to the 1870s, "parasite" was a rarely used term in biology. The organisms that are today classified as parasites were called "helminths" or "entozoans."[3] Starting in the 1870s, that changed, with a vast array of organisms suddenly classified as parasites. The reason was the development of germ theory. In miasma theory disease was diffuse and impossible to visualize. Germ theory gave it visible boundaries. A bacterium could be viewed under a microscope. With the ability to see disease's boundaries, and to identify it as an organism, came the ability to confer subjectivity and agency on it. Disease could be othered.[4]

Just as the political ideology of immunity was borrowed by biologists, the social discourse of the parasite was borrowed to explain the behavior of these organisms. Bacteria, parasitology implicitly argued, behaved like bad guests. They took food, energy, resources—life itself—from their host. They took what didn't belong to them. The host was entitled to throw these bad guests out.

On the surface, the deployment of the parasitic discourse in this context is an odd choice. If the point of the modern body is that it is well-bounded and autonomous, then why draw so much attention to organisms which, by definition, cross the boundaries of the body? The parasite lives in and off its host; its very existence testifies to the permeability of the membranes that immunization seeks to close off. The social meaning of parasite does not even map especially well to the biological relationship it was appropriated to describe. In the Ancient Greek usage of *parasitos*, the host's relationship to the parasite is ambivalent. The parasite pays for his meal with entertainment. He is indulged by the host, although, as he is not a guest, he is always threatened with eviction. No such ambivalence was present in the biological application of parasitism. Biological parasites were by definition disease agents. With the health of the host an absolute imperative, their eradication was a necessary reflex.

Applying a term anchored in class and social mores to biological relationships leads to confusingly moralistic judgments of natural behaviors. Cohen is particularly interested in the term, "obligate parasite," used for organisms that cannot survive outside the body of their host: "the idea that a parasite is obligated to its parasitism somewhat undermines the premise of the parasite, since its very nature requires it to be the bad guest. Indeed if it has no 'life' apart from the life that it 'manipulates' through the host's cellular processes, then it may not be either a good or a bad guest at all but something more like a symbiont."[5] Additionally, if what makes an organism a parasite is its misappropriation of a host's resources, then parasitism risks becoming a subjective judgment more than a biological fact. Leeches, for instance, may be considered parasites today, but were symbionts when doctors believed they could suck disease out of the body. The tapeworm has a similarly ambivalent status. An organism's parasitism is in the eye of the beholder, contingent upon the human host's estimation of how beneficial the relationship is.

Parasitism thus seems a confusing discourse to turn to in support of germ theory, immunity, and the modern body. But the contradictions latent in this discourse are precisely what make it work. The identification and eradication of parasites is part of a dialectical process through which the host is constituted. The host identifies something inside it that does not belong, pathologizes it, and purges it, and thus produces his or her own integrity—or at least a partial integrity that has to be continually reconstituted through the identification of new parasites and new acts of purgation. Just as the host of a dinner demonstrates mastery of their home by evicting parasites from a meal, the human subject gains mastery of the body by purging parasites from it. The modern body as a well-bounded and autonomous subject is constituted through gestures of biological othering and purgation.

Esposito puts forth a similarly dialectical understanding of the relationship between immunity and community. The immune subject is closed off from the vulnerability that characterizes community, but immunity is not a stable state that can be achieved. It is a never-ending process involving the constant identification of traces of the other inside the body. These openings to community are closed off through processes that are equal parts purge and assimilation: "The dialectical figure that emerges is that of exclusionary inclusion or exclusion by inclusion. The body defeats a poison not by expelling it outside the organism, but by making it somehow part of the body."[6] The immunization of the subject is a process that never fully eliminates the traces of the other. Community is an integral part of the dialectic. Immunity is not achieved; it is continually produced.

What this ultimately means is that the subject's autonomy *vis-à-vis* the collective remains uncertain. The biological theory of immunity brought medicine into line with the political project to atomize and autonomize the subject, but it did not succeed in closing the body off to its environment or to other people. If anything, by deploying a discourse of parasitism to explain the body's relationship to disease agents, biological immunity brought out in greater relief the always incomplete nature of immunity. The unwelcome guests of the body are never evicted once and for all: the vulnerability of community never entirely goes away. How the individual body fits in with the collective thus remains an open question.

The imperfectly immunized individual's relationship to the collective is further complicated by the fact that both Esposito and Cohen draw direct lines from the immunization of the individual body to the immunization of the body politic or the metaphorical body of the city. A group, a city, a state can be immunized by purging itself of its parasites, and thus enjoy its own kind of individualism. It is not clear what happens to the immunity of the members of such a collective, or how membership in an immunized collective body differs from community.

These questions relate directly to the discussion opened at the end of chapter 4 regarding the political capacities of noisy collectives. Rancière argues that a group is able to take part in politics only by suppressing noise and adopting an understandable voice. The group has to establish clear limits for itself, and a clear identity, and coalesce around a single subject position. In other words, Rancière requires the group to immunize itself. It must purge its parasites and clarify its borders if it wants to be listened to. I contrasted this model of the collective with Serres's parasitic collectives, whose boundaries are always unclear and whose speech is cacophonous. In this chapter I will look more closely at the question of the voice and noisiness of urban collectives, this time through the lens of the biopolitical ideologies I have just laid out.

I will begin by looking at French crowd theory from the early twentieth century. In the work of the proto-sociologist Gabriel Tarde, and that of the poet-philosopher Jules Romains, the body of the collective is a constant concern. These two thinkers ask what happens to the individual in a collective, and problematize the distinction between individual and group. They are both interested in the communication that takes place in and through groups, and how it relates to collective subjectivity. But what makes these writers particularly interesting for me is their engagement with parasites—mediatic, social, and biological. The groups they discuss are not the well-organized, univocal collectives of Rancière; they are noisy, nebulous, and unpredictable. Tarde and Romains demonstrate an openness to parasites that contrasts starkly with the purgative stance of immunity and the modern body.

Noise Makes the Body: Alternatives to Immunization

The end of the nineteenth century in France was a period marked by a flurry of writing on collectives. Gabriel Tarde (1843–1904) and his opponent, Émile Durkheim (1858–1917), were among the most prominent thinkers on the subject. Durkheim would ultimately emerge as the most influential of the two. He and Tarde took part in a well-publicized debate at the École des Hautes Études Sociales in Paris in 1903. Durkheim won that debate and Tarde's work was marginalized in France, though it would become influential in America, particularly at the University of Chicago. Tarde's thinking was rediscovered in France in the second half of the twentieth century, and has been acknowledged as an influence by Gilles Deleuze and Bruno Latour. Tarde has proved particularly influential in the study of digital social networks. Latour calls him "a thinker of networks before their time," and his writings have been referenced by Nigel Thrift and Tony Sampson, both of whom connect his concepts to disease metaphors (affective contagion in Thrift's case, virality in Sampson's).[7] Part of the reason Tarde's ideas struggled to find traction in his lifetime, and part of what has made them appealing today, is how radically they challenge the ideology of the immunized modern body. Tarde resisted the concept of a well-bounded, autonomous subject as well as the pathologization of parasites. His work represents an interesting alternative framework through which to engage with the biopolitics of the collective.

Durkheim promoted the idea that groups of people produced and were held together by "social facts," cultural norms and mores. Durkheim's understanding of how each person relates to the collective in some ways rejects the ideology of the immunized modern body. He criticized a Cartesian understanding of the purely rational individual, arguing that every person is influenced, often unconsciously, by the culture of their society and by their emotional ties to other people. Durkheim's self is open to its environment and context. He also refers to a "collective consciousness," implying that each member of a society participates in a shared subjectivity that supersedes their own. However, Durkheim also identified and promoted the "cult of the individual." Mirroring the analysis of Cohen and Esposito, Durkheim held that the late eighteenth century had seen the advent of a new secular religion whose gospel was the worship of autonomy, rationality, free expression, and equality. He argued forcefully that while each individual was shaped by their context, they were not subordinate to the collective and ultimately enjoyed a degree of freedom in how they responded to social facts. Individuals maintained their autonomy *vis-à-vis* the collective, and in fact could be completely disconnected from it. The rising suicide rate at the end of the nineteenth century was evidence. The proper response to this "anomie," he wrote, was not to combat individualism but instead to promote integration, a process through which individuals become emotionally invested in social facts. Durkheim did not believe the subject should dissolve into the group; individualism persists even in the most tightly knit society.

Tarde, by contrast, argued that groups were held together by imitation. There were no overarching social facts; rather, local interactions between members of a group radiated like soundwaves passing from molecule to molecule. Group-level behaviors were not the product of a shared consciousness, but rather epiphenomenal expressions of these local interactions. Tarde's collectives are more crowd than society. They are governed by unpredictable caprice rather than the relative stability of a social fact.

Tarde takes things one step further by suggesting that the same imitative processes are at work at different scales. If crowds are held together by the influence each member exerts on those in his or her immediate vicinity, so too is the human body held together by the influence each organ exerts on those nearby. Muscle tissue imitates muscle tissue and nerves imitate nerves. The cells inside the tissue of the body imitate one another, as do the molecules inside those cells. Every person is a crowd. Everything is dividual. Tarde also dematerializes the subject. His subject is embedded in virtual networks in addition to real space. "Not every meeting of the minds has physical contact as its necessary precondition."[8] There are no spatial limits to the subject. Tarde thus explodes the boundaries and integrity of the self. Not only is each person constantly exposed to the influence of their context, and not only does that context extend through networks to encompass the entire world, but the person itself is also implied to be illusory. There is no molar structure, only molecular interactions that produce moments of contingent organization.

Tarde's theories go against the premise of the immunized modern body, with its clear boundaries and autonomy. His work further contests the modern body through its embrace of contagion. Tarde uses imitation and contagion interchangeably to describe the interactions between members of a crowd. Contagion is not something that has to be eliminated to preserve the health of the body; contagion is, on the contrary, the cohesive force that holds the body together. Contagion binds a group just as it binds muscles and organs.

Tarde rejects the pathologization of parasites, and preserves the openness of the body. This is true not only of biological parasites, but also of mediatic ones. While Tarde describes the interactions between elements of a collective as "imitation," he does not mean that each person in a crowd faithfully reproduces the actions or emotions they perceive in those around them. The interaction is much messier than that. Tarde explains this dynamic using a sonic example: "One notes in passing the singular taste crowds have for broken windows, for noise, for puerile destruction: it's one of the many ways in which they resemble drunks, whose greatest pleasure, after emptying bottles, is breaking them. In this example, the first one to whistle probably did not realize what excesses he was going to provoke."[9] There are two kinds of mediatic parasite in play here. Tarde identifies crowds with noise. They are drawn to cacophony, and they produce it. The second kind is infidelity in transmission. Someone in the crowd produces a sound—a whistle—and that whistle propagates through contagion. The end result is not, as the word *imitation* might suggest, that the whole crowd whistles; the whistle cascades into a noisily unpredictable collective behavior that the first whistler never could have anticipated. While in this passage the end behavior is rioting, Tarde avoids the negative attitude toward the noisiness of crowds one finds in contemporaries like Gustave Le Bon, who likened crowds to "microbes that bring about the dissolution of infirm bodies or corpses," and believed it was necessary to protect against them.[10]

Tarde's theories were attacked by Durkheim, and quickly fell out of the sociological mainstream in France. One thinker who shared Tarde's openness to parasites, contagion, and the noisiness of the collective was the poet and philosopher Jules Romains (1885–1972). Romains is somewhat forgotten today. In his lifetime he was a prominent figure on the French literary scene, the president of PEN International from 1936 to 1941, and sixteen times nominated for the Nobel Prize in Literature. He is primarily remembered today as a playwright. *Knock ou la triomphe de la médicine* is still performed on French stages, and was adapted into a film in 2017 starring Omar Sy. Romains was, however, a prolific writer working in multiple formats. He considered himself a philosopher whose primary medium was literature. His first published poems appeared in the *Nouvelle Revue Française* accompanied by a note from André Gide announcing him as a great young talent. He published novels as well, including a Balzacian 27-volume series called *Les Hommes de bonne volonté* (Men of Good Will). The philosophy these texts transmitted was Unanimism, a millenarian philosophy that predicted the imminent death of individualism and the rise of new collective consciousnesses. That collectivism was based around the city, Paris in particular. Paris's streets, squares, and communication networks were what would allow the new consciousnesses to emerge.

Romains, like Tarde, was staunchly opposed to Durkheim's empirical sociology and the theory of social facts. In the final section of *Puissances de Paris* (1911), a collection of prose poems dedicated to various topoi in Paris (e.g., "La Place de l'Étoile," "La Rue Montmartre," "L'Omnibus"), he writes: "society is not just an arithmetic sum or a collective designation." He derides the "serious study of social facts" as a costly waste of time and money that can never produce a meaningful understanding of what the collective is. He promotes communal collectives, writing that it is an act of violence to "isolate [a group] from the fluid crowd" or to "exhort it to become a person."[11] Romains's writing, like Tarde's, is characterized by messy and open bodies, unstable selves, and noise in various forms. It speaks both to the body politics and sonic politics of early-twentieth-century Paris, and displays a strikingly positive attitude to the parasites of the city.

Corporeal metaphors mark Romains's writing about collectives from the very beginning. He claimed that his philosophy was inspired by an epiphany he had while walking down the rue d'Amsterdam with his friend, Georges Chennevière. He suddenly felt part of a vast organism: "In the rue d'Amsterdam I am like a cell in the body of a man or in the leaves of a tree. I am the only one conscious of this."[12] Romains had a degree in anatomy in addition to his doctorate in philosophy, and published a pseudo-scientific theory about the human body's ability to see through receptors in the skin (the theory was supposed to explain why sleepwalkers don't bump into the furniture). That theory was an example of his belief in the untapped potential of human bodies. Traces of his anatomical studies pervade his writing. In *Puissances de Paris*, he describes the different collectives produced by different locations in the city. The *unanime* of the rue Royale has "a hard soul [. . .] pressed by the lips of a wound." That of the rue Montmartre is "stretched, inflated. She knows that she is full of new births." The poet himself is part of the "flesh" of these groups.[13]

The anatomy of the collective body is the central concern of a novel he published the same year as *Puissances de Paris*. *Mort de quelqu'un* (literally, "death of somebody," but Desmond MacCarthy and Sydney Waterlow's 1914 English translation renders it as "Death of a Nobody") is the story of a lonely retiree living in Paris. Jacques Godard was once a maintenance man on the express train, but at the start of the novel he lives by himself following the death of his wife. His parents are still alive and live at the furthest end of France, in the village where Jacques was born. Godard's life, like that of the young girl in Chombart de Lauwe's map, mostly takes place inside a small triangle: the grocer, the cemetery where his wife is buried, his apartment in Ménilmontant. In its overall structure the novel is a simple allegory. Godard makes a spontaneous decision to break free from his normal routine; he goes to the Panthéon and decides, for the first time in his life, to climb it; there, atop France's shrine to the cult of the individual, he begins a journey to become the soul of a collective. He contracts pneumonia and dies. This man, too anonymous even to be remembered in the title of his own story, will be an example that anyone can spark an urban collective. His funeral draws out the residents of his building, obliging them to meet and speak to one another for the first time. It draws Jacques's father to the capital. It stops total strangers in the street and draws them into a crowd. This lonely man, killed by the frigid air atop the French Republic's temple of individualism, will be reborn as a crowd on a wide boulevard.

The novel is, of course, more complex than this didactic summary. The emergence of the collective is far from straightforward. Immediately following the discovery of Godard's body by his building's concierge, his neighbors gather in his apartment. This is unusual for them. They normally avoid each other as much as possible. In a scene that anticipates Le Corbusier's writings from later in the decade, and also calls to mind Marcel Proust's decision to line his bedroom walls with cork as a form of soundproofing, Romains writes: "the families kept to themselves and cursed the landlord for having put up such thin walls. In the evening when a family got to chatting around the table and they heard the murmur of their neighbors they broke off their conversation, grumbling: 'It's so unfortunate! We're not at home here. We have walls made of papier-mâché.'" When these people who can normally never be isolated enough come together in Godard's room, a transformation takes place. They begin to collectively embody their recently deceased neighbor. Conditioned by the shape of the room and the position of the furniture, they start adopting the habitual postures and movements of the man whose body lies before them. They even begin to sound like him, and speak phrases he once spoke. The narrator begins to refer to them as a group. The novel could end right there; the death of the individual brings together a collective who unite around his identity and become one entity. The end. Except the residents can't bear it. They are overcome by a "*trop-plein*," a surplus of energy, and several of them flee the room. "The group died a minute later."[14] Replacing the individual with a collective turns out not to be that easy.

For Rosalind Williams and Philippe Geinoz, what is missing here is the network. Williams emphasizes the importance of technologies of transportation and communication for Romains. These include the telegraph, the telephone, the automobile, and the wide streets and train networks of post-Haussmannian Paris. She sees Romains's writing as both advocating and acting out a process of assimilation into these networks: "The poet now understands his mission. He will participate in the efficiency and power of the networked city so that he becomes part of the infrastructure, at once technological and social, of modern life."[15] The idea that the subject becomes part of the infrastructure of modern life is at times literal in *Mort de quelqu'un*. Romains develops a mediatic version of an ontology based around being-for-others in which a character's physical existence is intertwined with their existence in media. Godard exists a little when his parents talk about him, and "still more when a letter came." When the concierge finds Godard's body, he hesitates to send a telegram announcing the news because to do so is to carry out a kind of execution. "If I didn't send the telegram? He would be dead only for me and himself." Jacques's father laments that he would still have a son if he hadn't received the message. The transmission of the news of Godard's death incorporates multiple networks and media. The concierge finds the family's address handwritten in the margin of a newspaper. He walks to the post office and dictates a telegram ("son died today at his home") which travels through electric wires to the far end of the country. Once there, the message is dictated to a messenger boy who recites it to himself while he runs to the family's house to complete the delivery.[16] Godard moves through a variety of media, and they play an important role in bringing together the collective that forms around his funeral.

However, Williams and Geinoz both underscore the efficacy and fidelity of these networks, whereas in *Mort de quelqu'un* they are full of errors. In the section where Godard's parents learn of his death, the narrator draws attention to loose ends, sloppiness, threats of illegibility that trouble the message as it passes from Godard's body to his childhood home. The narrator describes the post office in the provinces where the telegram arrives thus: "Its silence was not the same as any other silence. It existed apart, it came off the walls the way pulp comes away from a peel that's too rigid. It was light and always ready to bloom. Little vibrations must have been pullulating, too subtle to be heard, but occasionally loud enough to almost be noticed." There's a quiet noise resonating in this communication center. The message itself leaves the telegram operator nonplussed: he is uncertain if the "son" in question is the son of the Godard couple in his town, he misremembers Godard's name as "Jean," and when asked for the cause of death responds simply: "You know, in a dispatch . . ."[17]

Noise pervades the novel. While some of the characters see noisiness as an inhibitor to their coming together as a group, over the course of the story noise takes on increasingly positive connotations. Shortly after Godard's death, the same characters who previously wished their walls had better soundproofing to keep out the noises of their neighbors begin to be drawn out into the shared spaces of their building by noise. They step out onto the landing, "learning to live more in the staircase," as Georges Perec once wrote.[18] "Little groups prolixly lamented Godard," says the narrator. This prolix discourse—both excessive and insipid—becomes a dull hum, an asignifying noise. It draws more and more people out, and creates a new continuity between private and public space. This leads to even more noise.

Wind rushes through the newly cross-ventilated stairs, causing doors to slam shut and reopen. With each slam a glimpse of a resident's private space is offered to view—one learns that so-and-so has red tilework or a bed in their front room. The culmination of this process is the formation of a group, and when this group speaks, its voice comes out in an indecipherable noise.[19] It is no longer a question of individuals speaking; the group makes noise.

Noise is omnipresent in the climactic scene of the novel, Godard's funeral, and in a kind of epilogue in which a young man who attended the funeral experiences an epiphany while walking down a boulevard—a scene that reproduces Romains's account of his invention of unanimism. The young man remembers having walked that street in a funeral procession for one of his father's friends. He struggles to remember the dead man's name. He does what we all do in that situation, and tries every possible combination of letters he can think of: "Lenoir . . . Renoir . . . Gaspard . . . Bonnard . . . I definitely knew the old guy's name . . . Bonnard, Bonnet . . . Boulard." Two things happen here: first, the multiplication of ellipses breaks up the syntax of the young man's sentences; second, the words, by dint of repetition, begin to lose their referentiality. They are broken up into component phonemes. The losses of referentiality and syntax combine to turn Godard's name into a stuttering and meaningless noise. It is precisely this confusion that allows the collective spirit to find a new host. As the young man looks back on the events of one year earlier, he suddenly achieves a "superior lucidity" that sensitizes him to "a vast and vague noise." He immediately becomes an apostle for the noisy group age to come. Upon rereading the novel, ourselves sensitized to noise, we might notice that Godard's apartment was not entirely cut off from the world after all, but buzzed with a "hostile murmur."[20] It is perhaps his ability to coexist with this unwelcome guest (see the discussion of Émile Benveniste's etymology of *hôte,* discussed in chapter 6 below; Benveniste identifies the same root word for "hospitality" and "hostile") that predisposes Godard to trigger a collective.

In a preface to a collection of unanimist poetry, Romains boasted that "with his eyes closed he could tell the noise of one intersection from that of another."[21] This is an author who was deeply attuned to the noises of the city. In *Mort de quelqu'un,* aural noise and communicational interference are valorized rather than pathologized. Noisiness and collectivism produce one another, and both are encouraged. Romains demonstrates a similar openness to another kind of parasite: the biological parasite.

Romains repeatedly makes use of microbial metaphors. The novel's narrator compares Godard to "shredded algae" when people gossip about him in the village of his birth. Communal activity in the apartment is described as "the house [. . .] fermenting," implying that Godard's spirit is a kind of yeast. Godard's father compares his son's spirit to the rabies virus. Romains rejects the model of the plant cell with its hard cell wall (the image Le Corbusier would use for his ideal atomized society) by associating it and its "defined places, hard limits, a separation of beings so that they can never encroach upon one another"[22] with graves in a cemetery. He prefers three organisms that trouble a molar notion of identity and the boundaries of the self. He likes algae, a term referring to multiple phyla that are united less by common features than by their refusal to fit neatly into other classifications. Lacking the organs of plants but forming complex colonies that distinguish them from other eukaryotes, algae oscillate uneasily between molar and molecular levels of organization. Algae, yeast, and rabies are all characterized by their potential for disruptive effervescence: the gaseous and intoxicating products of fermentation, the foam at the mouth of the rabid dog, the algal bloom and its immense oxygen output. These organisms all produce an excess. They bubble up outside themselves.

Romains's preference for open bodies and ontologically ambiguous organisms joins up with his embrace of aural noise during the funeral scene. As Godard's neighbors carry his coffin into the church, they are greeted by the sound of an organ. This organ does not produce music, but a murmur that becomes a growl. "It wasn't coming from any specific part of the church; it filled it completely, the way a muzzle is filled with its howl." Mumbling, groaning, a scream: the church resonates with sublinguistic noises. The description echoes the passage in which Godard's "second life" begins (the moment his parents are informed by the young messenger boy of their son's death): it "began with some words stammered by a little boy in a kitchen, in front of a table with two bowls from which steam was rising; it drew itself out into a great cry; became a lamentation, and curled up in a ball as though to bite itself to death." And just as the mother's scream becomes an animal biting itself to death, the howling voice of the collective being born in the church quickly evolves into a bestial metaphor. The rumble of the organ "flowed around their souls, moving them, lifting them up, and drawing them into a kind of hot and vital current. They had the impression of being carried in the blood of a great being."[23]

Romains's metaphors are anatomically confused. The church is simultaneously the mouth of the beast in which its noise resonates and the veins in which its blood flows. The beast is a kind of ouroboros, the mythical snake consuming its own tail. Its articulation is hampered by its mouth being full of its own body. To this conjunction of a fluid cellular paradigm and a noisy aural one, Romains joins the gaseous image that I extracted from his biological metaphors (and that is also present in the steam rising from the bowls on his family's table). The scene concludes with the beast entering a frenzy, chasing its tail so fast that it becomes a whirlwind. The crowd experiences a kind of rapture as it enters the last stage of its "furious birth." Looking up into the vault of the church, they see smoke, "like from an overheated brake."[24] The sublimation of the individual into a collective is almost literal, the passage of a solid into a gas. But this gas is not Godard's spirit itself; it is, like the carbon dioxide produced by yeast or the steam rising from a bowl of porridge, a by-product, an excess. It is both part of the organism and outside it. Godard's bestial spirit grinds like the wheels of the express train he used to maintain, and out comes this smoke, a parasite that cannot exist without Godard but is not entirely part of him.

Romains and Tarde, both writing around the turn of the twentieth century, offer similar alternatives to the dominant biopolitics of their time. In contrast to the ideology of the modern body, immunized through the continual identification and purge of diverse parasites, Tarde and Romains defend open, amorphous, communal bodies. They problematize the idea of the individual and its enclosure, as Cohen puts it, "within an epidermal frontier that distinguishes the person from the world for the duration of what we call a life."[25] Their subjects are distributed through space and embedded in media. Their structure is ephemeral and arbitrary. They dissolve into microbial life forms and molecular interactions. Both of these thinkers embrace parasites rather than pathologizing them, and in so doing allow their subjects to remain permanently open to the other.

However, the question of the politics of these collective bodies remains unanswered. The modern body evolved alongside liberal democracy. It is an ideology shaped by, and one that shaped in turn, the values of individual autonomy and national sovereignty. How does the alternative biopolitics articulated by Tarde and Romains interact with these political values? Tarde and Romains both underscore that their collectives lack a unified voice, emitting noises instead. In Jacques Rancière's political theory, the lack of a voice disqualifies a group from agency in democratic society. He affirms that groups require clear boundaries and an identity. What political possibilities, if any, are available to the noisy, amorphous, open-ended collectives described by Tarde and Romains?

The Body Makes Noise: Violence When the Collective Speaks

Tarde notes the predilection of crowds for broken bottles and windows and puerile destruction. Gustave Le Bon, as I mentioned, would pick up on this theme to argue that the bigger the crowd, the more stupid and destructive it became. While Tarde is more ambivalent about the moral compass of crowds than Le Bon, he does acknowledge the collective's capacity to enter a purely destructive rioting mode. In his poetry, Romains largely avoids the politics of collectives. He studies them like a musicologist having his first encounter with an unfamiliar tradition: he notes their rhythms, their moods, their movements, their pitch. In his novels and essays, however, he was more willing to engage with politics. *Mort de quelqu'un* includes a scene in which the funeral procession is almost thrown off course while crossing paths with a riot. Godard's neighbors see police officers beating protestors, and many of them feel an urge to join the fray. There are echoes of General Lamarque's funeral, whose bloody, revolutionary aftermath is depicted in Hugo's *Les Misérables*, as well as of a number of other nineteenth-century funerals in Paris that were the pretext for street protests.[26] While Romains's focus in the novel, and ultimately that of his funeral procession, remains the messianic project of realizing collective consciousness, political mechanisms for crowd formation are alluded to, as is the possibility that the collective will participate in political violence.

Romains would reuse the image of strikers clashing with the army in his novel *Sur les quais de la villette* (1914), and he would continue to explore the relationship between politics and collectivism in his nonfiction writing. Violence is a recurring theme. In "Today's Problems" (1915) he initially asserts the political neutrality of unanimism by saying that it "favors neither the idolatry of forms of government, nor juridical means of oppression," but on the basis of this political agnosticism he goes on to write that a Prussian victory in the First World War, while not ideal, would be welcome if it led to the unification of Europe and supranational unanimism.[27] Romains points to military conquests by ancient Greece and Rome as a sign that the unanimist project might require some bloodshed.

Romains's advocacy of unity at all costs won him the praise of Action Française, the far-right French nationalist movement. The group stated that while they could not affirm with any certainty that the author held personal sympathy for their cause, the similarity of his program with theirs was unmistakable.[28] Romains himself would write admiringly of the Italian fascist party in "The Crisis of Marxism" (1933), suggesting that fascism was realizing the unanimist dream: "it seeks to put modern society on its feet, a society in which people, each in their place [*chacun à leur place*], finally declare they're happy to participate."[29] He would again make the argument that France should not allow nationalist pride to stand in the way of unanimism in the series of essays "The France–Germany Couple" (1935). In those essays Romains perversely sees the Nazi Party, despite its extreme nationalism, as a way of overcoming the various nationalisms of Europe. France, he argued, should work with Hitler rather than opposing him, to enable the rise of a pan-European collective. His arguments won him the praise of Joseph Goebbels, and in 1938 the German literary journal *Romanische Studien* dedicated a special issue to unanimism. In it, the Nazi linguist Edgar Glässer declared that Romains's unanimism shared all of its basic principles with Nationalsozialismus.

Romains sometimes praised fascist parties and sometimes backed away from the association. His hot-and-cold relationship with them reflects the lack of clarity in his thought, his struggle to balance competing goals, and his religious attitude to collectivism. His ambivalence about Europe being conquered by Prussia or Nazi Germany comes from a sense that groups are superior beings whose actions, like God's, are beyond his understanding. Consistent with the idea that a parasitic collective behaves in unpredictable ways because no single member of the group controls how other members use the quasi-object (Romains calls this unanimism's "subtle odor of anarchy"),[30] he refuses to predict or judge the behavior of collectives. As Leland Thielemann puts it in a scathing essay from 1941, "the unanimist phenomenon fascinates him so much that he can describe the unanimism of an army called out to put down a strike with as much empathy as he can that of the strikers. Unanimism would seem to have become a Good beyond ordinary good and evil."[31]

Romains's politics interest me for two reasons. The first is that this is another example of a discourse of parasitism intersecting with a fascist politics, but this time the relationship between the two is unusual. Esposito describes fascism as the *telos* of the ideology of the modern body, an antiparasitism taken to a self-destructive extreme. Romains's body politics, by contrast, is characterized by a radically welcoming attitude to parasites, preservation of the openness and amorphousness of the community, and staunch opposition to identity and nationalism. But Romains is always torn between these positions and his messianic desire for groups to crystallize and impose their will on the world. These conflicting urges manifest in the author's incoherent promotion of antinationalist, anti-authoritarian fascism. Romains's case suggests that alternatives to the immunized modern body can produce fascist ideologies as well, and vice versa, although this observation comes with the caveat that it is unclear what fascism means to Romains.

The second reason Romains's politics is of interest is because of the way he responded to the realization that fascism was not a desirable association for unanimism. In the 1940s, Romains, who would spend the Occupation in exile in New York, began to argue that unanimism was, contrary to what he had previously written, fundamentally incompatible with fascism. As Thielemann notes, Romains's strategy for doing this involved a significant reevaluation of the principles of unanimism. Previously, he had argued that unanimism might involve some violence, that violence was a product of how anarchic the groups were, and that lack of organization was precisely what made unanimism incompatible with authoritarianism. Now he sought to clearly separate his philosophy from any kind of destructive militarism, and to reconcile it to liberal democratic values. He retreated from his previous moral agnosticism.

In *A View of Things* (1941), he wrote that he had "always underscored the extreme importance—for better or worse—of the leader,"[32] a statement that does not match with what we find in *Puissances de Paris*, where groups are directed, if at all, by the form of the city streets, nor with the anti-individualism of *Mort de quelqu'un*, where the group's "leader" is a corpse whose name the group can barely remember. Romains over time adopted Durkheim's individualist paradigm, which he had criticized vociferously in his earlier writing. A unanimist group, he declared, could be brought about only through the spontaneous will of each individual member. The individual always maintained their autonomy *vis-à-vis* the collective, just as Durkheim's individual could always decide to reject the influence of social facts. Romains gradually abandoned the decentered, open qualities that characterize the groups in his early poetry and fiction, and replaced them with a structured model that makes unanimism difficult to distinguish from individualist society and its nations, political parties, and labor unions.[33] Romains's response to the recognition of the destructive potential of his collectives was, in other words, a movement toward the immunization of the collective.

Even among a partisan of unstable, communal models of relationality, there was a sense that the destructive power of a group correlated positively with its messiness. The immunization of the collective body was therefore unavoidable to make collectivism compatible with liberal democratic values. Romains accepted that his groups would have to become more rational and more univocal if the dangers of fascism and mob violence were to be foreclosed. Now, given how difficult it is to explain where the fascist elements of Romains's thinking come from, and how they relate to unanimism, it is questionable whether his diagnosis is the right one. Esposito's work would suggest that he had things backward. The idea, however, that the more open to parasites a group is, the more it tends to fascism and violence and, conversely, that immunization allows a group to participate in democracy, remains current. We see it in discussions of the use of social media in political organization and protest.

Tony Sampson, building on Tarde's theory of contagion, constructs a theory of communication and collective action that is welcoming to parasites. He gives a positive connotation to virality and microbial contagion, describing them as the connective tissue of networked society. Virality is "the very locus of the emergence of the dream of social action."[34] Like Tarde and Romains he connects biological discourses of parasitism to mediation, arguing that "nonlinear instabilities, interference, error, and aperiodic noise"[35] are essential to the way collectives coalesce and communicate. Sampson, however, does not allow noise to exist on its own terms. He treats it as a kind of undiscovered country which, with a bit more study, could be resolved into measurable components like affect. Understanding the emotions of group members, he suggests, would give an outsider a deterministic understanding of group behavior and allow the group to be better directed and organized, whether the end goal be political action or consumerism.[36]

Manuel Cebrian, Iyad Rahwan, and Sandy Pentland have likewise argued that network analysis pays too much attention to the viral spread of information and not enough to how information is received, processed, and translated into social action. They blame this for graph theory's failure to predict any social uprising or political movement. Their solution differs little from Sampson's. They propose a greater focus on incentive (in many ways a byword for affect: it includes interpersonal relations, emotional motivation, and social pressure). Their response is characteristic of a data analytics field that is obsessed with noise, but only as an error to be managed and minimized via ever-finer modes of quantification. Treating noise as a set of ultimately assimilable variables offers the promise of one day engineering the collective: "if we shift our efforts toward the mapping of incentives, then we may be able to better determine the suitability of content for recruitment to action and to create lasting social change."[37] Collective noise will, the implication goes, one day be so well understood that there will be no more noise, and the formation of collectives and the direction of their behavior will become formulaic. Provoking political opposition or obedience would simply be a matter of constructing the right meme and releasing it to the right part of the network.

These scholars are attempting to walk the same tightrope Romains tried and failed to walk a century ago. They try to reconcile a parasitic collectivism with liberal democratic ideals. They claim to embrace noise, but they treat it as something that can ultimately be understood—thus allowing decentered, open-ended communities to be mastered, no longer at risk of drifting into violent and destructive behavior. They paradoxically insist on the egalitarianism of community while also emphasizing the importance of a leader (Cebrian et al. distinguish between "political activists" and "the mass"). They ignore the possibility that more predictable channels might still be employed by multiple actors in contradictory ways, resulting in a cacophony of orders that could still engender unpredictable outcomes. They ignore the potential for subjectivity to circulate through the collective, and they ignore Serres's core argument: that there is no system without noise.

These approaches to collective politics are essentially attempts at reconciling parasitic collectivism with Rancière's theories. Rancière supports the idea that with enough planning and coordination, noise can be functionally eliminated from a collective, and that this is the key to effective political action. He supports both the idea that rationality and univocity grant a group recognition and agency in democratic society and the idea that a collective must immunize itself against its parasites. Whether these premises are valid, and whether these goals are attainable, are both open questions. In the next section I will examine Nuit Debout, a recent political movement based in Paris that sought in various ways to immunize itself. The movement foregrounded its decentralized organization and its lack of leadership, while also carefully controlling its communication in the hope of avoiding being dismissed as a disorganized mob. As we will see, that needle proved difficult to thread, and it did so for reasons that were largely outside the movement's control.

Nuit Debout and the Impossible Task of Speaking as One

On February 17, 2016, France's labor minister, Myriam El Khomri, presented the first draft of Law 2016-1088 to parliament. The text, which was branded the *Loi Travail* and the *Loi El Khomri*, outlined an overhaul of the French employment system. The reform elicited strong opposition from labor unions, student groups, and opponents of then-President François Hollande. That opposition coalesced on March 31 into a demonstration in the Place de la République in Paris. Protestors began occupying the square in nightly assemblies during which they discussed the labor law and other challenges facing French workers. The assemblies and the movement associated with them came to be known as Nuit Debout. Over the following weeks, Nuit Debout protests would spread to other cities in France, and the movement would gradually gain international attention as a spiritual successor to the Occupy Wall Street protests that originated in New York and the Spanish *Indignados* protests of 2011.

Nuit Debout was a protest movement that paid particular attention to mediation and noise. Suspicious of how traditional mainstream media would report on their activity, the group produced its own journalism outfits—Radio Debout and TV Debout—that were broadcast on online streaming services like Mixlr, YouTube, and Periscope. These channels allowed members of the movement to speak to an outside audience without the filter of journalists attempting to interpret their message. The movement also deployed a system for managing internal noise. Each speaker at a general assembly was allotted two minutes. The listeners were instructed to listen silently and to respond, if necessary, using soundless hand gestures adapted from a system used by the *Indignados* protests in Spain. Instead of clapping to show approval, people were asked to wave their hands in circles above their heads. Joining one's hands above the head indicated a request for silence.

These rules reflected several underlying strategies of the movement. While the group promoted the parity of all speakers and participants,[38] and privileged the collective will, it nevertheless insisted on univocity. The integrity of individual speech was protected through the strict enforcement of a space of silence around the speaker. The group also underscored the importance of creating near-unanimous consensus in collective decisions, encouraging assembly leaders not to adopt resolutions that were passed only by simple majority. When the group spoke, it had to do so with one voice.

There is a clear Rancièrian conceit in Nuit Debout's approach to communication. Sophie Wahnich, a historian of the French Revolution, argues that Nuit Debout "affirm[ed] that democracy is the art of deliberation."[39] While the movement was motivated by frustrations with electoral politics,[40] it embraced Enlightenment ideas about politics as rational debate between autonomous individuals, and reproduced democratic institutions like the Assembly. Nuit Debout bought in wholeheartedly to a concept of democracy founded on the syllogistic linking of politics to speech, speech to the individual voice, the individual voice to the absence of noise.

The most spectacular demonstration of the movement's sonic politics was its orchestra. The Orchestre Debout met for the first time on April 20, 2016. The musicians were a mix of amateurs, professionals, and students, and at that first performance they played the first, second, and fourth movements of Antonin Dvořák's *New World* symphony. Over the next year the orchestra would play over a dozen concerts, performing symphonies, choral music, and opera from the classical repertoire. In the initial call for musicians, the organizers concluded with the note "No solo, no ego: we are a collective." (Note, however, that it did play with a conductor.) Orchestral music was a metaphor for the movement: a symbolic space where individuals possessing distinct voices could harmoniously combine into a euphonic whole. As John Spitzer and Neal Zaslaw demonstrate, the orchestra has, since the seventeenth century, been a popular metaphor for politics, and vice versa. Nuit Debout's deployment of an orchestra, in addition to cultivating an intellectual (and therefore serious and rational) aura, is of a piece with French Revolution-era use of the orchestra as a metaphor for the unity that could arise from "voluntary contribution to the common good."[41]

The orchestra also typically imposes a certain regime of listening. The audience in the concert hall is silent while the conductor's baton is raised. This is different from, say, the rock concert, where the audience is expected to produce noise throughout the performance.[42] During Orchestre Debout's first performance, the musicians stood while the audience sat cross-legged. Most listened in silence, reproducing the dynamics of Nuit Debout's general assemblies but reframed as a spectacle rather than as a democratic deliberative process. The orchestra in this way served as a symbolic complement to the rules governing speech, mediation, and the orientation of collective will within the movement. It helped to establish a silent buffer around the center of the square in order to enable a mode of collective discourse and decision-making founded on the inalienability of the individual and his or her voice.

In practice this strategy was not very successful. Despite the best efforts of organizers, noise crept in. *Le Parisien*, in its guide to the gestures used during general assemblies, notes that "certain signs are poorly understood by the participants, who, for example, confuse the gesture for applause with the one for voting yes."[43] Orchestre Debout's first concert was interrupted by applause shortly after it began, and at several moments individual spectators or passersby could be heard shouting out. The sound of cars circling the Place de la République was omnipresent.

More interesting, though, than this internal noise is the noise that characterized how the movement was heard and understood by people outside it. Despite the tight control it exercised over media channels through Radio and TV Debout, the movement was repeatedly criticized by external commentators for a lack of clarity about its motivations and demands. In *Le Nouvel Observateur*, Éric Aeschimann described Nuit Debout as "surrounded by a silence that's filled with respect, but also confusion," and asked: "What does this movement want? What is it expressing? Where is it going?"[44] Geoffroy de Lagasnerie criticized its failure to make demands.[45] Despite carefully crafting a space for a univocal speech to be heard, Nuit Debout was perceived as a movement completely devoid of speech.

One objection that might be made here is that the perplexity of mainstream media commentators or of the political establishment cannot be taken at face value. There are perhaps political reasons for those entities to play dumb. The point, however, is ultimately moot. Regardless of whether the commentariat, politicians, or the wider public could theoretically have deciphered Nuit Debout's discourse, the fact remains that despite the ample steps taken by the movement to safeguard the univocity of the messages it articulated, those messages nevertheless arrived at their destination muddled. Nuit Debout could control the way its voice was emitted, but not the channel it passed through nor the recipient to whom it was addressed. It could not force its messages to be heard.

This fact is further exemplified by another demonstration in Paris against the *Loi Travail*: the demonstration of May 1, 2016. The march was part of the traditional May Day *Fête des travailleurs*. It was organized by a collection of national labor unions with the participation of Nuit Debout. Participants were called to assemble in the Place de la Bastille and to march to the Place de la Nation. Following the march, Nuit Debout would hold a General Assembly in the Place de la République to consolidate the day's message. This march had a strong commitment to the power of discourse and the voice. In the call to strike issued by the union confederations, the unions demanded the renewal of dialogue between their leadership and the government. Marchers held banners expressing their opposition to the *Loi Travail*, and chanted slogans in unison like "Withdrawal, withdrawal of the labor law. No amendments, no negotiation."

But the nature of the demonstration changed when it reached the Boulevard Diderot. A group of several hundred people wearing balaclavas moved to the front of the march and tossed projectiles at the police officers assembled there. Similar developments had taken place at demonstrations against the *Loi Travail* throughout the six weeks preceding the first of May. Only four days prior, 214 people had been taken in for questioning and 78 police officers had been wounded when fighting broke out during nationwide protests. In all of those cases the ethereal and imprecise weapon of choice for the police was the tear gas grenade, a weaponized form of the smoke that accompanies the corporealization of the collective in *Mort de quelqu'un*. It is a weapon that fills space and reduces visual fidelity. Protestors threw back firecrackers, an explosive of pure noise.

Now, there was ambiguity about the identity of the perpetrators of this violence. According to the Interior Ministry they were "*casseurs*," hooligans with little to no ideological connection to the protest. They were, in the estimation of Olivier Cahn, primarily members of the "black bloc," a group of organized provocateurs with anarchist political leanings who infiltrate protests in order to provoke violence from crowd-control police officers.[46] They pose as radical members of whatever protest they happen to have infiltrated, in the hopes of causing so much chaos that police become confused and attack peaceful protestors. The goal is to actualize and mediatize state violence, and to radicalize nonviolent members of the march by subjecting them to that violence. Others rejected this explanation. A group of students from a high school in Paris's 4th arrondissement admitted that they had organized themselves outside of the union structure but described themselves not as nihilistic outsiders keen for a fight, but as ideological extremists for whom violence was a means to put pressure on the government. Demonstrators affiliated with the Confédération générale du travail, one of the union organizers of the march, suggested that the police had provoked the violence themselves as a way to justify dispersal of the march. Cahn insinuated that police had deliberately failed to arrest the *casseurs* at previous clashes so that they could continue to act out, providing an excuse to break up the demonstration.

Ultimately, whether or not the violent elements in the May 1 demonstration and in other demonstrations associated with the anti-labor law movement were "*casseurs*" in the full sense is not interesting. What matters is precisely the confusion their activity produced. What matters is that these agitators, working on the "margins of the demonstration" (as the police put it), were able to co-opt the messaging of the movement so fully that their noise became inseparable from the voice of the collective. The carefully articulated demands of the protestors became unintelligible amidst the noise of fighting, despite the careful attention paid by union leadership and by Nuit Debout to the clarity and univocity of their speech. While the *manifestation* was designed to clarify a set of demands (*manifester* comes from the Old French for "to show plainly"), because it relied on the open media channel of the street it gradually elided into its etymological cousin: *infestation*. It opened itself to parasitism.

There were two primary consequences of this parasitism. The first was the obfuscation of the group's message in the mediatization of the demonstration. Newspapers including *Le Figaro*, *Marianne*, *Huffington Post*, and *Libération* focused their reporting on the violence that had disturbed the march. Philippe Brochen, reporting for *Libération*, concluded that the demonstration took on the meaning imposed by the parasitic *casseurs*: "We can now say that this demonstration against the labor law has transformed into a movement against the police."[47] The second consequence was the evacuation by police of the very space cultivated by Nuit Debout to render its speech audible. Starting at around 10 p.m., supposed *casseurs* began to launch projectiles at police forces on the periphery of Nuit Debout's evening assembly in the Place de la République. Within an hour the police had launched tear gas into the square and were forcing its evacuation. *Le Monde* described protestors racing to disassemble sound equipment that had been put in place for the night's speeches. The mediatic apparatus constructed to transmit the individual voice was obliterated as a consequence of the ultimate uncontrollability of noise.

Is It Possible to Speak without Being a Host?

The experience of Nuit Debout is consistent with the basic observation made by Michel Serres about parasites: they cannot be eliminated from the channel. The movement tried to speak clearly, but was unable to prevent parasites from eroding its borders and identity, and muddling its message. The protestors, like street artists, found that as soon as they tried to adopt a voice, parasites rushed in to stop communication. Other demonstrations associated with the anti-labor law movement produced similar outcomes; indeed, problems with protecting the univocity of political demonstrations are not limited to that movement, nor to demonstrations in Paris. The same scene has played out in protests around the world.

The ubiquity of this dynamic represents a challenge to Rancière's concept of politics. Rancière's politics is a struggle to escape from noise and be heard. Once a group enters the *partage du sensible*, its demands can be answered by institutions. The demonstrations described above tried to do just this: the trade union confederations sought to reopen dialogue with the government by using street protests as a way to make themselves and their complaints manifest. The problem is that entering into dialogue with the government necessitates the adoption of a position of emission within a communicational framework. The group must become a subject and address a message. As Serres describes, to do so is to open oneself to parasitism. This produces a vicious circle: the *demos* must emerge from the realm of noise and adopt a voice in order to be recognized by the state, but the act of adopting a voice is the very means by which it becomes susceptible to noise. If an audible voice and a clear message are the preconditions for political agency, then effective protest is not just "paradoxical," as Rancière calls it, but functionally unattainable.

Zeynep Tufekci points out that governments around the world are increasingly conscious of this dynamic, and have weaponized it: "The internet's relatively chaotic nature, with too much information and weak gatekeepers, can asymmetrically empower governments by allowing them to develop new forms of censorship based not on blocking information, but on making available information unusable."[48] This is the thinking behind the accusation that French police deliberately refuse to arrest *casseurs* so that they can continue to disrupt protests. If effective political action by the people requires communication, intractable governments need neither respond to nor silence dissidents; they can simply drown them out.

How should one react to this? Should one, *à la* Rancière, continue to search for an ephemeral space in which a message can pass, and hope that the parasites will stay away until it does? In doing so, one risks saying something very different from what one means to, or never being able to say anything at all. Or should one abandon discourse altogether and remain a parasite? Should speech be left to the suckers in charge, and should the rest of the population embrace the power of interference? During the 2013 demonstrations in Taksim Square in Istanbul, police accused demonstrators of verbally abusing them, as a pretext for dispersing a protest. Following the evacuation of the square, the performance artist Erdem Gündüz reentered it and stood still and silent. Several hundred people eventually joined "the standing man." By not making a sound, the crowd made it impossible for police to misrepresent their speech. But they also surrendered any hope of expressing their grievances against the state. They literalized the silence Nuit Debout was accused of.

Is there a way out of this bind? In chapter 6 I will argue that there is, and that moving beyond the aporetic antagonism between host and parasite requires a reconsideration of what it means to be a host, and a radically different attitude to biological, social, and mediatic parasites. As a way of laying out the terms of that argument, in this section I want to examine the biopolitical dimension. In this chapter my focus has been on how the voice and its synecdochal identification with a certain thinking of the political subject interact with biopolitics. I have juxtaposed the ideology of the immunized modern body, which is inextricable from Enlightenment individualism and rationalist politics, and a more open, communal thinking of the self. The first of these pathologizes parasites; the second is more indifferent to them. The first is identified with a voice; the second is cacophonous. The first, according to Esposito, leads to the violence of authoritarianism, while the second, as Tarde and Romains show, leads to the disorganized violence of riots. While the second of these two conceptions of the body has its problems, I believe it ultimately represents the path to a more humane and equitable urban politics.

In a recent overview, Alfred Tauber documents the major shifts taking place currently in biological theorizations of immunity. Very different conceptions of bodily boundaries, identity, and environment are emerging. At the risk of repeating the sleight-of-hand exchange through which science borrows concepts from politics and in turn naturalizes political ideologies, I want to use these shifts in thinking about immunity as a frame of reference to explore alternative notions of political subjectivity. This field that for so long has provided a reference point for what makes the self individual ironically now asserts the openness of all bodies. It has almost become a *munology*, a theory of the mutual indebtedness of all life.

Tauber's *Immunity: The Evolution of an Idea* traces the development of immunology from preliminary work by Claude Bernard, who "set the theoretical stage for the autonomous organism," to Élie Metchnikoff, who introduced questions of agency, and then to Frank Macfarlane Burnet, whose work "formally introduced the 'self' into the immunological lexicon." With his Clonal Selection Theory, Burnet posited a mechanism by which the immune system could distinguish between the body it was defending and intruders, with defensive mechanisms activated only for the latter. This mechanism is known as self/nonself discrimination. Explaining how the body recognized itself became a rich field of study. The idiom of the immune self rapidly took off in immunology, and soon a wide variety of terms from the philosophical discourse of the self—agency, the individual, tolerance, perception and recognition, and foreign or the other—were imported to explain it. (Over the course of his book, Tauber metaphorizes the immune system as the body's police, *gendarmerie*, armed forces, and passport control.) "Protection, autonomy, and individuality" became immunology's chief values and concerns.[49]

Tauber's account of the history of immunity shows that the medical production of the healthy body is always intertwined with its discursive production. The immune self is a metaphor. It is also, he argues, an inadequate metaphor that has failed to account for much of the observed activity of the immune system. Developed to explain the active immune system (the immune system destroying a pathogen), the self/nonself discrimination paradigm has had difficulty explaining the behavior of the resting immune system. It is also ill-equipped to account for autoimmunity and pregnancy. Moreover, the immune self is not a theoretical model in the true sense, and the term has not been formally defined. It is more of a "guiding paradigm or a basic presupposition of the science." With this in mind, Tauber argues for the notion of immune selfhood to be discarded in favor of "a new understanding, one that encompasses a complex diversity of organisms living together in a cohesive ecology."[50]

Tauber's advocacy of an ecological approach to the body derives both from his belief in the immune self's shortcomings as a theoretical guide and from more general shifts in the disciplinary boundaries of biology. Changes in the fields of developmental biology and ecology have led to the rise of hybrid research areas—the "eco-evo-devo synthesis." Researchers in these areas hold that the body is not autonomous from its environment, nor is it just in its environment. It develops "*with* and *through*" its environment.[51] Development is plastic, with developmental routes and even the genetic code of a given body shaped by the environment. In turn, developing bodies have been shown to alter their environments to create a milieu that favors them. These discoveries have pushed some researchers to redefine the boundaries of the developing body to include its environment. Tauber writes: "one might even argue that drawing the boundary of an organism's physiology at the 'skin' or exterior membrane is arbitrary."[52]

The holistic concept of the individual self has been further problematized in the other direction. Whereas the germ theory that shaped early immunology considered microbial life purely from the point of view of the threat it posed to human bodies—that is to say, as a parasite—researchers have begun to rethink the parasitic status of these organisms.[53] Viruses have been shown to constitute "a stable part of the human meta-genome, dubbed the 'virome.'" Chronic infection is part of the resting state of the healthy body, not just a mark of its catastrophic failure. The human gut is populated by "approximately 1000 major bacteria groups," and at least 150 species within play partner roles in its function.[54] The gut microbiome not only helps bodies to survive, but can also affect what have traditionally been defined as core components of identity. Changes in the gut microbiome correlate with depression, anxiety, schizophrenia, and autism as well as sexual preference. These interactions problematize the distinction between human body and microbe. As Margaret McFall-Ngai tells Tauber, even symbiosis—if we think of it as maintaining an organismal boundary between two subjects, and especially if we think of it as a hierarchical relationship between host and symbiont—is inadequate for describing the interactivity of life. She suggests that "instead of the 'host organism,' vertebrates are more accurately viewed as 'a carriage of complex consortia.'"[55]

These discoveries lead Tauber to conclude that the centerpiece of twentieth-century immunology, the immune self with "the cardinal features of Western notions of individuality," selves that "both defend and champion their own autonomy,"[56] is untenable. Pervasive symbiosis unmoors any concept of individuality, and forces us to rethink life as an unstable, connective, unbounded substance.

Tauber's argument here bears a strong resemblance to one made by Jacques Derrida in a somewhat different context. Derrida's target was J. L. Austin's speech act theory, and in particular Austin's use of the term "parasite." Austin had argued that linguists should start by explaining "serious" speech acts, where people meant what they said, before considering "parasitic" speech acts like citation, fiction, and irony, where they didn't. Derrida argued that a workable theory of language could not possibly be developed in isolation from communication's failures. Meaning was always contingent, regardless of the seriousness of the speaker. He wondered what attracted Austin to the terminology of parasitism in the first place. Derrida offered the following explanation of where parasites come from:

> It should also be remembered that the parasite is by definition never simply external, never simply something that can be excluded from or kept outside of the body "proper," shut out from the "familial" table or house. Parasitism takes place when the parasite (called thus by the owner, jealously defending his own, his *oikos*) comes to live off the life of the body in which it resides—and when, reciprocally, the host incorporates the parasite to an extent, willy nilly offering it hospitality: providing it with a place. The parasite then "takes place."[57]

Parasitism comes not from the outside but from the host, when he or she adopts a specific stance, calling the parasite a parasite. Through the act of naming the parasite the host defines some resource as his or her own, asserting the existence of boundaries and of a property that falls within those boundaries. Parasitism does not "take place" unless the host starts by giving it a place. The parasite does not attack the boundaries of the host; the host becomes bounded through the act of identifying the parasite.

It is very striking to read Tauber's citation of McFall-Ngai alongside Derrida's text. We begin to see in her language the process Derrida describes happening in reverse. Her decision to disavow the discourse of the "host organism" is directly tied to an ontological disavowal of organismal boundaries and hierarchies. This is interesting not just as a felicitous convergence of two thinkers working in two different domains with the same terminology, but also as an example in Tauber's text of how the production of the scientific body is always also a discursive process.[58] The words scientists use and the philosophical precepts they underpin structure the conceptualizations of life that empirical science is capable of giving us.

Tauber drives this point home by critiquing experimental protocols grammatologically. Criticizing immunologists for employing terms borrowed from Cartesian representationalism, he describes the science as "locked into a semantic impasse where 'meaning' cannot emerge." He criticizes scientific reductivism for modeling itself on outdated linguistic theories: "the grammar of reductive analysis (e.g. stringing words into sentences), although necessary, is hardly sufficient for constructing coherent narratives."[59] The same applies to systems biology, which he says has not grappled with the assumptions underlying its informatic theories of meaning.[60] He is critical of experimental methods and theoretical models that relegate environmental effects and the emergent characteristics of complex systems to the category of "noise" to be disregarded. Ultimately, he says, "without a philosophy and accompanying language to address the nature of form, establishing a truly novel science cannot proceed." No amount of computing power can overcome "a seventeenth-century philosophy having reached its conceptual limits."[61]

However, while Tauber's text elucidates the need for a radically new thinking of the body, it also demonstrates the difficulty of putting that thinking into words. At multiple points he deconstructs the terminology of immunology only to immediately redeploy it in a new context. The worst example of this is in his discussion of Thomas Pradeu's continuity thesis, which he presents as an alternative to the immune self. Tauber praises it for the fact that "notions of selfhood play no role in" it, but in the very next sentence he writes: "regulation is determined solely within the dynamics of the system it*self*."[62] Earlier in that paragraph, and then repeatedly in the next two pages, he uses terms like "self-regulated" and "self-reactive" for this immune system that is supposedly *sans* self. Part of this can be chalked up to Tauber parroting Pradeu who, he says, "pushes the 'immune self' out the front door," only to open "the back door to welcome its twin, 'individuality,' back into immune theory" (phrasing that is overdetermined given the importance of hosts, hospitality, and the home to immunological discourse). But this accusation could just as well be redirected at Tauber, who describes his task in his introduction not as the deconstruction of identity but as "a displacement of one form of identity for another." How he envisions this other identity is at times revolutionary (necessitating a "new biology"), and at other times difficult to distinguish from the identity it is replacing. When he writes: "instead of insularity *dialectics* determines identity,"[63] one could fairly ask how "self" and "nonself" are not dialectical. Tauber repeatedly derides the Cartesianism of twentieth-century immunology, but his Hegelianism is just as limiting.

With this criticism, I do not mean to dismiss Tauber's text. My point, rather, is to draw attention to the magnitude of the challenges one faces in trying to escape the ideologies of self, individuality, and identity. While Tauber's analysis of recent scientific research compellingly signals the need for new ways of thinking the body and the environment, finding a vocabulary to visualize those new ways of thinking is no small task. Just as immunology's conceptualization of the body as an immune self was never just scientific but also discursive, developing new conceptualizations of the body, a new biopolitics, necessitates transformations of discourse. Changing the way one relates to biological parasites requires changing the way one relates to mediatic ones as well.

In chapter 6 I will discuss this discursive dimension and what it might mean for the social politics of the city. I will look at how Derrida's work on linguistic parasites and hospitality intersects with Gilles Deleuze's writings on literature, subjectivity, cartography, and the body. These texts have influenced contemporary thinkers like Rosi Braidotti, who has advocated a posthuman ethics centered around a "non-unitary, nomadic or rhizomatic"[64] view of the body and an embrace of *zoe* as a life force that traverses organismal and species boundaries.

Returning to Nuit Debout and street politics, what do the new approaches to immunity offer? Many of Nuit Debout's participants accepted the imperative to make their movement into a host. They tried to purify the movement of its parasites. They tried to speak with one voice so that their demands would be heard and answered by those in power. They failed. The borders of the movement and the clarity of its message could not be adequately policed. Parasites continually found their way in. But parasites, Derrida argues, do not come from the outside; they are discursively produced as part of the process through which an entity establishes itself as a host. Nuit Debout's parasites did not originate outside the movement; they were generated by the movement's own efforts to establish boundaries for itself and adopt a voice.

Disavowing the host position, it follows, would mean no parasites are produced. That is not to say that there would be no *casseurs*, no confusion, no cacophony. It would mean that the movement would adopt a radically different understanding of its boundaries, and of what its language was meant to accomplish. The movement could have undergone an eco-evo-devo synthesis. Instead of attempting to clear a discursive space in the city, to create a hole in the environment, Nuit Debout could have developed with and through its environment. Applying ecological thinking to the movement would mean thinking of *casseurs* not as parasitic outsiders who needed to be purged to protect the integrity of the *manifestation*, but as part of complex consortia shaping the milieu of the protest in intersecting and ever-evolving ways. It would mean getting rid of the almost-brand name identity, Nuit Debout, which implies clear temporal, spatial, and corporeal limits, and instead treating the movement as a process. What would a movement conceived along these lines accomplish? What would its speech mean? A movement that does not seek to reify itself as host, and consequently does not distinguish between its voice and the noise around it, would pose a challenge of listening. Rather than making demands, it would invite interpretation.

6 Underground

What would it mean to construct a city that does not pathologize its parasites? Is it possible to welcome parasites, to make them at home with us? Does doing so make parasites disappear from the equation, giving rise to some new kind of equality, or is it just a compassionate rebranding of the hygienic ideology that has always sought to eliminate parasites from the city? Is there any way out of the antagonistic host/parasite dialectic that pervades our conceptualization of the city and locks us into a static, self-annihilating struggle between meaning and noise? Answering these questions requires us to ask what it means to offer hospitality.

For Jacques Derrida, hospitality is not part of ethics or an ethics among others; it is ethics itself. "As it concerns *ethos*, that is to say dwelling, being at home, the place where the family lives, and how one exists in those places, how one relates to oneself and others, to others as kin or others as foreigners, *ethics is hospitality*."[1] Derrida divides hospitality into two parts. The first of these he derives from Émile Benveniste's etymology. In ancient Greece, foreigners were entitled to certain rights. These included a safe welcome should they come into contact with a Greek citizen. But not every foreigner held these rights. Only the *xenos*, the foreigner who spoke Greek, was to be allowed into one's home. (In Latin, *xenos* was translated as *hostis*.) Not only that; the foreigner would have to have a recognizable name, a family, the possibility of one day receiving his host in return. Thus, the right to hospitality began with a question: *who are you?* Only those who could answer it properly would be welcomed. This kind of hospitality, which is legally defined, Derrida calls the right to hospitality.

Derrida contrasts this right to hospitality with what he calls the law of hospitality. The law of hospitality, despite the implications of its name, is not juridically or legally defined. It is closer to a commandment, a suprajuridical obligation. The Law of hospitality, which he sometimes capitalizes, tells us to welcome the other, the foreigner, regardless of his or her legal status, regardless if they have a right to be welcomed. The law of hospitality is absolute and unconditional: "Absolute hospitality requires that I open my home and that I give, not just to the foreigner (who has a family name, the social status of foreigner, etc.), but to the absolute, unknown, anonymous other, and that I *give place* to them, that I let them come, that I let them arrive, and take place in the place I offer them, without asking of them either reciprocity (entering into a pact) or even their name."[2] Absolute hospitality is offered to anyone, anything, man, woman, animal. Even to the dead. It is offered without questions, without identification, without any attempt to establish the subjectivity of the other. It is an act of pure generosity.

For Derrida, these two aspects of hospitality cannot stand alone. The right to hospitality, taken on its own, results in a tautology. A *xenos* is a foreigner who speaks the local language. If we understand speaking a language to mean something more than simply understanding a lexicon, i.e., sharing the local culture enough to understand how the lexicon is being used, then the *xenos* is not actually foreign at all. If he speaks the language, he is already one of us. The home is therefore only ever really opened to the self. The true other, the *barbaros*, the foreigner who doesn't speak the local language, does not share in the right to hospitality. Indeed, according to Benveniste, ancient Greeks encountering a *barbaros* were required to kill them. The right to hospitality sees to it that the other is never welcomed. Hospitality is never truly offered; the home is opened only to those who already have the legal right to access it.

Absolute hospitality is equally empty in isolation. If hospitality is offered to any and all, if anyone can enter my house without asking, if everyone can make themselves at home, then what makes the home mine? If all property is common property, then there is no property at all. In order for my welcome to make sense as an act of hospitality, there must be a possibility that the *étranger* (both stranger and foreigner) will not be welcomed. Before I can be generous, I must possess something to be generous with. "No hospitality [*pas d'hospitalité*], in the classic sense without sovereignty of oneself over one's home, but since there is no hospitality without finitude, sovereignty can only be exercised by filtering, choosing, and thus by excluding and doing violence."[3]

Hospitality thus makes sense only when these two terms are put into opposition. The law of hospitality can be meaningfully obeyed only by transgressing the rules governing the right to hospitality. The right to hospitality "is both what makes hospitality possible, or the hospitable relationship to the foreigner possible, and what limits and prohibits it."[4] If there is no framework in place establishing that my home belongs to me, and that other people can't enter it without my permission, there is no way for me to offer my home. One cannot be generous with a space to which everyone already has unconditional access. Hospitality is thus predicated on a right to exclude rather than a right to welcome. The law of hospitality makes sense only within the context of its necessarily imperfect translation into hospitality rights and laws. It makes sense only within a juridical framework, underpinned by violence, that defines and defends the right to property.[5] Hospitality necessarily contradicts itself.

Derrida titles his second lecture on hospitality *Pas d'hospitalité*, meaning both "no hospitality" and a step of, from, or toward hospitality, an increment of hospitality. Hospitality approached one step at a time. The parasite plays a key role in allowing hospitality to take place. Hospitality makes sense only if it simultaneously asserts the existence of a boundary, and allows someone who belongs on the other side of it to cross. Managing this unstable liminality is the parasite's function. This is visible in the original usage of "parasite." As I explained in chapter 1, in ancient Greece, a parasite was a poor man allowed to dine at a wealthy man's feast in exchange for entertaining the guests. He ate at another man's table in another man's home. He was offered hospitality, a conditional hospitality imbricated in an economic power relation. But his hospitality was not the same as that offered to the other guests. The parasite was a guest named as an outsider, an unwelcome guest who was allowed to stay, but bore the brand of his structural exclusion from the meal. He thus served as a kind of emissary of the excluded multitude, allowing the true guests to understand themselves as guests. By making exclusion present, he materialized the host's power to exclude. By being unwelcome, he gave the welcome meaning.

This is what Derrida is referring to when he writes: "parasitism takes place when the parasite (called thus by the owner, jealously defending his own, his *oikos*) comes to live off the life of the body in which it resides—and when, reciprocally, the host incorporates the parasite to an extent, willy nilly offering it hospitality: providing it with a place. The parasite then 'takes place.'"[6] The parasite doesn't invade the meal. The host offers him a place. He then accuses the parasite of taking that same place. He asserts (it is the owner who names the parasite as such) that the parasite is eating somewhere he doesn't belong (*para-sitos*, eating next to). In so doing he gives the guests living proof that there is a here distinct from there, a here that belongs to someone and not to someone else. The parasite reveals the home to be bounded, reveals the meal to be property, reveals the host to be master of both. As Mark Wigley writes in *The Architecture of Deconstruction*, the parasite may appear to destabilize the home, but while "the sense of place is always as infected as that of the house, [. . .] it is not lost with the disruptive return of what is buried within it. On the contrary, it is produced by that very return."[7] The parasite ultimately gives rise to place rather than undermining it. It (and not the guests) is what makes the host a host.

The structural importance of the parasite to hospitality and to the architecture of the home is why circumventing the limitations of the host/parasite dialectic is more complicated than welcoming the parasite. Without an unwelcome guest, being a welcome guest means nothing. Welcoming a specific parasite does nothing to undermine the structural exclusion that renders hospitality possible; welcoming all parasites, and thus embracing absolute hospitality, makes hospitality meaningless. The parasite, by giving rise to a boundary while crossing it, allows the gesture of hospitality in all its paradox to take place. Derrida's understanding of the parasite as that which gives rise to the boundary leads him to ultimately concede the structural inevitability of parasites. Parasites give rise to home, to property, to place, to structure. His position on this point is very similar to that of Serres, who calls the parasite the clinamen that allowed civilization to begin.[8] Coming to terms with the parasite would undo those foundations and challenge what it means to be human.

In *Of Hospitality* Derrida leaves his audience in an uneasy ethical position *vis-à-vis* parasites. Having drawn attention to the arbitrary violence of the parasite's exclusion, he does not broach the radical position that would overturn that violence, instead offering conditional hospitality as a contingent and ephemeral gesture of goodwill. He put this progressivist position in clear terms in a 2001 interview with Giovanna Borradori, which Borradori aptly titled "Autoimmunity." Derrida states:

> An unconditional hospitality is, to be sure, practically impossible to live; one cannot in any case, and by definition, organize it. [. . .] And I well recognize that this concept of pure hospitality can have no legal or political status. No state can write it into its laws. But without at least the thought of this pure and unconditional hospitality, of hospitality *itself*, we would have no concept of hospitality in general and would not even be able to determine any rules for conditional hospitality (with its rituals, its legal status, its norms, its national or international conventions).[9]

Derrida presents absolute hospitality as an abstract benchmark against which to judge our shortcomings as hosts and those of the various laws that govern the right to hospitality.

Derrida's political texts on hospitality are pragmatically incrementalist. His writing on hospitality in language, by contrast, is more radical. In 1971 he gave a lecture titled "Signature Event Context" at a conference on communication. Its primary focus was a major lacuna in the work of the speech act theorist J. L. Austin. Derrida's criticism centered on Austin's decision to explain how communication takes place by starting with what he called "serious" acts of communication while setting aside "parasitic" uses of language like quotation, fiction, misunderstanding. Derrida argued that it was not possible to found a communication model on the exclusion of parasites, because parasites were a constitutive feature of communication. They served as the condition of possibility for meaning. He argued that language should not be understood as a dialectical opposition between "serious" meaning and "parasitic" iteration. Rather, meaning and parasites were always active in different proportions. Derrida's lecture was criticized in 1977 by John Searle, prompting a response titled "Limited Inc a b c." The title alludes to the importance Derrida would give to economic metaphors throughout his text. Economics comes from *oikos* (the home) and *nemein* (management). Derrida's use of economic metaphors in this text reflects his belief that one cannot talk about communication without talking about the home, property, ownership. One cannot talk about language without talking about hospitality.

Derrida's use of economic metaphors is also provoked by Searle, who defended Austin by arguing that his exclusion of parasites from speech act theory was no different from the reductivism common in the production of economic models. Searle suggests that parasitic language can eventually be accounted for in speech act theory through "the introduction of technical terminology of the welfare economics sort." Derrida retorts that what is at issue is not a different economics, a more humane economics, an economics that offers the parasite a bit more to eat. What is at issue is the persistence of the *oikos* itself.

> An economics taking account of effects of iterability, [. . .] an economics calling into question the entire traditional philosophy of the *oikos*—of the *proper*: the "own," "ownership," "property"—as well as the laws that have governed it would not only be very different from "welfare economics": it would also be far removed from furnishing speech acts theory with "more elegant" formulations of a "technical terminology." Rather, it would provoke its general transformation.[10]

Derrida draws together the hospitable undercurrents of "parasite" and the economic metaphors deployed by Searle, and argues for the kind of wholesale transformation in the economics of language that he would advocate in a more tepid way in his political texts. Accounting for the parasites of language is not merely a question of granting them social security benefits. The parasite can either remain the excluded term, an emissary of the outside allowed into the home, a pathological element that the host both excludes and allows to stay because its unwelcome presence is the very thing that gives meaning to his or her mastery, home, property; *or* hospitality can be discarded altogether: the home can be offered to all, eliminating concepts of place, property, self. The alternative is not between classical economics and welfare economics; the alternative is between economics and something entirely different.

The abolition of hospitality is a radical project. Perhaps it is, as Derrida says, unrealizable. Possibly it seems like a disproportionate response to the injustice that underpins any act of hospitality. And yet Derrida affirms that at the very least we must be able to think such an abolition if we are to even open the possibility of a more just practical ethics. Now, one could argue that if discarding hospitality implies the destruction of hierarchies, even accepting that they may be founded on violence, then the result would be the flattening of everything, the descent into static, the triumph of noise under another name. But that is not necessarily the case. The choice is not simply between, on the one hand, hierarchized systems whose order, however fleeting, is founded on an interminable project of self-purification involving violent acts of exclusion and, on the other, entropic egalitarianism. Doing away with the host/parasite dialectic does not have to mean unleashing anarchy. It can instead unlock new modes of meaning-making. We do not need to demolish the city, but to deconstruct it.

Communication or Reading?

What was Derrida's issue with Austin's speech act theory? Austin attempted to bracket parasitism and to found a theory of speech acts on supposedly serious speech. Searle, in Austin's defense, called the move temporary, saying it was necessary to understand how speech worked before looking at special cases where it didn't. In Derrida's view, a gesture like that was not possible. One could not exclude parasitism to explain communication, because parasitism was not a special case, an occasional hiccup in the otherwise successful ordinary functioning of communication, but rather something that was always lurking in every act of communication: "As soon as a possibility is essential and necessary, *qua possibility* (and even if it is the possibility of what is named, *negatively*, absence, 'infelicity,' parasitism, the non-serious, non-'standard,' fictional, citational, ironical, etc.), it can no longer, either de facto or de jure, be bracketed, excluded, shunted aside, even temporarily, on allegedly methodological grounds."[11]

In other words, parasites could not be avoided by making language stay "'at home,' by and in itself, in the shelter of its essence or *telos*." They were internal to language, its "positive condition of possibility."[12] Derrida's thinking about communicational parasites is identical to Serres's. For both writers, the essential error is the assumption that the parasite represents an external and occasional violation of otherwise stable norms of communication. Both reframe parasites as the condition of possibility of meaning rather than meaning's antagonist. Reframing parasitism in this way means that what needs to be explained is no longer how language sometimes goes awry, but instead how it is possible to communicate at all. (I note similarities with how the key question in the biological theory of immunity shifted from how the body destroys disease to how it manages to not destroy itself.)

Accounting for parasites as intrinsic to language is one of the principal goals of Derrida's deconstructive hermeneutic: "The parasitic structure is what I have tried to analyze everywhere, under the names of writing, mark, step, margin, *différance*, graft, undecidable, supplement, *pharmakon*, hymen, *parergon*, etc."[13] The sheer number of these terms, with the "etc." at the end pointing to the inability to ever close the list, is a shorthand for how Derrida understood language. Meaning is never stable or self-contained. It is never present. It is always deferred, displaced. One can access it only partially and through a process that opens up new voids in meaning. Derrida's account of language is antithetical to a communication model like Claude Shannon's, wherein there is an emitter who possesses a concept, translates the concept into language, and passes it through a channel where it is modified by parasites before arriving at a receiver, who must then filter out the effect of the parasites (the noise) to access the concept as it originally was. Derrida opens "Signature Event Context" by declaring his skepticism of informatic theories of communication and of communication itself.

Derrida's alternative to communication theory leans heavily on his thinking of hospitality as *ur*-ethics. Quoting Emmanuel Levinas, he writes that "language *is* hospitality." Whereas Austin and Searle, Derrida implies, extend only conditional hospitality to the parasites of language, deconstruction offers them absolute hospitality. There is no noise of language in deconstruction, in the sense that meaning-making does not involve the abjection of anything. The interpreter is not trying to reconstitute the speaker or writer's "original" meaning, and there is no noise reduction protocol. Everything is offered a place at the table of signification.

Reciprocally, hospitality is language for Derrida, or at least, the practical ethics of relating to the other is inextricable from how one relates to language, how one produces meaning, how one writes and reads. "We have come to wonder," he writes, "whether absolute, hyperbolical, unconditional hospitality doesn't consist in suspending language, a particular determinate language, and even the address to the other."[14] Conditional hospitality begins with a question: "who's there?" (Or "who's coming?" or "*qui vient?*" as the arrival of the other is perpetually deferred, always on the horizon.) It begins with a demand for dialogue, a requirement that the other prove their identity, their subjectivity. Conditional hospitality implies communication. Absolute hospitality requires the suspension of communication, a different way of being in language. It implies a refusal to distinguish between meaning and noise, speaker and listener, self and other, host and parasite. The radical openness to the parasites of the home that Derrida describes in his essays on hospitality is directly connected to the radical openness to the parasites of language he displays across all of his writings.

The idea of a hermeneutic that does not distinguish between meaning and parasite has been elaborated by a number of theorists and philosophers of language. The majority of them connect it to literature or literarity. Derrida, though he writes extensively about literary texts, carefully avoids reifying literature as a distinct category of writing, with all the word entails about canon and high culture. Deconstruction is not a literary theory. Any text can be deconstructed; not just poetry. And yet, as Wigley notes, Derrida's texts "repeatedly invite [an association with literature] through a sustained privileging of the literary as a strategic response to the traditional subordination of writing." Like Derrida, I do not want to privilege literature, or to suggest that novels and poetry enact absolute hospitality in an uncomplicated way. But literarity—not as an attribute exclusive to novels and poetry, but as a way of engaging with textuality across media—can potentially offer a space in which to think through the aporias of hospitality and the deconstruction of architecture. While Derrida is ambivalent about literature as an institution, he does privilege reading and writing as ways of engaging in deconstruction, especially as it relates to architecture and the home. Wigley detects a pervasive desire in Derrida's writings to construct an "elsewhere" or a "non-site" without boundaries as an alternative to place. Such an alternative would avoid the violence that underpins the constitution of the *oikos*. But this non-site must not simply be a different place or a new space; it has to fall entirely outside the logic of place and space. It must not be recuperable by cartography. Derrida puts forward "spacing" (*espacement*) as a way of conceptualizing this non-site: "the 'becoming space' of that which is meant to be without space." The method he identifies for spacing is writing: "What Derrida locates in the unmappable territory that binds philosophy and the spatial arts in convoluted and surprising ways, the atopic spatiality in which one cannot 'make a diagram . . . draw a sort of chart, or cartography of their positions,' is 'writing.'"[15]

Derrida also speaks of the necessity of dislocation, of approaching philosophy through literature or art as a way of creating the spacing necessary to effectively critique it. With that in mind, it is worth considering theories of literarity—not in order to elevate literature as a model for architecture or urbanism, but to dislocate the questions of architectural and urban parasites, and to understand what it is that takes place in reading and writing that allows one to access Derrida's theoretical non-site.

In *The Noise of Culture*, William Paulson distinguishes between two kinds of reading. The first is informatic, communicational reading—the kind one does with an instruction manual—where meaning and noise are distinct categories, with the reader seeking to filter out the latter to access the former. The second kind is literary reading. In literary reading, "all information is aesthetic."[16] There is no distinction between meaning and noise. The literary reader must create an *ad hoc* interpretive framework capable of producing a meaning that cannot help but be original to that particular act of reading. The reader does not seek to minimize or eliminate noise; instead, noise and content join together as one, inviting the reader to engage in a creative and ephemeral process of reorganization. An absolute hospitality of reading takes place where host and parasite cease to exist as distinct categories.

The French philosopher Maurice Blanchot advances much the same idea of what makes literary reading special. Like Paulson he distinguishes between "the nonliterary book [that offers itself] as a tightly woven net of determined significations, a set of real affirmations" and the literary work that "has no guarantee in the world, and when it is read, it has never been read before." Blanchot's work is notable for his insistence that literary reading transforms not only the text but the people involved in it. For Blanchot, literary reading is anathema to individualism. It demands the dissolution of the self, of the subject. Writer and reader cease to occupy their respective positions of emitter and receiver in a communicative framework, and slough off their individuality. The reader must lose "his personality, his immodesty, his stubborn insistence upon remaining himself in the face of what he reads," and in the process he must destroy those same qualities in the author, or at least divorce the author's identity from the text.[17] When this happens, a new kind of space is opened up: a literary space. This is a space that is no one's property, to which no one has a preferential right.[18] It is a space without hosts or *oikos*. It is a space where shifting meanings produce themselves through the encounter of beings that have lost their singularity. Blanchot's notion of a deindividualizing literary space echoes Derrida's assertion of a fundamental link between the practical ethics of hospitality—the boundaries of the home and the relationship to the other—and the philosophy of language.

Gilles Deleuze makes much the same argument, though his emphasis is on writing rather than reading. For him, literarity is incompatible with the boundedness and subjectivity of the host. It "strips us of the power to say 'I.'" Deleuze contrasts two visions of the self. The first possesses properties and characteristics in a stable way. He calls this the organismal self. It has form and occupies a place. It is persistent. The second vision, which he prefers, is the self as a matrix of intensities and virtualities. This is really no self at all. The self is an illusion of organization that masks the molecular interconnectedness of things. The first vision of the self is concerned with being, whereas the second is concerned with becoming. "To become is not to attain a form (identification, imitation, Mimesis) but to find the zone of proximity, indiscernibility, or indifferentiation where one can no longer be distinguished from *a* woman, *an* animal, or *a* molecule—neither imprecise nor general, but unforeseen and non-preexistent, singularized out of a population rather than determined in form." Becoming is always incomplete. Deleuze understands literature as an act through which both writer and language engage in becoming: "In writing, one becomes-woman, becomes-animal or vegetable, becomes-molecule to the point of becoming-imperceptible." Language likewise loses its solidity. Literarity "opens up a kind of foreign language within language, which is neither another language nor a rediscovered patois, but a becoming-other of language, a minorization of this major language."[19] Once again we have the idea that literarity is opposed to communication, and erodes any possible distinction between meaning and noise. Deleuze uses the terms *mots-souffles* and *mots-cris*, breath-words and howl-words, signification that lies between speech and noise.

Deleuze's alternative to the self is also relevant for its biological dimension. While he does not refer to parasites, he does connect his notion of literature to the body and the concept of health. His idea of health is anti-hygienic. He is opposed to the hermetic detachment of the body from its disease-generating context. Instead he advocates merging the body with the "symptoms" (the affects and intensities) that pervade the environment: "The world is the set of symptoms whose illness merges with man. Literature then appears as an enterprise of health: not that the writer would necessarily be in good health [. . .], but he possesses an irresistible and delicate health that stems from what he has seen and heard of things too big for him, too strong for him, suffocating things whose passage exhausts him, while nonetheless giving him the becomings that a dominant and substantial health would render impossible."[20] Deleuzian health is not robustness or sovereignty; it is fragility, a permeability of the body *vis-à-vis* the world around it. Literature is one way of engendering this counterintuitive health.

Roberto Esposito draws on both Deleuze and Blanchot in his theory of textuality. Esposito believes that literature gives us access to a "being that is both singular and plural—to the non-person inscribed in the person, to the person open to what has never been before."[21] By dispensing with personhood and the autonomy of the subject, literature opens a way out of immunity and into a different kind of collective configuration.

Though they use different terms, these thinkers share the idea that literarity obliterates the distinction between meaning and noise and, in the process, engenders the dissolution of the subject. Literarity creates an unbounded space, or operates a spacing, allowing for new kinds of encounter and relationality. In these ways it offers an alternative to the host–parasite dialectic, with its subjects, boundaries, and meanings. But how to translate literarity to the city or to architecture remains an open question. How does one write or read a city literarily? Bearing in mind Derrida's warning about a conflation of literarity with the institution of literature, we can say that rendering Paris literary is not just a matter or representing it in novels or poems. In chapter 4, I criticized Réda and Vasset's decisions to transmit their experiences of Paris in single-authored printed books, which structurally inhibit certain kinds of collective appropriation and encounter to which the texts otherwise might have given rise. And yet, at the same time, as the city is always mediated, it is impossible to distinguish between interventions in the "real" city and in the virtual, mediated one. A printed book can still intervene in how its readers listen to and interpret urban space. Ross Chambers has argued that Baudelaire's prose poetry was an attempt to aestheticize urban noise. For Baudelaire, he writes, the question was not "how to produce harmonious verses that deny the presence and power of noise and seek to cancel it out, but rather how to incorporate this defining noisiness of urban life into an aesthetics that might somehow be capable of doing justice to noise's pervasive and inescapable, if mostly ignored, presence. How to envisage a noisy form of beauty, or the beauty of noise?"[22] This is a kind of literarity of the city, but carried out in poetry rather than in the built environment. Literature is not incapable of participating in literary urbanism, but neither is it the only medium that can. The question still remains: how do the other media of the city, how do architecture and urban planning, engage in literarity so that they, too, can do justice to the inescapable presence of the parasite?

Excavating Literary Paris

Deleuze writes that literarity gives us access to "an eternity that can only be revealed in a becoming or a landscape that only appears in movement."[23] A Paris that appears only in movement is difficult to describe. Trying to communicate it makes it disappear. In the opening to "Limited Inc a b c" Derrida wonders how his interlocutor, Searle, can have so much confidence in his ability to discern serious speech from the nonserious. He contrasts it with his own sense that the "terrain" of their debate is "slippery and shifting, mined and undermined. And that this ground is, by essence, an underground."[24] There is a reference here to Heidegger's writing on *Grund*—both ground and reason. Heidegger observes in *The Principle of Reason* that philosophy is preoccupied with the image of itself as a practice of identifying stable ground on which to build ideas and epistemologies, but it fails to take any account of that metaphor and, in doing so, leaves itself fundamentally groundless. Beneath its rationality is a void. In *Of Grammatology*, Derrida picks up Heidegger's argument, stating that philosophy is founded on an abyss. Derrida also frequently deploys the image of the crypt, a haunted cavity buried beneath an apparently stable edifice. The crypt, as a space where something is "encrypted," conveys the sense that the emptiness beneath philosophy's foundations is a secret, a shame, something that has to be encoded so that the public cannot read it. The crypt, Wigley writes, conceals the violence at the founding of the institutions whose edifices tower over the abyss. By questioning the stability of the ground beneath Searle's argument, Derrida is laying bare not only the violence Searle has wreaked on Derrida's own reading of Austin, but also the institutional violence latent in Searle's promotion of a "politically neutral 'space of theory,'" and questioning both the rationality of that argument and the informatic premise that clear communication can take place.[25]

He is also making use of one of his preferred images for deconstruction: shaking an edifice to test its foundations. Deconstruction is an opening of the crypt, a dive into the abyss to see how deep the instability runs. Taking my cue from that image, I will conclude this book in the underground spaces of Paris. The city's underground spaces are, depending on where and how one looks, exquisitely alien and cryptlike (the subterranean aquifer where Gaston Leroux's Phantom of the Opera lives hidden, or the catacombs that in the 2014 horror film *As Above, So Below* contain the door to Hell) or rational and cartographic to the point of being inconceivable outside of their map (the metro). For that reason, they are a privileged site for exploring the tension between an informatic vision of the city as a medium of communication and the disorienting, unstable, and desubjectifying vision of it as a literary space.

The tension between these two visions of the underground is present in Victor Hugo's *Les Misérables*. Hugo imagines lifting the city off the ground like the lid of a jar to reveal the vast underground network of the sewers. Viewed from high above, the nest of tunnels and tubes resembles an "eccentric oriental alphabet, as intricate as a thicket, against a background of shadows."[26] Underground Paris is not quite a language. It is a strange and foreign text, authored by no one and addressed to no one, muddled and obscure and written in shadow. This is a Paris where meaning and noise have joined. It is illegible, but it nevertheless calls out to be read. It is a true cryptogram.

Hugo goes on to demonstrate that reading the city literarily is not easy. In the passages that follow, he digs through the mud of the sewers looking for truth, and tries to force the city to become legible. He looks for referents: "There, the bottom of a bottle indicates drunkenness, a basket-handle tells a tale of domesticity."[27] The noisy and disorienting space becomes an opportunity for Hugo not to lose himself, but to show his mastery. He imposes epistemological order. He points out the core of an apple eaten during a literary debate; whatever literary connections it once had are gone, and now it is just an apple core. Hugo's attitude is paradigmatic of the way Parisians and the city's planners have long approached the underground of their city, a space that condenses both the possibility for estrangement, confusion, and the loss of self on the one hand, and the desire to maintain order and individualism through mastery of the city's networks on the other.

Marc Augé explores this duality in *In the Metro*. The metro, though it is one of the spaces in the city where people are forced into closest contact with alterity, has become a way for Parisians to reinforce their individual selves. "Nothing is so individual, so irremediably subjective, as a single trip in the subway, [. . .] and yet nothing is so social as one such trip."[28]

Reading is central to the experience of the metro, he writes, and there is always the possibility that a traveler might lose him- or herself in doing so, but for the most part, users of the metro engage in informatic readings that reinforce the self. They build memories and routines around the metro. They build their identity on it. They internalize the map. One might think of one's metro stop as an extension of one's home, or a metonym for one's neighborhood. Station names bring to mind the things one has done after getting off the train at those stations. The subway map is a "Carte du Tendre," a map of the user's heart. The metro, though it might be a labyrinthine space, is there to be deciphered, and a person becomes a true Parisian by learning to extract information from it.

Consistent with Augé's argument, learning to read the Paris metro map is a key initiatory scene in immigrant narratives. The protagonist of Camara Laye's *L'Enfant noir* (*The Dark Child*) is given the map at the end of his coming-of-age story as he boards a plane from Guinea to Paris. "But the map meant nothing to me," he says. "The very idea of the *métro* was extremely vague."[29] Rachid Boudjedra's *Topographie idéale pour une agression caractérisée* (*Ideal Topography for an Assault*) recounts the fate of a Berber migrant who spends hours wandering helplessly in the metro network because he cannot read the map. When he finally finds his way out, he is murdered. In these novels, the challenge to render the messy spaces of the city legible is the challenge to become assimilable into the urban community—with violent death lingering in the distance.

The urge to express one's mastery of the city through mastery of the underground sign system is also present in various contemporary practices of urban exploration. Who knows how many people descend into the city's network of catacombs, metro tunnels, sewers, abandoned quarries, and maintenance tunnels? Some do it for the thrill, some to take pictures, some to party. The most famous and probably best-organized of these groups is Les UX, Urban eXperiment. UX began in 1981; today there are approximately 100 members, divided into a variety of cells. It was started by a group of high-school friends who, following a dare, camped out in the Panthéon until after it had closed for the night. They first became known to the public in 2004, when police were informed that the group had been hosting an underground film festival (in the full sense of underground) in a cavern beneath the Palais de Chaillot. They gained greater notoriety in 2006, when they revealed that over the course of a year they had covertly restored the broken mechanism in the clock of the Panthéon. The director of the Panthéon called the police, took the group to court, and hired a technician to break the clock again. The group will not reveal what other elements of the city's cultural heritage they are maintaining in secret.

Part of the appeal of UX is the sense of wonder they provoke. There is an audacity to the group's activities that cannot help inspiring one to look at the city anew, to question if all is as it seems. But another part is the envy their mastery of urban networks inspires. A key moment in the group's development was a heist in the early 1980s that resulted in the acquisition of three maps of Paris's tunnels from a government telecommunications office. Those maps give the group its power. The group's goal, moreover, is not to disturb or estrange the city, but to make it more efficient. Their spokesman, Lazar Kunstmann, has said that the group is motivated by frustration with the government for allowing minor elements of the cultural heritage to decay when small amounts of money would suffice to protect them. The group once left a memo on the desk of the security director of a major Parisian museum detailing lapses they had found in the museum's security. Les UX inspire a sense of mystery in those who have never explored the city's underground tunnels, but their work relies on cartographic mastery of those spaces, and seeks to render them more rather than less informatic. They want the city to work like clockwork.

It is clear from these examples that while the underground spaces of Paris might still be jumbled, much work has been done to put these spaces on the map, to regularize them and rationalize them, to sift through the mud and reestablish a hierarchy between sense and nonsense, information and noise, host and parasite. It is possible to imagine a future where the city's underground is as well mapped as its aboveground. An underground transformed into a roster of places, destinations people go on the weekend: the UX cinema, raves and dance parties in abandoned caverns, the swimming pool the politician Nathalie Kosciusko-Morizet proposed installing in the abandoned Arsenal metro station. It is easy to imagine a top ten list of "Best places to experience loss of self in Paris."

And yet, while the underground spaces of Paris increasingly resemble those above ground, they are still the places where we are best able to glimpse the abyss at the foundations of the city. The hollow space beneath the rationalized, informatic city. The crypt in which is hidden the violence of the urban order. While many underground practices and artworks seek to drive this void ever further down, further out of sight, one text that does not is Rachid Boudjedra's *Topographie idéale pour une agression caractérisée*, which I mentioned briefly above. This is a text in which the political and ethical stakes of the conflict between informatic urbanism and a desubjectifying, literary urbanism are laid starkly bare. The novel shares, to an almost uncanny degree, a vocabulary with Deleuze and Derrida. Published in 1975, it belongs to the same decade as "Signature Event Context," "Limited Inc a b c," and *Capitalism and Schizophrenia*. The novel bridges those texts, bringing issues of hospitality and language together with Deleuze's definition of literarity and his concern with nomadism, cartography, and the body. Boudjedra's book poses questions that traverse literature, urbanism, and ethics. How does one abolish the communicational framework of the modern city, and replace it with literarity? How does one engage in absolute hospitality? How does one deconstruct the city without demolishing it? These questions, as Derrida admitted, are perhaps even more vital when it comes to architecture and urbanism than when it comes to language. This is because while we are always in mediation, the city is the medium we inhabit *par excellence*. The city is the medium where we are most directly confronted by the ethical stakes of our relationship to the parasite. It is where parasitism meets up once again with the meaning it once had: Who eats? Who is at home? Who is welcome?

The Hospitality of Reading

Topographie idéale pour une agression caractérisée follows an anonymous Berber migrant who has just arrived in Paris by train after immigrating from rural Algeria. Unable to read or speak French, he becomes lost in the metro and spends hours boarding trains at random, trying to find the station whose name is scrawled on a piece of paper he carries with him throughout his journey. Most of the people he encounters treat him roughly, but occasionally someone stops to give him directions or escort him part of the way. Ultimately, when he emerges into the city streets, he is murdered. A group of racist hoodlums carrying knives and bike chains beat and stab him to death in a bloody anti-immigrant orgy.

Viewed from one angle, the novel is almost an allegory of the laws of hospitality. Boudjedra makes numerous references to ancient Greece: he calls the metro a labyrinth, implying that the migrant is one of the sacrificial youths sent from Athens to its conqueror, Crete, to be devoured by the Minotaur. He repeatedly alludes to Odysseus's time as an *hôte* on the island of the lotus-eaters. These references elevate the novel's plot above the anecdotal *fait divers* and tie it directly to the foundation myths of hospitality. Echoing Derrida and Benveniste, Boudjedra emphasizes language as the determining factor in the welcome offered to the stranger. The novel's protagonist is trapped in the metro because he does not speak French. He cannot read signs, he cannot understand the map, he cannot ask for help except through gestures, and he cannot understand the instructions people offer him. He is bewildered by the images that cover the metro walls, mistaking a tampon advertisement featuring a smiling woman for a sign welcoming "all the miscreants of the earth."[30] His native language, "the language of the Piton," is a rural dialect, so he cannot even converse with other North African immigrants in the lingua franca of Arabic. He is thus not a *xenos*, the foreigner who speaks the local language and must be welcomed, but a *barbaros*, the foreigner who doesn't, and therefore must be killed on sight.[31] (The point is driven home when he stops to admire an advertisement for Barbary figs.)

The novel's emphasis on the estranging power of language is underscored by its style. The text is composed of run-on sentences that stretch for pages, fragments, and stream-of-consciousness passages interrupted with punctuation mid-clause. Boudjedra's vocabulary is rich. The narrative voice uses free indirect discourse, and constantly switches among different points of view. It is not always clear whose thoughts it is relating, how faithfully it relates them, or when it should be read as an omniscient third-person perspective. The question is rendered more complicated by the presence of a diegetic, unreliable observer in the form of a police investigator attempting to reconstruct the chain of events leading to the migrant's death. The narrator also repeats entire passages verbatim. The effect of all of this, as Mireille Rosello has argued, is that it is easy for the reader to lose his or her place, so to speak.[32] The reader enters an alienating textual space akin to the labyrinthine metro, and experiences disorientation alongside the migrant.

It is tempting to say that the novel's form forces the reader to experience the migrant's estrangement, and thus teaches him or her how it feels to be a *barbaros*. However, there are two reasons why that argument does not work. The first, on which Rosello focuses, is that the stakes facing character and reader are wildly different. Whereas the former is lost in a new country, with his survival dependent on deciphering the underground sign system, the reader can always put down the novel. The reader can always walk away, but the character cannot. While the migrant's dominant emotions are fear and confusion, the reader is likely to feel some pleasure at working through a stylistically challenging work of fiction—how often do people look forward to "getting lost in a good novel" over vacation?

The second reason is that while Boudjedra's text is challenging, it is not illegible. Indeed, for the fluent Francophone, it cannot help being legible. The novel forces the reader to recognize that fact by consistently providing word-for-word transcriptions of texts that baffle the migrant, such as the names of metro stations and the captions on advertising posters. "He doesn't understand any of the writing (LOTUS: SAVOIR-VIVRE IS IN THE DETAILS) superimposed on the image (LOTUS IS AS SOFT AS A BABY'S SKIN)."[33] Before he or she knows it, the reader has read the text that mystifies the character. The narrator also provides detailed ekphrastic descriptions of posters and photographs the character encounters. The Arabic loan word *lascar* is parsed with a full dictionary definition.[34] A reader familiar with the Paris metro has more than enough information by the end of the novel to reconstruct the protagonist's journey station by station. The techniques Boudjedra uses to alienate his readers from French, confusing as they may be, are conventional tropes of European modernism. Stream-of-consciousness writing, interminable sentences, lack of narrative structure, and the use of free indirect discourse hardly qualify as experimental to a reader familiar with Joyce, Proust, Faulkner, and Woolf. (Boudjedra's references to Odysseus/Ulysses are just as much citations of Joyce as they are of Homer.) The text does not force the fluent Parisian to experience illiteracy; rather, it rewards the highly literate reader, turning the migrant's painful confusion into a pleasurable puzzle. On that basis, as Rosello says, it is almost grotesque to talk about the novel's form as a proxy for the migrant experience.[35]

Rosello concludes that the gap between reader and migrant is ultimately unbridgeable. There is no way for the migrant to meet the reader on equal terms. There is no way for him to assimilate. The narrator, too, makes this point. Boudjedra describes the "good immigrants" who speak fluent French, marry French spouses, and smoke French cigarettes but remain ineluctably foreign due to their accent, skin color, or some other marker of otherness. Learning to read signs is not enough for assimilation. As Derrida writes, language is not just a lexicon; sharing a language means sharing a culture. The *barbaros* does not cease to be foreign just by learning a grammar.

Another way to put this is that there is no way of arriving in Paris. The labyrinthine metro is not the final test before the migrant enters the city. It is one out of many labyrinths that collectively serve to perpetually defer arrival. Even if the migrant were to escape it unharmed, which the protagonist of the novel doesn't, what lies beyond are more labyrinths: the factory, the slum, the streets, the bureaucracy. This is why the novel's narrator repeatedly states that the salient feature of the metro map is not the lines representing the paths of the trains but the circles demarcating the zones. These circles do not converge on a center, he says, but signify that the city has no center, only an infinite series of barriers one inside the other. In this respect the prophetic statement of the *lascars* is true: the migrant will come back home, or he will die in transit. He can never arrive in the sense of making the new city his home. He can never escape his journey except by turning back. (And even then he is likely doomed to more aimless wandering if we judge by the example of the *lascars*: having gone to Paris for work, and subsequently returned, they spend all their days drinking and playing games, living off the savings from their factory jobs and telling tall tales of life in the big city. They, too, are still in transit.) Derrida could be describing this novel when he writes in *The Monolingualism of the Other*:

> The monolingual of whom I speak speaks a language of which he is *deprived*. The French language is not his. Because he is therefore deprived of *all* language, and no longer has any other recourse—neither Arabic, nor Berber, nor Hebrew, nor any languages his ancestors would have spoken—because this monolingual is in a way *aphasic* [. . .], he is thrown into absolute translation, a translation without a pole of reference, without an originary language, and without a source language [*langue de départ*]. For him there are only target languages [*langues d'arrivée*], if you will, the remarkable experience being, however, that these languages just cannot manage to reach themselves because they no longer know where they are coming from, what they are speaking *from* and what the sense of their journey is. Languages without an itinerary and, above all, without any superhighway of goodness knows what information.[36]

In the end, Boudjedra's novel seems to offer little solution to the dilemma of hospitality. The migrant can never fully arrive at his destination, much less assimilate, and the citizens there can do virtually nothing to welcome him. He can never learn the local language, and the reader can never forget it enough to truly empathize with him. We are left with what Derrida called the apparent impossibility of hospitality: "these interminable, uncrossable thresholds, and these aporias."[37] How does one act if hospitality is impossible? For Boudjedra, who said he hoped his novel would make young North Africans realize that "emigration is a trap,"[38] the solution might be to stay at home. Rosello is well aware of the aporia at the heart of Derrida's hospitality, and its consequences for the inhabitants of former colonies.[39] She acknowledges that the reader of Boudjedra's novel and the Parisians who populate it are incapable of welcoming the migrant. Instead, she advocates an "aesthetics and ethics of accompaniment." We can "be with" the migrant, she writes. We can "stay with, live with, and share, pointlessly perhaps, his painful experience of disorientation even if it means witnessing, somewhat helplessly, the violence that the community to which 'we' belong is capable of inflicting on migrants."[40] Such an ethics does nothing to bridge the gap between citizen and foreigner, but it is a way of not capitulating to that gap.

The paradoxical nature of hospitality may in fact foreclose the possibility of properly welcoming the migrant, but that does not mean other solutions are not available. The starting premise of Rosello's argument is that the novel's complex form is a performance of the migrant's disorientation in the city. As a result, the way one reads the novel is an analogue for the way one welcomes the migrant. However, it is important to be clear about what kinds of literacy are engaged by the novel. For Rosello, the literacy in question, the illiteracy that marks the migrant's otherness, is informatic: "The text that we watch like an image represents a type of image that is meant to be read and interpreted as a set of instructions."[41] Both novel and map are presented as instruction manuals, texts from which one extracts information. If the migrant can receive the message, he can arrive at the city (both as place and community). If he can enter the communicational framework, he can cross the threshold.

By conflating novel and map, Rosello glosses over the important differences between informatic reading and literary reading. The novel, as a literary work, invites a different attitude to meaning and noise than the informational map. Rather than trying to read the novel like a map in order to share in the migrant character's experience of disorientation, we could consider Boudjedra's extremely literary style as an invitation to read the map and the underground network differently. The migrant is marked as inescapably other because he cannot make the map legible, he cannot decipher its code and cannot separate noise from content enough to access the instructions it is presumed to contain. That does not mean he lacks the ability to read it literarily, to flatten the distinction between noise and content, and allow ephemeral meanings to emerge through his encounter with the text.

Indeed, that is a skill he demonstrates at multiple moments. Here is a description of his attempt to understand an advertisement for Lotus brand toilet paper.

> What adds to his perplexity not understanding the relationship between the plant that only grows in his region, close to the sea, and this child, this bowl, this paper unrolled like a ribbon on the carpet, going off in search of complicated interpretations, telling himself that the child is perhaps a victim of some magic spell involving lotus leaves or fruits (*lotos*, in his language) and camphor and sweet almond oil and alum that he was forced to swallow and which has made him euphoric and cheerful, but not at all grasping what role the paper has played in this ritual ceremony. The stylized drawing of the lotus leaves that takes the place of the letter o reinforces the poetic onslaught whose magic tends to erase from people's minds any comic or upsetting reaction.[42]

The migrant is incapable of making the poster legible. He cannot understand the text exhorting him to buy Lotus (despite the presence of lexical and visual cognates) and he lacks the cultural literacy to know what the toilet paper is for. He does not realize that he is looking at an advertisement, and therefore cannot understand himself (or the consumer) as its target. But his various illiteracies do not stop him from reading the image. A new meaning, or series of meanings, emerges through his encounter with it. In the ensuing passage the image becomes a work of literature, joining the canon of works about the lotus plant. The narrator references Odysseus (and even includes a parenthetical citation), and from there the reader is free to make connections with the texts on the lotus-eaters by Tennyson, Joyce, etc. Although (or because) he cannot make the text legible, he reads it literarily.

Now, Boudjedra's narrator dismisses the value of this reading on the grounds that the poetic associations the image inspires for the protagonist are the advertisement's goal: "Advertisers employ a multiform spectrum where everything counts: the image, the sound, and the interpretation creating an entire poetic and harmonious forest around the word *lotus* with the sole object of hiding the disgust such an image ought to provoke from anyone."[43] Seeing the brand's logo and thinking of Odysseus is a naïve failure to see through the advertisement's manipulative strategy. Poetry has become a marketing tool. In my view, Boudjedra's anticapitalist skepticism of the reading his protagonist is capable of ultimately underestimates the transformative potential of literarity as Paulson, Blanchot, Deleuze, and Esposito understand it. For those thinkers, literarity is not just a mode of free association through which a given text is personalized. It is, on the contrary, a radical process of depersonalization. Truly literary reading cannot be recuperated by consumer capitalism because it leaves behind no consumer in its wake, no person to do the buying. Truly literary reading defies the narrator's skepticism and opens up new horizons within Boudjedra's novel.

I have described how the protagonist of this novel is structurally prevented from ever "arriving" in Paris because he cannot speak the local language. He is a *barbaros*, so he can never be welcomed. However, if we follow Deleuze's understanding of literarity, the terms of the problem change. According to Deleuze, literarity "opens up a kind of foreign language within language." This results in "language as a whole [. . .] being toppled or pushed to a limit, to an outside or reverse side that consists of Visions and Auditions that no longer belong to any language."[44] The language of literature is foreign to every reader, even to the author. Distinctions of belonging and exclusion fall away.[45] Everyone is a *barbaros* in literature.

There are hints in Boudjedra's novel that literary reading could offer an alternative to the structural exclusion effected by the informatic city. The protagonist at times feels welcome in the underground. He realizes that "he's not so bad off in this extreme confusion of space and names."[46] Abandoning his *telos* and giving up his quest to extract meaning and himself from the channel might open new modes of being and relationality. The Parisians around him are likewise tempted to break off their commutes and "transcend themselves, to propel themselves toward forbidden spaces."[47] Literary spaces, perhaps. The appeal of a disorienting and desubjectifying experience of the underground is constantly at war with their "propensity to close, enclose, and shut away everything in an assemblage of lines segments angles and curves." They are torn between a need to stratify and order and an ever-present urge to discard the map and lose themselves. They wonder what would happen if they stopped experiencing these "semblances of space" as analogues of "real, hatched, striated, sectioned, dislocated space."[48]

The reference to "striated space" in that quotation is just one of many occasions where Boudjedra's novel reproduces, and at times even anticipates, critical terms used by Deleuze and Félix Guattari. In addition to striated space (*l'espace strié*) and smooth space (*l'espace lisse*), these include the binary oppositions sedentarism/nomadism, and the organism/Body without Organs. Boudjedra's Deleuzian vocabulary, like his allusions to the temptation of self-transcendence, point to utopian horizons in his narrative that might be accessible if the underground were to become literary.

Deleuze and Guattari define striated space as cartographic space. It is associated with the grid or diagram. Things within striated space take on position, order, and form. Smooth space, by contrast, is a vector space. Things within it have direction and intensity, but not dimensions:

> Smooth space is filled by events or haecceities, far more than by formed and perceived things. It is a space of affects, more than one of properties. It is *haptic* rather than optical perception. Whereas in the striated forms organize a matter, in the smooth materials signal forces and serve as symptoms for them. It is an intensive rather than extensive space, one of distances, not of measures and properties. Intense *Spatium* instead of *Extensio*. A Body without Organs instead of an organism and organization.[49]

Striated space is associated with sedentarism and the organism, and smooth space with nomadism and the Body without Organs. Sedentarism refers both to a static appropriation of space and to a way of traversing space focused on arriving at a given destination. Sedentarism includes practices like migration that are not literally sedentary but take for granted the existence of points A and B and the ability to move from one to the other. Sedentarism transforms space into place. Nomadism is a smoothing practice. The nomad lives in the "intermezzo." He or she does not move between points, but generates paths. While the nomad may come to a stop during his or her journey, those stops are subordinate to the line, to the journey itself, rather than the other way around. These two pairs of terms are of obvious relevance to Boudjedra's protagonist. He is a nomad who becomes a migrant. He trades the path for its own sake for a destination. While he is tempted to engage in nomadism in the metro, privileging movement itself over the destination, he ultimately stays true to the sedentarist project of leaving the metro and establishing residency. He judges that mastering striation, allowing himself to be put on the grid, will confer power and belonging on him.

That brings us to the third pair of terms: organism/Body without Organs. One of *Topographie*'s recurring motifs is the notion that once the migrant enters the metro, he is destined to leave or lose (part of) himself in there. The narrator repeatedly quotes a fictional advertising slogan that says: "a tomato that goes in the oven risks leaving its skin behind." The *lascars* in the protagonist's village who have been to Paris know from experience that their compatriot will inevitably lose something: "his leg, his virtue, his native language, his eyes, his skin, his faith [. . .], his cells, his liver, his lungs and other testicles."[50] It appears that their prophecy is fulfilled at the end of the migrant's journey, when his body is beaten and stabbed to the point of unrecognizability. Given the racist violence of that act, it is hard to see the prophecy as anything other than a threat echoing Boudjedra's own interpretation of his novel. Don't emigrate to France, young Africans, or you'll end up mutilated.

But we could also understand the *lascars*' warning in another way: as a statement that the protagonist will have to become a Body without Organs, which Deleuze and Guattari define in the following way:

> A body without organs is not an empty body stripped of organs, but a body upon which that which serves as organs [. . .] is distributed according to crowd phenomena, in Brownian motion, in the form of molecular multiplicities. The desert is populous. Thus the body without organs is opposed less to organs as such than to the organization of the organs insofar as it composes an organism. The body without organs is not a dead body but a living body all the more alive and teeming once it has blown apart the organism and its organization.[51]

The Body without Organs is not death, but a radical alternative to the self. It rests on the idea that the body is not an autonomous, stratified, and individual thing, but a matrix in which a potentially endless variety of intensities can intersect and combine. It's a connective body. A Tardian body: "Dismantling the organism has never meant killing yourself, but rather opening the body to connections that presuppose an entire assemblage, circuits, conjunctions, levels and thresholds, passages and distributions of intensity, and territories and deterritorializations measured with the craft of a surveyor."[52] The Body without Organs is about becoming, not being. It preexists being in a certain respect. Multiple Bodies without Organs exist *in potentia* for everyone and everything, and more can always be made. But they are not things, states, or places. They are not skins to put on. They are not a space, but a "spatium": a void in the body that has not yet been opened. A spacing. The Body without Organs is "nonstratified, unformed, intense matter, the matrix of intensity."[53]

It is possible to imagine a different version of Boudjedra's novel in which the protagonist remains permanently in transit as a nomadic Body without Organs, instead of losing his life at the moment he arrives at his destination. A version in which the protagonist, instead of being structurally excluded because of his inability to be anything other than a parasite in the communicational and hospitable framework of the city, instead encounters the city in a literary way. Instead of undertaking a doomed project to establish himself as a subject with place, limits, and identity, so that he can request hospitality in the home whose address he carries in his pocket, he might find himself in a city where unbounded, plural matrices combine and conjugate, where bodies do not have forms but allow different intensities to pass, where static modes of being are replaced by combinatory practices of becoming.

The alternative to individualism and self I have described here is similar in many respects to the one developed by Rosi Braidotti. Just as I have drawn attention to the role of the parasitic discourse in the assertion of a hegemonic, hierarchical, exclusive host, Braidotti critiques a pathologization of "others" that subtends the circumscription of subjectivity in post-Enlightenment Europe. "Universal 'Man,'" she writes, "is implicitly assumed to be masculine, white, urbanized, speaking a standard language, heterosexually inscribed in a reproductive unit and a full citizen of a recognized polity." This restrictive normativity excludes not only humans who fail to match the description but also "our genetic neighbors the animals and the earth as a whole." As an alternative, she draws on Spinoza and Deleuze and Guattari to instead argue for a monistic, nondialectical, nomadic, and rhizomatic alternative to the self. Against monadic and agential theories of the self she emphasizes "the priority of the relation and the awareness that one is the effect of irrepressible flows of encounters, interactions, affectivity and desire, which one is not in charge of."[54]

There are clear resonances between my reading of Deleuze and Guattari and Braidotti's, and her work in this area is especially valuable for the constant attention she brings to the ethical implications of occasionally abstract rhetoric. She is engaged on behalf of the marginalized others of

Enlightenment individualism, and her appreciation for nonhuman life and the planet are especially relevant given biological science's historic role in justifying individualist theories of the self and its more recent shift toward problematizing those same theories. She calls for a reconciliation with the organisms that likely first come to mind when we hear the word "parasite."

But there are important differences between her argument and mine. The biggest of these is her commitment to subjectivity. "One needs at least *some* subject position,"[55] she writes in *The Posthuman*. Her reasoning is that subjectivity is necessary to maintain "political and ethical accountability," reflecting her wariness of a politically neutral posthumanism. There are strong similarities here to the ethical dead end in which Jules Romains found himself, caught between his certainty that the posthuman collectives at the heart of unanimism would have their own ethics beyond what an individual could conceive, and his desire for the new ethics to flatter the sensibilities of the old.[56] By trying to maintain a system of accountability while simultaneously discarding conscious agency, Braidotti opens the door to the return of many of the power structures, spatial boundaries, and dialectical oppositions her monistic approach is meant to circumvent. The self/other dialectic is allowed to persist, reframed as a connective relationship rather than an oppositional one. Though Braidotti's insistence on the flows and becomings of her subjects goes a long way toward blurring boundaries, there is a sense that although the parasite may have been reframed as symbiont, it remains separate from its host.

It is not surprising that Braidotti's preservation of subjectivity brings with it cartographic metaphors, whose connections to Enlightenment practices of subjectification, localization, and citizenship go unexamined. She calls herself a "tracker and cartographer" who is "committed to the task of providing politically informed maps of the present."[57] Describing her writing as a map that allows us to localize concepts gives it an uncomfortably informatic overtone, despite her critique of the informatics of neoliberalism. This impression is strengthened by her call for "an understandable language"[58] in which to visualize posthuman subjects. She prefers serious speech to parasitic ambiguity. Her attraction to informatics and cartography culminates in a striking embrace of the "smart city" model of urbanism. Despite the many problems and contradictions latent in smart city urbanism, Braidotti praises smart cities as open-source utopias in which the public gains complete access to knowledge and administrative power.[59]

So, while I share Braidotti's vision of a Deleuzian nonself, I find her preservation of subjectivity problematic. Serres and Derrida together show that the subject position is deeply intertwined with a communicational model of language that necessarily entails the production of boundaries and the pathologization of parasites. In "Il faut bien manger" (the title can be translated as "one still has to eat" or "one has to eat well"), an interview with Jean-Luc Nancy, Derrida anticipates Braidotti's pragmatic justification for preserving the subject. The concept of the subject is often a political "calculation" whose motivations he understands but which, he feels, preempts a true confrontation with ethical questions: "I believe that in ethico-political terms there is no responsibility or decision without an encounter with the incalculable or the undecidable." He goes on to criticize supposedly post-subjective philosophies that "reconstitute under the name of subject, or under the name of Dasein, an identity that's illegitimately delimited."[60] Like Derrida, I do not believe it is possible to neatly dissociate subjectivity from theories of self and individualism, as Braidotti attempts to do. On the contrary, I find the gradual passage from the subject to a surveillant and informatic urbanism that takes place in her work telling. It is emblematic of subjectivity's inextricability from processes that striate space and erect boundaries around the self. Braidotti's work shows that disavowing the rhetoric of self and individualism on its own is not enough to create a city without parasites. Doing so while keeping subjectivity does not lead to a radical transformation of the city, but instead has as its logical endpoint the same informatic urbanism that individualism leads to. A true transformation of urban space requires moving beyond the subject and the self to find a radically different thinking of being and relationality.

In summary, I have opposed the informatic city wherein information, resources, and bodies are communicated from defined place to defined place, individual subject to individual subject, to a literary city in which no distinction is made between signal and noise, or host and parasite. The latter entails openness and fluidity of bodies, structures, and spaces. I have contrasted two ways of reading Boudjedra's novel. The first is an informatic reading in which the novel's style is experienced as an imperfect performance of the protagonist's failed reading of the metro map. This approach to the novel demonstrates the aporias of hospitality, and leaves both reader and characters helpless to prevent the foreigner's violent elimination from the city. The second is a literary reading that breaks down the identities of reader, characters, and author. This second reading, though its outcome is not explored by the narrative, offers the hope of an alternative to the violence that inheres in every conditional expression of hospitality, and a possible path to an absolute hospitality.

I have drawn attention to moments in the novel where the protagonist appears to engage in a literary reading of his environment as a way to show that literarity is more a stance of the reader than a characteristic of texts. Surrounded by informatic readers and by texts conceived to communicate information, the protagonist can still experience literarity. It is important, however, not to put too much stock in these moments. The implication that Boudjedra's protagonist might have had a different fate if he had simply read the underground literarily is dubious, if not offensive. While the novel encourages its reader to treat the ethics of reading as a proxy for ethics *tout court* (and while Derrida offers some justification for this perspective), Rosello rightly warns against an "over-emphasis on textuality"[61] where metaphors are used to gloss over the brute, material conditions of life. A Body without Organs is still a body. Perhaps the character "is not so bad off" in the underground, and perhaps he could stay there in some metaphysical sense, but he still eventually has to eat. Changing the way he conceptualizes his peregrination in the metro does not stop him from feeling exhaustion. Nor is it likely to stop the racist young men he meets from perceiving him as a parasite or a *barbaros*. Focusing on what one character—especially a supremely marginal one in sociopolitical terms—can do to render urban space literary allows a kind of neoliberal individualism to creep back in. Literary reading, like meditation, begins to tip over into a discourse of spiritual personal hygiene. Loss of self as self-care. If we understand literarity as a personal change in perception rather than a systemic one, then it is an abstract, rarefied mental exercise whose application to the violent realities of urban politics is grotesque.

I do not believe that a few fleeting moments of literary experimentation redeem Boudjedra's character's journey. He dies, brutally and pointlessly, and if literarity interrupts his journey to death, it does not do so nearly enough. I do not see this novel as a model to follow, and I am not particularly moved by the idea of literary reading as a private mode of resistance within and against a structurally informatic urban environment. What I want to know is: what would have happened to this character if he had arrived in a structurally literary one? To save the literary city from being an empty spiritual exercise or a lofty mode of self-care, we must explain how it moves beyond the individual. For the literary city to truly be a connective space, it has to be a collective one. It cannot be the parasite alone who transcends the host/parasite dialectic, especially when it is the host who calls that dialectic into being. I believe it is important not only to observe that it is possible for each of us to engage in literary readings of the city, but also to ask how the city can be written literarily. I have read this novel against itself, trying to find the contours of a world that is present, if at all, only as a fleeting moment of doubt. I want to ask now: what would it mean to create literary cities, to engage in literary urbanism? In what ways can a city be structured to favor literary practices and experiences? Is there an architecture that structurally favors relationality and becoming? Is there an architecture without *oikos*, a deconstructive architecture?

D.S.

The challenges of translating literary concepts into architecture are what Derrida ran aground on in his attempt to design a garden at La Villette in Paris. In the 1980s, the architect Bernard Tschumi was commissioned to transform the immense grounds of Paris's disused abattoir into a park. The abattoir had been created by Haussmann. Five slaughterhouses in the city were closed in favor of an immense complex outside the city walls. In a short 1929 article accompanying photographs by Éli Lotar of the abattoir, Georges Bataille writes: "Nowadays the slaughterhouse is cursed and quarantined like a boat with cholera aboard. The victims of this curse are neither the butchers nor the animals but those fine folk who have reached the point of not being able to stand their own unseemliness, an unseemliness corresponding in fact to a pathological need for cleanliness."[62] Bataille understands the slaughterhouse as an urban parasite, a disease agent banished to the boundaries of the city to protect the health of the residents, who are scared of coming into contact with the bloody mess that makes their meals and their survival possible. The hearth, the feast, the hospitable meal, are separated from the blood and guts and the extinction of life that they call for.

Tschumi was confronting a prime symbol and expression of the antiparasitic ideology in Paris. The goal he set himself was to avoid antiparasitism. Importantly, he understood this task in communicational as well as in bio- and sociopolitical terms. He set out to "dismantle meaning."[63] Like Derrida, he believed that breaking out of the informatic, communicational framework was inextricable from a reconciliation with other kinds of so-called parasites.

Tschumi's debt to Derrida was such that he invited him to participate in the design of the park. With some reluctance, Derrida said yes. Tschumi teamed him with the architect Peter Eisenman. Eisenman would describe their collaboration as "a double parasitic laziness."[64] Derrida believed architecture was an especially apt target for deconstruction, not least because "deconstruction" is an architectural metaphor. He recommended that the two should focus on translating into architecture the concept of *khôra* or *chora*. This word is used by Socrates in Plato's *Timaeus* to mean place in multiple ways. In ancient Greece the *khôra* was the space outside the city proper. Plato used it as a third term in his theory of form: *khôra* mediated between the ideal and the real. It was a kind of conceptual opening in which the passage from ideal to real could begin to take place. Derrida defines it to mean "place in general, the residence, the habitation, the place where we live, the country. It has to do with interval; it is what you open 'to give' place to things, or when you open something for things to take place."[65] It means place, but also a kind of spacing.

Julia Kristeva understands *chora* as a space that opens the possibility for subjectivity and meaning. The "semiotic *chora*" is where the infinite potential for signification is located. It is a space inhabited by language, but it cannot be accessed through language (it is similar to Derrida's concept of arche-writing). In her essay "The Subject in Process," in which she summarizes her theory of subjectivity as something that is constantly undergoing redefinition, she suggests that the semiotic *chora* is best accessed through music or architecture. The "*chora* is the non-verbal semiotic articulation of the process; music or architecture might provide metaphors better suited to designate it than the grammatical categories of linguistics which it actually reorganizes."[66] Eisenman picked up on this meaning and contributed the obvious pun, adding an L to *chora* (the title of the book the two would publish is *Chora L Works*). He suggested using music rather than language as the point of reference for their design. Etymologically, chorus and *khôra* are not related, but chorus does bear a relationship to place. It comes from a word for a circle of dancers, the same root as choreography. It is an ephemeral place that arises through the coming together of a community around music. It may come from a root meaning to enclose, or a root meaning to enjoy. An enclosure for rejoicing, or, taking some liberty with synonyms, a pleasure garden.

How do you produce an architecture that embodies these terms? An ephemeral, musical architecture that is neither abstract nor real? The task is paradoxical. Architecture is the concrete medium *par excellence*. Buildings are made to be stable, they are built of boundaries, they are places. How can architecture exist in the interval between concept and reality without tipping over into the latter? Some commentators on *Chora L Works* argue that there is no answer to these questions. They treat Derrida's collaboration with Eisenman as a kind of performance art piece or practical joke in which the philosopher demonstrates, by failing to design anything, that architecture is incapable of operating as the medium of deconstruction. As Brendon Wocke puts it: "An architectural construction is necessarily complete, monolithic (and thus opposed to the 'openness' required by the notion of the *chora*)," and so "the garden finds itself constructed not as a built environment but as the acme of an aesthetics of absence."[67]

And yet, Derrida himself repeatedly states in *Chora L Works* that that was not his purpose. In an interview with Jeffrey Kipnis, one of the book's editors, after the collaboration ended, Derrida insists that he had found the beginnings of a deconstructive architecture in his mind, but could not quite seize it.[68] I detect genuine embarrassment rather than performative auto-estrangement in his conversation with architecture students at The Cooper Union, during which he repeatedly expresses his difficulty understanding how to write in architecture. He cannot read an architectural diagram or calculate the loadbearing capacity of a wall. Architecture, he says, is like speaking a foreign language for him. Such gestures are common in Derrida's writing; he often said he was not a philosopher, distancing himself from the discipline the better to deconstruct it, but in this exchange his tone lacks ironic self-assuredness.

The explanation Derrida gives Kipnis for his failure to build anything with Eisenman supports the idea that he was not content with publishing a book. He said their design failed for reasons that were "cultural, political, social, economic, financial, material and architectural." It is one of architecture's chief virtues, he says, that it is forced to confront such obstacles, and he declared that this is what makes architecture "more affirmative, consequential, and effective than deconstruction in discourse."[69] Unlike the writer of deconstruction, the deconstructive architect must put their money where their mouth is and affirm something, do something:

> And what I finally began to understand is that what they were doing, or what Peter is doing, not only is properly traditional, deconstructive, but shows that if deconstruction means something or is at work somewhere, that it does not consist only in semantic analysis, discursive statements, but does something, and I always repeat that deconstruction is not negative, it is affirmative, it does something, it affirms something. If deconstruction affirms something, is at work and leaves a trace, it does so through that form of architecture. But perhaps the traditional architecture is not right anymore. Perhaps once you have interrupted something in the tradition of architecture having to do with philosophy or theology, perhaps what you do is not architecture anymore.[70]

Derrida asserts that the discipline of architecture is ill-equipped to carry out deconstruction. The architecture of monumentality, starchitects, and planning commissions is too cartographic, informatic, and individualist. But Derrida does not say that deconstruction cannot take place in the built environment. On the contrary, he vigorously defends deconstruction's capacity to affirm. It is possible to build deconstructively. A new kind of architecture, capable of realizing a deconstructive city, can conceivably

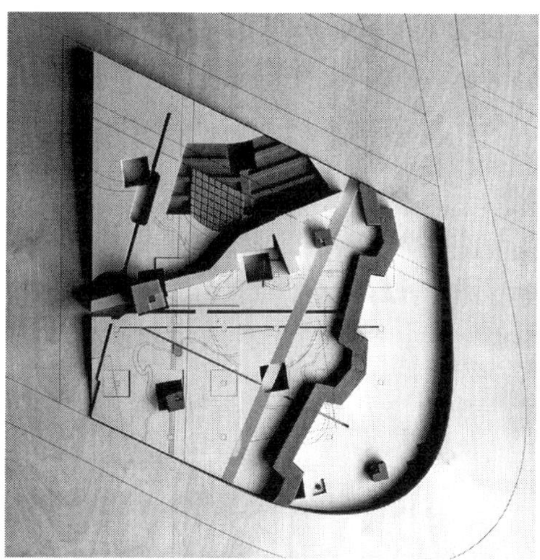

Figure 6.1
Model produced by Eisenman Architects for the collaboration with Derrida at La Villette, courtesy Eisenman Architects

emerge. Tschumi referred to the park at La Villette in just such terms, declaring his goal to be "architecture against itself."

Derrida describes his design as an image in a dream that he could remember but not put into words. The fact that he and Eisenman did not build anything puts us in a similar position. It is possible to get some idea of how Derrida and Eisenman envisioned this new architecture by studying the rejected plans they include in their book (though the task is made somewhat more difficult by the presence of ten square holes punched through the text, corresponding to ten square shapes in the planned garden. This makes it impossible to read some of the words in the book). The model put together by Eisenman's firm resembles a lyre or harp, or an open grand piano. The pedestrians are like the wind or fingers playing on the strings of the architecture, unlocking resonances and harmonies that are latent in it but imperceptible without the encounter between building and body. Structurally this is a chaotic space (some linguists suggest that *khôra* and chaos share a root). There is no focal point. The space is divided by irregular shapes that do not quite fit together. This is not a place with defined uses, but a zone where unpredictable events can take place. Derrida repeatedly alluded to the labyrinth both for its pragmatic effects (disorienting the pedestrian) and its classical baggage (Ariadne's dancing ground in Greek mythology). Mirrors and glass are used to create spaces of encounter and disorientation, and they make it difficult to fully apprehend the space visually. To destabilize the architect's position as author and authority, the pair imagined an unfinished space that could be overwritten by its users. They talked of using a mix of solid materials like stone and steel, and soft ones like sand. This would allow visitors to leave their own traces in the garden.

We can see from these elements that deconstruction in architecture is not just a play with the syntax or symbolism of shapes and materials—the vernacular, to use the linguistic metaphor architects employ. Architecture as a discipline is also being deconstructed. Derrida and Eisenman point toward a collaborative, open-ended, multisensory, and ephemeral architecture. Jennifer Bloomer calls it a minor architecture, an allusion to Deleuze's minor literature and another music metaphor.[71]

How such values might translate in the built environment can be teased out further through analysis of some of the buildings that have been constructed in the Parc de la Villette since Derrida and Eisenman abandoned their project. La Villette is today the site of the Cité de la Musique and Paris

Philharmonic, a campus of music-related buildings. These structures partly realize the choral architecture dreamed of by Derrida and Eisenman.

Christian de Portzamparc's Cité de la Musique opened in 1995. It houses the national music conservatory, the museum of instruments, a library, and exhibition and teaching spaces. Portzamparc referred to his design as an oneiric city, a labyrinthine dreamscape in which you can never quite figure out where you are or how it relates to where you've been. The Cité's website proudly boasts that it takes musicians two weeks to find their way around. For Portzamparc, architecture is a durational artform that can be perceived only in movement. Both he and the Cité's co-founder, the composer Pierre Boulez, have pointed out its similarity to music in this regard. The modular design of the central concert hall plays with movement and ephemerality. All of its elements can be rearranged to accommodate diverse musical needs. The form of the room is indeterminate: it is rectangular at ground level but ellipsoidal at the balcony. Attention to the acoustics of space is paid in all zones of the Cité, including the museum of instruments, which hosts a performance every day. The museum, typically a space for looking at objects, becomes an aural one as well, and the acts of looking and listening begin to be confounded. The ocularcentrism of architecture as a whole is challenged in these buildings.

Jean Nouvel's Philharmonic opened in 2015. It was built at the very edge of La Villette, practically straddling the *boulevard périphérique*, the boundary of the city. That road embodies the historic schism between central Paris and its poorer suburbs. Nouvel's Philharmonic was intended to eat into that barrier. The Philharmonic's programming reflects the desire to reach across cultural boundaries and bring in new audiences, with Maghrebi music, jazz, pop, and contemporary experimental work in addition to the classical repertoire.

The building was conceived as a bridge between city and nature as well as between inside and out. Nouvel described it as a new hill, a third Butte alongside the Buttes-Chaumont and Montmartre. The rooftop viewing deck is nine stories up, and open to the public five days a week. It offers one of the few true 360-degree views of Paris from a perspective where it is virtually impossible to see where the city ends and the suburbs begin. The exterior walls are tiled with tessellated aluminum birds. These create a mirror effect, distorting the already unpredictable curves of the building. It is as if at any moment this murmuration could disperse, and the building would vanish into the sky. Inside, the building shares many features with Portzamparc's. The concert hall is fully modular. Carrying on the natural theme, the balconies form floating clouds. But their shape is functional as well, with the curves carefully calculated to make the room acoustically viable regardless of its configuration.

It is quite easy in these descriptions to hear echoes of Derrida and Eisenman's design. These buildings are not fixed in place, but constantly in movement. They embrace the notion of an ephemeral choral architecture that emerges through the coming together of people around music. One notes recurring motifs, like the labyrinth and the mirror. These buildings are designed to disorient in diverse ways. They break down some of the city's boundaries and power structures. They challenge the dominance of the visual by making the aural and the acoustic the organizing principles of their designs. In these ways they inadvertently fulfill some of the goals of Derrida and Eisenman's stalled project. In others, however, they fall short. They do nothing to undermine the architect's status as authority, and they were designed by the most famous of France's brand-name architects. Another more fundamental issue concerns noise. One of the major technical feats of Nouvel's Philharmonic is that the concert hall almost floats in space. Its walls are broken up with pockets of air that sonically insulate the interior of the building from the sound of the highway just outside. This is a clear example of anti-parasitism. It reflects an assumption that visitors to the concert hall will engage in listening that gives meaning to some sounds and pathologizes others. Derrida defines *chora* as an opening, and in many ways Nouvel and Portzamparc's buildings are open: to the public, to nature, to the unexpected. But the Philharmonic's attitude to noise belies that openness, creating an interior both physically and symbolically cut off from the city and suburbs the building purports to unite. Despite the building's sensitivity to the links between sound, architecture, and sociopolitics, and its commitment to welcoming new people into sonic spaces with a reputation for exclusivity (i.e., the classical concert hall), this fundamentally remains an architecture of enclosure. The building would be more choral, more deconstructive, more literary, if the listening regimes it cultivated had more in common with those cultivated on its rooftop Belvédère, where the sound of instruments blends with sounds of cars, birds, wind in the trees, echoes off the pavement.

These buildings demonstrate both the difficulties and the potential of architecture that is not built on anti-parasitic ideologies. They are reminders that while Paris has been dominated by anti-parasitism for much of its history, there have always been pockets of smoothness in the city, moments of absolute hospitality. There have always been meals where anyone was welcome, moments when meaning and noise fell away and what Deleuze calls the outside of language was glimpsed.[72]

The buildings in La Villette use music as their guide for approaching this ideal, emphasizing the sonic and communicative meaning of parasite. In other places in Paris the biological meaning of parasite is privileged, and ecology is the frame. In 2016, XTU Architects were awarded a contract as part of Réinventer Paris, a municipal call for proposals to design innovative buildings on public land. Their design, originally titled InVivo and now called Alguesens, centers on four buildings. The Tree House, Plant House, and Algo House combine housing for students and researchers with diverse plant ecosystems. The walls of Algo House are green and lined with algae. The fourth building houses earthworms. The design also includes plans for a facility called La Paillasse, a word that can mean both straw mattress—implying a makeshift home—and laboratory bench. La Paillasse is imagined as a collaborative space of work and experimentation. It will be overseen by a group of nonprofit organizations and research institutes, including the Centre Michel Serres (a school for interdisciplinary research) and the street art organization Le MUR.

This design does not entirely succeed in transcending the host/parasite dialectic. For one thing, while the buildings are conceived to accommodate the nonhuman, opening up the idea of which bodies the city is for, the presence of algae, trees, and worms on the site is justified on anthropocentric, economic grounds. These species are expected to serve the human residents. The algae will cool the building, and be harvested for scientific research. The trees will clean the air. The worms will decompose human waste. The hospitality offered to these organisms is conditional. The nonhuman has to pay its way. Even setting those issues aside, as of this writing, construction on the site has not yet begun, and the complex may yet turn out, like Derrida and Eisenman's, to be an unrealized concept. Nevertheless, these buildings, with their green walls and ecologically diverse spaces, do at least strive toward an architecture that does not pathologize parasites. In

Figure 6.2
Alguesens, formerly titled InVivo, a laureate of the Réinventer Paris competition, by XTU Architects

this design, every barrier has become a biome. The city is conceptualized on the presumption of symbiosis: on a belief that life works together, not against. The city is understood to be not just for us, however "us" might be defined. This proposal may not fully escape the host/parasite dialectic, but it helps us to visualize a city that welcomes even the lowliest life, and not because humans can extract value from it somehow.

The pathologization of parasites, as I have demonstrated over the course of this book, takes place in many ways and in many domains of the city. From the closing off of domestic space to the outside world, and to one's neighbors, to citywide policies governing the housing of immigrants; from home media technologies to the design of building façades; from advertisements in public spaces to illicit forms of writing like graffiti and street art; from urban cartography to wandering and urban sport; from democratic politics and the concept of the political subject to the riot; from public hygiene to the questions of where a body ends and what it means to be human; from communication to literature. The pathologization of parasites underpins fundamental structures of the modern city and of modern politics (the latter deeply tied to the symbolic space of the *polis*). No longer pathologizing parasites entails major transformations across all areas of urban life. I have argued that such transformations are desirable, because of the violence that underpins the host/parasite dialectic and because they offer a way to combat the inertia of a politics where one of the most powerful tools available to both governed and governors is static.

Derrida's position regarding hospitality is that laws and regulations will always on some level betray the absolute Law of hospitality, but he is pragmatically willing to defend laws that are more hospitable. In *Cosmopolites de tous les pays, encore un effort!* he calls on municipal governments around the world to turn their cities into sanctuary cities as a counterweight to national anti-immigrant laws. While Derrida's political incrementalism can be frustrating when it is contrasted with the radicalism of his thinking on language, I respect his refusal to let the ideal be the enemy of the good and his willingness to speak in concrete terms. Looking at the examples discussed in this book, we can likewise identify flawed and pragmatic policies that would make cities more open to so-called parasites. That would include removing rather than reinforcing barriers—whether in the form of walls and gates, social pressure, or governmental policy (rent escalation, limited transport infrastructure, redlining, tightening immigration controls, anti-refugee laws). Or rethinking who has access to urban channels like the building façade—not only in legal terms but also in terms of the social factors that, for example, underpin the gender disparity in practices like street art. They might include finding different ways of engaging with city-based political movements that do not involve an expectation that inherently cacophonous forms of protest attain clarity in their messages and boundaries. Or exploring nonanthropocentric approaches to architecture and urbanism that recognize the connectivity demonstrated by life at every level of complexity. Actions like these would create more absolutely hospitable cities where fewer of those at the communal table are identified as not having a right to be there.

I offer these practical steps as expressions of, rather than replacements for, the conceptual transformation in urbanism I have advocated throughout this chapter. When Derrida says that without "the thought" of pure and unconditional hospitality, "we would have no concept of hospitality in general and would not even be able to determine any rules for conditional hospitality," he is, to be sure, backing away from the radical implications of absolute hospitality in practice.[73] But he is also reminding us that concepts set the terms of the ethical and the political. Thinking the city in frameworks other than the pathologization of parasites opens up radically different ethical and political horizons. How the city as an aesthetic work, as an environment, and as a space of encounter is thought, written, read, and interpreted bears a direct relationship to the kinds of ethical and political practices possible within and through it. In Derrida's writings on hospitality, more important than any policy position is an openness to *ce qui vient*, to who or what is coming. A willingness to be surprised, a welcoming posture toward the unexpected, a readiness to open the door. Cultivating such an attitude in all domains of the city is a step toward creating a Paris without the parasite.

Notes

Chapter 1

1. Département des Hauts-de-Seine, *Projet de plan de prévention du bruit dans l'environnement* (Compiègne: Imprimerie de Compiègne, 2016), 6.

2. Laetitia Van Eeckhout, "Paris part en guerre contre le bruit," *Le Monde*, 10 March 2015.

3. Henri Lefebvre, *Le Droit à la ville* (Paris: Anthropos, 1968).

4. Michel Serres, *The Parasite*, trans. Lawrence W. Schehr (Minneapolis: University of Minnesota Press, 2007), 79 (translation modified).

5. Friedrich Kittler and Matthew Griffin, "The City Is a Medium," *New Literary History* 27, no. 4 (1996): 722.

6. Scott McQuire, *The Media City: Media, Architecture and Urban Space* (Thousand Oaks, CA: SAGE Publications, 2010), 18–19.

7. De Waal writes: "interface is a particularly apt term because it shifts attention from the spatial aspect [. . .] to the question of the relationships themselves. Who is relating to whom? How are these groups brought together? Who is excluded?" Martijn De Waal, *The City as Interface: How New Media Are Changing the City* (Rotterdam: Nai010 Publishers, 2014), 21.

8. Thank you to Thomas Y. Levin for suggesting this example.

9. Mark Nunes, *Error: Glitch, Noise, and Jam in New Media Cultures* (New York: Continuum, 2011), 3.

10. Michiel de Lange and Martijn de Waal, eds., *The Hackable City: Digital Media and Collaborative City-Making in the Network Society* (Singapore: Springer, 2019), 3.

11. Nunes, *Error*, 3.

12. McQuire criticizes scholars who treat computing as a rupture in the history of urbanism, noting that pronouncements about some new technology revolutionizing the experience of space and time in the city have been a "recurrent theme" for two centuries (McQuire, *The Media City*, 24). To give a Parisian example, in 1901 Gabriel Tarde wrote: "It fell to our century, by the means of perfected locomotion and instantaneous transmission of thought across all distances, to give to the public, to every public, the unlimited reach it was capable of." Gabriel Tarde, *L'Opinion et la foule* (Paris: Éditions Félix Alcan, 1901), 10–11.

13. Jussi Parikka, *Insect Media: An Archaeology of Animals and Technology* (Minneapolis: University of Minnesota Press, 2010), xxvi–xxvii.

14. Roland Barthes, *The Eiffel Tower and Other Mythologies*, trans. Richard Howard (Berkeley: University of California Press, 1997), 9.

15. Shosana Zuboff, *The Age of Surveillance Capitalism* (London: Profile Books, 2019).

16. Maurice Blanchot, *L'Espace littéraire* (Paris: Éditions Gallimard, 1955).

Chapter 2

1. Martin Heidegger, *Poetry, Language, Thought* (New York: HarperCollins, 1971), 146.

2. Michel Pinçon and Monique Pinçon-Charlot, *Paris mosaïque: promenades urbaines* (Paris: Calmann-Lévy, 2001), 249.

3. François Loyer, *Paris Nineteenth Century: Architecture and Urbanism*, trans. Charles Lynn Clark (New York: Abbeville Press, 1988).

4. Sharon Marcus, *Apartment Stories: City and Home in Nineteenth-Century Paris and London* (Berkeley: University of California Press, 1999), 20–21.

5. Marcus, *Apartment Stories*, 139. 1850 was not special in itself, except as a round number and the death year of Honoré de Balzac—a figure whose writings are the best example, Marcus says, of chaotic, socially mixed, semipublic apartment life.

6. "The great novelty of urban life [. . .] does not consist in having thrown the people into the street, but in having raked them up and shut them into offices and houses. It does not consist in having intensified the public dimension but in having invented the private one." Franco Moretti, *Signs Taken for Wonders: On the Sociology of Literary Forms* (London: Verso, 2005), 127.

7. Walter Benjamin, *Reflections*, ed. Peter Demetz (New York: Schocken, 1986), 216.

8. Edmond de Goncourt and Jules de Goncourt, *Journal des Goncourt* 1 (Paris: Bibliothèque Charpentier, 1888), 346.

9. Monique Eleb and Anne Debarre, *L'Invention de l'habitation moderne, Paris, 1880–1914* (Paris: Éditions Hazan, 2000).

10. Sun-Young Park, *Ideals of the Body: Architecture, Urbanism, and Hygiene in Postrevolutionary Paris* (Pittsburgh: University of Pittsburgh Press, 2018), 10–11.

11. Quoted in David Harvey, *Paris Capital of Modernity* (New York: Routledge, 2006), 251.

12. The term comes from Allan Sekula, quoted in Scott McQuire, *The Media City: Media, Architecture and Urban Space* (Thousand Oaks, CA: SAGE Publications, 2010), 40.

13. Aimée Boutin, *City of Noise: Sound and Nineteenth-Century Paris* (Urbana: University of Illinois Press, 2015), 72.

14. Pierre Pinon, *Paris, biographie d'une capitale* (Paris: Éditions Hazan, 1999), 228–229.

15. Quoted in Jean-Louis Cohen and Monique Eleb, *Paris Architecture 1900–2000* (Paris: Éditions NORMA, 2000), 12.

16. Quoted in Fabienne Chevallier, *Le Paris moderne: histoire des politiques d'hygiène. 1855–1898* (Rennes: Presses Universitaires de Rennes, 2010), 65.

17. Chevallier, *Le Paris moderne*, 62–63.

18. Pinon, *Paris*, 247.

19. This rupture remains true, and is explicitly foregrounded in Paris's strategic plan published in 2015: "The city block and neighborhood have become essential points of intervention for responding to the different challenges of the sustainable, resilient, inclusive city." Mairie de Paris, *Paris intelligente et durable: Perspectives 2020 et au-delà*, api-site-cdn.paris.fr/images/89758, 22.

20. Eleb and Debarre, *L'Invention de l'habitation moderne*, 251–256.

21. Boutin, *City of Noise*, 74.

22. Pinon, *Paris*, 240.

23. Eleb and Debarre, *L'Invention de l'habitation moderne*, 286.

24. Le Corbusier, *Urbanisme* (Paris: G. Crès, 1925), 203.

25. Quoted in Marc Perelman, *Le Corbusier, une froide vision du monde* (Paris: Michalon, 2015), 132.

26. Le Corbusier and Amédée Ozenfant, "Une ville contemporaine," *L'Esprit nouveau*, no. 28 (1925): 2393.

27. Le Corbusier, *Urbanisme*, 244.

28. Le Corbusier, *Urbanisme*, 207.

29. Le Corbusier, *Toward an Architecture*, trans. John Goodman (Los Angeles: Getty Publications, 2007), 83.

30. Le Corbusier, *Toward an Architecture*, 168.

31. Le Corbusier, *Toward an Architecture*, 276.

32. Le Corbusier, *Toward an Architecture*, 268–269.

33. Le Corbusier, *Toward an Architecture*, 261. Le Corbusier did express a hope that the shared sporting fields in his housing developments would help workers bond with their bosses, putting a stop to labor unrest. Simone Brott, "The Le Corbusier Scandal, or, was Le Corbusier a Fascist?," *Fascism* 6, no. 2 (December 2017): 219. But this exception did not apply to everyone. The artist's house (Le Corbusier, *Toward an Architecture*, 264) is drawn as a detached and walled-off property not connected to a larger development, reflecting the independence of the artist. Residents of the Villa apartments at the upper end of Le Corbusier's housing spectrum would each benefit from a private hanging garden, a sports room inside the apartment, and a delivery service for food, sparing them the need to frequent the agricultural fields and shared green spaces. The height of luxury is never having to leave one's room.

34. Le Corbusier, *Toward an Architecture*, 269.

35. Le Corbusier, *Urbanisme*, 202–203.

36. "In 1962, an aerial view of Paris revealed to him the 'scandal' and 'sickness' of houses that 'see each other, hear each other.'" Simon Richards, *Le Corbusier and the Concept of Self* (New Haven: Yale University Press, 2003), 238.

37. Quoted in Richards, *Le Corbusier and the Concept of Self*, 107. The quote comes from Le Corbusier's Divine Proportion conference.

38. "The *hum* then to fill all the holes, the emptiness. Musical hum, colorful hum, damasked hum, embroidered or batiked hum. A little racket, a big racket, reading the newspaper (description of other people's actions), cinemas, dance halls, . . . Pigall's . . . to escape, to never come face to face with oneself. 'If I were to come face to face with my soul (vision of horror)? What would I say to him? Watch out!' Thus do they structure their diversions to never meet themselves." Le Corbusier, *L'Art décoratif d'aujourd'hui* (Paris: G. Crès, 1925), 30–31.

39. Le Corbusier, *Toward an Architecture*, 172.

40. Le Corbusier and Ozenfant, *L'Esprit nouveau*, no. 28, 2317.

41. Anthony Vidler, *Warped Space: Art, Architecture, and Anxiety in Modern Culture* (Cambridge, MA: MIT Press, 2001), 118–122.

42. Beatriz Colomina, *Privacy and Publicity: Modern Architecture as Mass Media* (Cambridge, MA: MIT Press, 1996), 312.

43. Quoted in Colomina, *Privacy and Publicity*, 311; original emphasis.

44. Le Corbusier, *Toward an Architecture*, 172. He also says to teach your children to keep the floors perfectly tidy for the same reason; obviously, not all of his recommendations are feasible.

45. Colomina, *Privacy and Publicity*, 283.

46. Colomina, *Privacy and Publicity*, 326.

47. Colomina, *Privacy and Publicity*, 323.

48. Perelman, *Le Corbusier*, 116.

49. Le Corbusier, *Toward an Architecture*, 109; emphasis added.

50. "*Sur les quatre routes* has three pages of dedications to fascist groups including L'Action Française; to the Legion of Xavier Vallat, Commissioner-general for Jewish Questions; to Pétain; and to Pierre Caziot, Secretary and signatory to the Jewish laws." Brott, "The Le Corbusier Scandal," 209.

51. François Chaslin, *Un Corbusier* (Paris: Éditions du Seuil, 2015), 217.

52. Richards, *Le Corbusier and the Concept of Self*, 43–44.

53. Brott, "The Le Corbusier Scandal," 211–213.

54. The three books, all published independently of one another, were Perelman's *Le Corbusier*, Chaslin's *Un Corbusier*, and Xavier de Jarcy's *Le Corbusier, un fascisme français* (Paris: Albin Michel, 2015).

55. Jean-François Gravier, *Paris et le désert français* (Paris: Éditions du Portulan, 1947), 60.

56. Gravier, *Paris et le désert français*, 111.

57. Gravier, *Paris et le désert français*, 82.

58. Gravier, *Paris et le désert français*, 224.

59. Roberto Esposito, *Terms of the Political: Community, Immunity, Biopolitics*, trans. Rhiannon Noel Welch (New York: Fordham University Press, 2013), 84–86.

60. The population in 1965 was 36,500. Matthew Taunton, *Fictions of the City: Class, Culture and Mass Housing in London and Paris* (London: Palgrave Macmillan, 2009), 106.

61. Christiane Rochefort, *Les Petits Enfants du siècle* (Paris: Grasset, 1961), 124–125.

62. Colin Jones, *Paris: Biography of a City* (New York: Penguin, 2006), 517.

63. Jane Jacobs, *The Death and Life of Great American Cities* (New York: Random House, 1961).

64. Ken Knabb, ed. and trans., *Situationist International Anthology*, revised ed. (Berkeley: Bureau of Public Secrets, 2006), 2.

65. Taunton, *Fictions of the City*, 122.

66. Pinçon and Pinçon-Charlot, *Paris mosaïque*, 249.

67. Pinçon and Pinçon-Charlot, *Paris mosaïque*, 243.

68. Éric Hazan, *Paris sous tension* (Paris: La Fabrique Éditions, 2011), 100.

69. A few years ago, while I was in Paris on a research trip, I got a message from some American friends who were staying in an Airbnb in the 17th arrondissement. They invited me to meet them at their apartment for a bottle of wine. When I arrived at their building, I discovered it was the night of the Fête des Voisins, and all the permanent residents were chatting in the lobby. One of them, thinking that I was a neighbor he hadn't met, offered me a glass of wine and we began talking. I met most of the residents before my friends started worrying and came downstairs to look for me. That experience is one example of the unpredictability still present in the managed public life of the Fête, and the potential for a foreign element to sneak into private space.

70. Levin points out that this shot is made especially deceptive by the absence of the conventional signatures of surveillance footage: the images are in high definition, without grain or the artefacts of VHS tape. And yet, the mode is unquestionably surveillant in the hermeneutic it forces the viewer to adopt. The camera is not keyed to any action and its focus is everywhere at once. The viewer is not watching; he or she is looking, and waiting. Thomas Y. Levin, "Five Tapes, Four Halls, Two Dreams: Vicissitudes of Surveillant Narration in Michael Haneke's *Caché*," in *A Companion to Michael Haneke*, ed. Roy Grundmann (Malden, MA: Wiley-Blackwell, 2014).

71. Roland-François Lack, "Three Filmmakers in Romainville: Haneke, Bosetti, Feuillade," *The Cine-Tourist*, www.thecinetourist.net/three-filmmakers-in-romainville.html.

72. Le Corbusier loved automobiles. He designed his Villa Savoye with a driveway whose curvature matched the turning radius of the 1927 Citroën; the Voisin manufacturer sponsored his plans for the reconstruction of Paris; and in *Urbanisme* he holds out an almost messianic hope for the car: "The automobile has killed big cities," he writes. "The automobile must save them." Le Corbusier, *Urbanisme*, 263.

73. Michael Cowan, "Between the Street and the Apartment: Disturbing the Space of Fortress Europe in Michael Haneke," *Studies in European Cinema* 5, no. 2 (2008): 127.

74. Brianne Gallagher, "Policing Paris: Private Publics and Architectural Media in Michael Haneke's *Caché*," *Journal for Cultural Research* 12, no. 1 (2008).

75. Kevin Stoehr, "Haneke's Secession: Perspectivism and Anti-Nihilism in *Code Unknown* and *Caché*," in *A Companion to Michael Haneke*, ed. Roy Grundmann (Oxford: Wiley-Blackwell, 2010), 490.

76. © Christian Blondel—Atelier des 4 Lunes.

77. Some commentators assume that Majid's son is behind the tapes, or that he is working in concert with Georges's son, whom he meets at the end of the film. In the end, any assignation of responsibility can only be theoretical and unsatisfying; the shots achieved by the surveillant would necessitate a quantity of camera equipment unlikely to remain hidden. That they do is, ultimately, enabled by the fact that the camera is Haneke's own, and exists outside the diegetic realm of perception.

78. Roland-François Lack notes that the son's school, like the rue Brillat-Savarin, is a geographical *petit fait faux*: the name given to the school is that of a real school, and the location shot is a school as well, but they are not the same place.

79. Le Corbusier, *Toward an Architecture*, 109. Katherine Shonfield writes about a similar phenomenon in 1960s London. Through a reading of two Roman Polanski films she draws attention to the anxiety surrounding formaldehyde-based sealants. These products were supposed to reestablish the hermeticism of the home's walls, which had been compromised by the adoption of cavity walls. Insulation was marketed as a way to keep things out of your home, but it was itself an "alien viscous substance" liable to release fungus or toxic fumes into the living space. This is a perfect example of an anti-parasitic architecture creating the conditions for parasites to enter the home. Katherine Shonfield, *Walls Have Feelings: Architecture, Film, and the City* (London: Routledge, 2000), 57.

Chapter 3

1. Michel Serres, *The Parasite*, trans. Lawrence W. Schehr (Minneapolis: University of Minnesota Press, 2007), 12.

2. Daniel Dennett uses the architectural metaphor of the theater to explain Cartesian epistemology. Daniel Dennett, *Consciousness Explained* (New York: Little, Brown, 1991), 107.

3. Serres, *The Parasite*, 11–13.

4. Xavier Prou, interview by Mark Jenkins, *UK Street Art*, 29 July 2008, www.ukstreetart.co.uk/blek-le-rat-interview/.

5. Brassaï, *Graffiti* (Paris: Flammarion, 2002), 10.

6. Victor Hugo, *Notre-Dame of Paris*, trans. John Sturrock (New York: Penguin, 1978), 189–198.

7. Marshall McLuhan, *Understanding Media: The Extensions of Man* (Cambridge, MA: MIT Press, 1994), 9.

8. Hugo, *Notre-Dame of Paris*, 237.

9. Neil Levine, "The Book and the Building," in *The Beaux-Arts and Nineteenth-Century French Architecture*, ed. Robin Middleton (Cambridge, MA: MIT Press, 1982), 138–173.

10. Martin Bressani and Marc Grignon, "Henri Labrouste and the Lure of the Real: Romanticism, Rationalism, and the Bibliothèque Sainte-Geneviève," *Art History* 28, no. 5 (2005): 716.

11. Bressani and Grignon, "Henri Labrouste," 723–725. The effect is reinforced by the presence directly in front of the library of the Panthéon, Paris's mausoleum of Republican heroes.

12. Bressani and Grignon, "Henri Labrouste," 732.

13. Bressani and Grignon, "Henri Labrouste," 743.

14. Bressani and Grignon, "Henri Labrouste," 728.

15. "In the Second Empire, when little carving was done, the smooth, continuous stone façades of the apartment houses were acknowledged as a quality finish. This combination of quality and simplicity came to be seen as 'modern' and equated industrialism with the classical style." Anthony Sutcliffe, *Paris: An Architectural History* (New Haven: Yale University Press, 1993), 88.

16. François Loyer, *Paris Nineteenth Century: Architecture and Urbanism*, trans. Charles Lynn Clark (New York: Abbeville Press, 1988), 239.

17. Quoted in Sutcliffe, *Paris*, 121; emphasis added.

18. Le Corbusier, *Toward an Architecture*, trans. John Goodman (Los Angeles: Getty Publications, 2007), 112.

19. "The determinant surface of the cathedral is ordered around squares and circles." Le Corbusier, *Toward an Architecture*, 139.

20. Jay David Bolter and Richard Grusin, *Remediation: Understanding New Media* (Cambridge, MA: MIT Press, 2000).

21. Annette Fierro, *The Glass State: The Technology of the Spectacle, Paris, 1981–1998* (Cambridge, MA: MIT Press, 2003), 9.

22. André Breton, *Nadja* (Paris: Éditions Gallimard, 1964), 18.

23. Chareau's building was transparent in another way: to avoid attracting too much scrutiny from stylistically conservative neighbors, the home has a hidden entryway, and its façade is not visible from the street.

24. Walter Benjamin, *The Arcades Project*, 2nd ed., trans. Howard Eiland and Kevin McLaughlin (Cambridge, MA: Harvard University Press, 1999), 180. Émile Zola took a more perverse view of glass architecture in his 1872 novel *La Curée*. The novel tells the story of Aristide Saccard, a government employee turned social-climbing real-estate speculator, and his wife, Renée, a modern-day Phèdre who falls in love with Saccard's son from his first marriage. Saccard fantasizes about covering Paris in an immense glass roof. His own home has a glass *serre*, which is one of the sites of his wife's incestuous love affair with Saccard's son. For Zola, glass architecture evokes disciplinary hypervisibility and taboo exhibitionism. Émile Zola, *La Curée* (Paris: Pocket, 1990).

25. There are examples of glass architecture that predate modernism, like Baltard's iron and glass pavilions for the Les Halles market in the center of Paris and Jourdain's imposing *art nouveau* department store, La Samaritaine. These buildings were scandal-makers in their day, but did not provoke wholesale change in the use of glass in the rest of the city.

26. Quoted in Anthony Vidler, "Books in Space: Tradition and Transparency in the Bibliothèque de France," *Representations*, no. 12 (1993): 115.

27. Fierro, *The Glass State*, 7.

28. Vidler, "Books in Space," 131–132.

29. Anthony Vidler, *The Architectural Uncanny: Essays in the Modern Unhomely* (Cambridge, MA: MIT Press, 1992), 220. Colin Rowe and Robert Slutzky drew attention to the ambiguity of transparency, as well as the ubiquitous and uncritical use of the term in modern architecture, in "Transparency: Literal and Phenomenal," *Perspecta* 8 (1963): 45–54.

30. Fierro, *The Glass State*, 27.

31. Vidler, *The Architectural Uncanny*, 220.

32. Banishing Paris's skyscrapers to one suburb has not been completely successful at hiding them from view. Sutcliffe recounts the scandal produced by the appearance of these buildings at the end of the Champs-Élysées: "Telephoto pictures were used on television and in the press to exaggerate the towers and diminish the Arc de Triomphe, which seemed to be at the mercy of devouring Behemoths." Sutcliffe, *Paris*, 175. Buildings that seek transparency often end up achieving the opposite.

33. Pierre Pinon, *Paris, biographie d'une capitale* (Paris: Éditions Hazan, 1999), 301.

34. Vidler, *The Architectural Uncanny*, 220.

35. Fierro, *The Glass State*, 5.

36. Brassaï, *Graffiti*, 11–12.

37. Brassaï, *Graffiti*, 137.

38. Bolter and Grusin, *Remediation*, 34.

39. He enjoys the experience of pareidolia, his mind's eagerness to interpret accidental scratches as facial forms, and he writes: "It is often no easy task to tell apart a chance resemblance from one that already bears the sovereign stamp of thought." Brassaï, *Graffiti*, 30.

40. Serres, *The Parasite*, 79.

41. "The whole substance of the wall stirs with a life of its own. Its cracks, gashes, and mold bring out similarities which, if come upon by chance, help man to get back in touch with himself." Brassaï, *Graffiti*, 141.

42. Le Corbusier, *Toward an Architecture*, 109.

43. Mona Abaza, "Walls, Segregating Downtown Cairo and the Mohammed Mahmud Street Graffiti," *Theory, Culture and Society* 30, no. 1 (2012): 128.

44. Serres, *The Parasite*, 11.

45. Abraham Clet, "Florence Street Sign Art by Clet," *Visit Tuscany*, Accessed 4 April 2020, https://www.visittuscany.com/en/ideas/florence-street-sign-art-by-clet/.

46. ZEVS, "ZEVS: Visual Kidnapping," *Ping Mag*, 11 August 2008, http://pingmag.jp/2008/08/11/zevs-visual-kidnapping/.

47. Invader, *L'Invasion de Paris* 2 (Paris: CTRL + P, 2012), 70.

48. Serres, *The Parasite*, 95.

49. Serres, *The Parasite*, 13.

50. Lewis Carroll, *Alice's Adventures in Wonderland and Through the Looking Glass* (London: Puffin Books, 1997), 180.

51. Serres, *The Parasite*, 228.

52. JR, "Group Action Guidelines," *Inside Out Project*, Accessed 2 April 2020, http://www.insideoutproject.net/sites/all/themes/insideout/documents/Group_Action_Guidelines.pdf.

53. JR, "Use Art to Turn the World Inside Out," *TED*, YouTube Video, 24:09, 5 March 2011, https://www.youtube.com/watch?v=0PAy1zBtTbw.

54. Brassaï, *Graffiti*, 19.

55. Alfred Delvau, *Les Murailles révolutionnaires* (Paris: Joubert, 1851), 3.

56. The May 1968 graffiti is collected and translated in Ken Knabb, *Situationist International Anthology*, revised ed. (Berkeley: Bureau of Public Secrets, 2006), 445–457.

57. Nioucha Zakavati, "Street art féministe: Visite guidée à la Butte-aux-Cailles, un 'musée à ciel ouvert,'" *TV5Monde*, 9 August 2019, https://information.tv5monde.com/terriennes/street-art-feministe-visite-guidee-la-butte-aux-cailles-un-musee-ciel-ouvert-313316.

58. The growing number of nonmale street artists in Paris might be a positive consequence of the institutionalization of street art, as it is now easier for artists to work in broad daylight. To the extent these artists take advantage of this freedom to undermine the dominant trends and themes of street art, they create a new layer of parasitism. A practice like street art is on the side of neither host nor parasite; the transformation of an old parasite into a new host opens the door to new forms of parasitism.

59. Brassaï, *Graffiti*, 137.

60. Lachlan John MacDowall and Poppy de Souza, "I'd Double Tap That!! Street Art, Graffiti, and Instagram Research," *Media, Culture and Society* 40, no. 1 (January 2018): 3–22.

61. "L'Invasion des 'Space Invaders' se poursuit, Le 1.000e installé à Paris," *Le Parisien*, 8 June 2011, www.leparisien.fr/flash-actualite-culture/l-invasion-des-space-invaders-se-poursuit-le-1-000e-installe-a-paris-08-06-2011-1485931.php.

62. Frédéric Keck, "Space Invader rencontre King of Kowloon," *Esprit* 8 (August/September 2011): 175–178.

63. Jussi Parikka, *Digital Contagions: A Media Archaeology of Computer Viruses* (New York: Peter Lang, 2016). Aram Bartholl's art installation *Dead Drops*, which began in New York and spread to a number of cities including Paris, similarly makes street art into a vector for computer viruses. Bartholl cements USB flash drives in walls, creating a digital sharing network physically embedded in the matter of the city. Anyone can plug a computer into the drive, adding files to it or copying files left behind by previous users. This method of file transfer offers almost nothing in the way of protection from computer viruses.

64. Jeff Hemsley and Robert M. Mason, "The Nature of Knowledge in the Social Media Age: Implications for Knowledge Management Models," *Journal of Organizational Computing and Electronic Commerce* 23, no. 1–2 (2013).

65. Jacques Derrida, *Dissemination*, trans. Barbara Johnson (London: Continuum, 2004).

66. Invader's maps are a wink to museum maps, but if Invader turns the city into a museum—a place where people shuffle from artwork to artwork, photographing each so that they can score points when they upload their photos to the

internet—his museum is inside out. The original name of the Musaeum, opened by Ptolemy in Alexandria, evoked the cave wherein dwelt the Muses. The museum was, by implication, a secluded enclosure. Invader (and street artists in general) subvert the implication that the museum is inside.

67. GeoCities was the most literal example of the way in which urban geography served as a metaphor for understanding the internet in the 1990s. The now-defunct website not only encouraged its users to think of their websites as residences "under construction," but also used real-world toponyms like Hollywood and Nashville to thematically sort the content being shared in the network. Richard Vijgen's 2013 online art project, The Deleted City, was an attempt to produce a geographic map of the millions of archived pages from the platform.

68. Shoshana Zuboff, *The Age of Surveillance Capitalism* (London: Profile Books, 2019), 141.

Chapter 4

1. Georges-Eugène Haussmann, *Mémoires du Baron Haussmann* 2 (Paris: Victor-Havard, 1890), 53.

2. Min Kyung Lee, "The Bureaucracy of Plans: Urban Governance and Maps in Nineteenth-Century Paris," *Journal of Urban History* 46, no. 2 (2020): 250–252.

3. Gilles Palsky, *Des chiffres et des cartes: naissance et développement de la cartographie quantitative française au XIX siècle* (Paris: Ministère de l'enseignement supérieur et de la recherche, comité des travaux historiques et scientifiques, 1996), 18.

4. There are traces of this in Hugo's *Notre-Dame de Paris* in the chapter "A bird's eye view of Paris," in which he visualizes the city from above. He attributes the aerial perspective to a bird, underscoring its nonhuman quality, but what makes it nonhuman is not really how animal it is but how technical it is. Hugo situates Paris on an orthogonal grid and uses cardinal directions to orient the reader. He provides an overwhelming litany of place names—one street "was called the Rue de la Harpe on the left bank, the Rue de la Barillerie on the Island, the Rue Saint-Denis on the right bank, the Pont Saint-Michel on one arm of the Seine and the Pont-au-Change on the other"—the sort of information one finds on a map, not in the mind of a bird. Victor Hugo, *Notre-Dame of Paris*, trans. John Sturrock (New York: Penguin, 1978), 160.

5. Lee, "The Bureaucracy of Plans," 254.

6. One of Haussmann's first acts as prefect in 1853 was to commission what at the time was the most complete cadastral map of Paris. Scott McQuire, *The Media City: Media, Architecture and Urban Space* (Thousand Oaks, CA: SAGE Publications, 2010), 45.

7. Lee, "The Bureacracy of Plans," 248–249.

8. Jorge Luis Borges, "On Rigor in Science," in *Dreamtigers*, trans. Mildred Boyer and Harold Morland (Austin: University of Texas Press, 2014).

9. The airplane was one of Le Corbusier's recurring aesthetic models, and a centerpiece of his reimagining of urban traffic.

10. Anthony Vidler, *Warped Space: Art, Architecture, and Anxiety in Modern Culture* (Cambridge, MA: MIT Press, 2001), 320. Vidler emphasizes the continuity between twentieth-century mapping techniques and the political function of cartography in the seventeenth century later in the same essay: "Le Corbusier has simply substituted the airplane's eye for that of the absolute monarch," 320.

11. Paul-Henry Chombart de Lauwe, *Paris et l'agglomération parisienne* (Paris: Presses Universitaires de France, 1952), 107.

12. Éric Hazan, *Paris sous tension* (Paris: La Fabrique Éditions, 2011), 100.

13. Guy Debord, "Théorie de la dérive," *Les Lèvres nues*, no. 9 (1956).

14. Debord, "Théorie de la dérive." Another way to understand the paradoxical nature of SI's psychogeographic maps is to think of them in the framework of Deleuze and Guattari's notion of smooth and striated space. In *A Thousand Plateaus*, striated space is defined as cartographic space: organized, legible, gridlike. SI, however, seems intent on producing the conditions of smooth space through a process of mapping. Gilles Deleuze and Félix Guattari, *A Thousand Plateaus: Capitalism and Schizophrenia*, trans. Brian Massumi (Minneapolis: University of Minnesota Press, 1987), 592.

15. Debord, "Théorie de la dérive."

16. Gilles Ivain, "Formulaire pour un urbanisme nouveau," *Internationale Situationniste*, no. 1 (1958): 18; original emphasis.

17. Internationale Lettriste, "Projets d'embellissement rationnels de la ville de Paris," *Potlatch*, no. 23 (1955).

18. Oulipo, an abbreviation of *Ouvroir de littérature potentielle*, is a still-active group of authors who impose mathematical and algorithmic constraints on their texts. Georges Perec's *La Disparition* (1969), written without any word containing the letter "e," is a famous example.

19. Jacques Roubaud, *The Great Fire of London: A Story with Interpolations and Bifurcations* (Champaign, IL: Dalkey Archive Press, 1991), 97.

20. Joshua Armstrong, "Empiritexts: Mapping Attention and Invention in Post-1980 French Literature," *French Forum* 40, no. 1 (Winter 2015).

21. Jacques Réda, *La Liberté des rues* (Paris: Éditions Gallimard, 1977), 56.

22. Walking a pet tortoise was, according to Benjamin, an ostentatious way of setting one's pace in Paris's shopping arcades in 1839. Walter Benjamin, *The Arcades Project*, 2nd ed., trans. Howard Eiland and Kevin McLaughlin (Cambridge, MA: Harvard University Press, 1999), 422.

23. Federico Castigliano, "Le Divertissement du texte: écriture et flânerie chez Jacques Réda," *Poétique* 4, no. 164 (2010). Filippo Zanghi, *Zone indécise: Périphéries urbaines et voyage de proximité dans la littérature contemporaine* (Villeneuve d'Ascq: Presses Universitaires du Septentrion, 2014), 117.

24. Karen O'Rourke, *Walking and Mapping: Artists as Cartographers* (Cambridge, MA: MIT Press, 2013), 88. Another precursor discussed in O'Rourke's book is Stephan Barron and Sylvia Hansmann's drive across France along the path of the Greenwich Meridian in 1989.

25. The project commissioned by Louis XIV would be completed in 1718. A second, more detailed map commissioned by the Corps des Ponts et Chaussées was begun in 1733 and would be published in 1744. A third project, more massive still, was ordered by Louis XV in 1747, and would map France at the scale of 1 to 86,400.

26. Michael Biggs, "Putting the State on the Map: Cartography, Territory, and European State Formation," *Comparative Studies in Society and History* 41, no. 2 (1999): 389.

27. Jean-François Rémy Duclos, "La Revanche du flou: Jacques Réda à l'épreuve de la cartographie dans *Le Méridien de Paris*," *French Studies* 68, no. 1 (2014): 56.

28. Jacques Réda, *Le Méridien de Paris* (Paris: Fata Morgana, 1997), 37.

29. Duclos, "La Revanche du flou," 50.

30. Réda, *Le Méridien de Paris*, 33.

31. Réda, *Le Méridien de Paris*, 68.

32. Jacques Réda, *L'Adoption du système métrique* (Paris: Éditions Gallimard, 2004).

33. "Réda's metric system does for verse what the Dibbets system does for space." Duclos, "La Revanche du flou," 59.

34. Réda, *Le Méridien de Paris*, 13.

35. "I start heading south, in search of the second plaque that I know has been placed close by: at the corner of the avenue and a rue Binet [. . .] but it's impossible to go to it in a straight line. With ease the longitude line crosses through a succession of obstacles—fences, walls—that prohibit a body in motion from following its trajectory." Réda, *Le Méridien de Paris*, 12.

36. Réda, *Le Méridien de Paris*, 17–18, 23.

37. Réda, *Le Méridien de Paris*, 24–25.

38. "Our differences in age, language, clothing, and social status were enough to make me completely invisible in their eyes." Réda, *Le Méridien de Paris*, 22. In another scene Réda worries that a group of homeless men who are camped near a plaque will speak to him if he goes over to look for it. Réda, *Le Méridien de Paris*, 12.

39. Philippe Vasset, *Un livre blanc* (Paris: Librairie Arthème Fayard, 2007), 78.

40. Vasset, *Un livre blanc*, 20.

41. Églantine Colon argues that Vasset's engagement with the political takes place almost against his will. The political continually interrupts the author's "neutral," documentary project: "*Un livre blanc* is [. . .] constantly traversed by a tension between the desire for a neutral description of urban peripheries, and the unavoidable perception of the socio-spatial antagonisms that have structured these spaces." Églantine Colon, "Neither *lieux de mémoire*, nor *non-lieux*: Towards a Concept of Precarious Spaces in Philippe Vasset's *Un livre blanc*," *French Studies* 71, no. 1 (2017): 72–73.

42. Vasset, *Un livre blanc*, 68.

43. Jacques Rancière, "Onze thèses sur la politique," *Filozofski vestnik* 2 (1997): 100.

44. "Political argumentation is at the same time the manifestation of the world in which it is an argument, addressed by a subject qualified to do so, about an identified object, to a recipient who is obliged to see the object and hear the argument that he would 'normally' not have a reason to see or hear. It's the construction of a paradoxical world that brings together two separate worlds." Rancière, "Onze thèses," 101.

45. Rancière offers several examples. Among them is Olympe de Gouges, who during the French Revolution protested that if women could be put to death by the state then they necessarily must be citizens, in which case they deserved the rights the new republic had conferred only on men. Jacques Rancière, *Dissensus: On Politics and Aesthetics*, trans. Steve Corcoran (London: Continuum, 2010), 76–77.

46. Vasset, *Un livre blanc*, 10.

47. Rancière, "Onze thèses," 100.

48. Vasset, *Un livre blanc*, 23.

49. Vasset, *Un livre blanc*, 24–25.

50. When the site was active it contained a variety of media connected to Vasset's project, including film. Were it still active, it would complement the book in important ways. However, the fact that the site needed to be maintained by the author, and that it thus could go completely dead, is itself the problem. It echoes Vasset's

refusal to open his project up to reappropriation by other practitioners. Zanghi, *Zone indécise*, 20–21.

51. Vasset, *Un livre blanc*, 24.

52. Vasset, *Un livre blanc*, 54.

53. Réda, *Le Méridien de Paris*, 68. Earlier in the text Réda has a more skeptical view of games. He describes his task as "a sort of treasure hunt [. . .] that amuses me less and less," 28. Part of the problem with Réda's game is that it has only one player, and it's not much fun.

54. Vasset, *Un livre blanc*, 50.

55. Guy Debord, *La Société du spectacle* (Paris: Éditions Buchet-Chastel, 1967), para. 29.

56. Memes are often inspired by a source text, but a meme is characterized by inter-referentiality rather than by referentiality. An example is "Hey Girl Ryan Gosling," a meme that envisions Gosling as a perfect boyfriend, sometimes quoting Third Wave feminist theory, and is held together by a basic image template and the phrase "Hey Girl." As Gosling has pointed out, this is a phrase he never said. The images are just referencing each other.

57. "Since the logic of contemporary participatory culture is based on the active involvement of users, incompleteness serves as a textual hook for further dialogue, and for the successful spread of the meme." Limor Shifman, *Memes in Digital Culture* (Cambridge, MA: MIT Press, 2014), 87–88.

58. *The Office*, season 6, episode 1, "Gossip," dir. by Paul Lieberstein, written by Paul Lieberstein, aired 17 September 2009, NBC.

59. While Sampson criticizes the use of the term "viral" and its negative connotations of disease, he remains married to the contagious paradigm throughout his work. While hoping for "a kind of network virality that surpasses linguistic categories of disease," his substitute is "new exploitable social assemblages of affective contagious encounter." Tony Sampson, *Virality: Contagion Theory in the Age of Networks* (Minneapolis: University of Minnesota Press, 2012), 3.

60. Kenneth Frumkin, "Bilateral Calcaneal Fractures and 'Free Running': A Dangerously Cool Emerging 'Sport,'" *Annals of Emergency Medicine* 46, no. 3 (2005): 300. See also Jason R. Miller and Sébastien G. Demoiny, "Parkour: A New Extreme Sport and a Case Study," *Journal of Foot and Ankle Surgery* 47, no. 1 (2008): 63–65.

61. Jeffrey Kidder, "Parkour, the Affective Appropriation of Urban Space, and the Real/Virtual Dialectic," *City and Community* 11, no. 3 (2012): 241.

62. "There are no fundamental differences, everything is real but probably a little more 'practiced,' maybe a bit more 'polished,' we keep the best sections but we also

keep in a few 'messed up' sections, like in the Matera video, to keep the authenticity and the sense of difficulty; that's essential. We don't want to lure people in by making them think it's easy, it's doable, when in fact we've worked at it." Author's interview with Parkour Paris. Ironically, the addition of failed stunts might make the videos more "contagious," as they render them more "incomplete" in Shifman's terms.

63. "In that moment, you are the king of your own little world in which this was the obstacle and you overcame it. For that obstacle at that time, you own it. And then you go on to another obstacle." Kidder, "Parkour, the Affective Appropriation of Urban Space," 245. Savile draws attention to the use of the Budo term "the way" in Parkour circles. Stephen John Savile, "Playing with Fear: Parkour and the Mobility of Emotion," *Social and Cultural Geography* 9, no. 8 (2008): 911.

64. "The imagined potential of PK vision is perfectly summed up by a traceur who chimed in during my interview of someone else, 'The way you perceive objects around you changes a lot. You'll never look at the world the same way again. [. . .] Instead of challenges you begin to see opportunities where challenges are. [. . .] You can't help it. You just see stuff and you're like, 'Oh man, I want to do parkour.' More accurately, nontraceurs see neither challenges nor opportunities. The urban environment is not filled with 'obstacles' at all; it is filled with forms and shapes largely deprived of any creative human uses. The environment may afford vaults and wall climbs, but most people fail to perceive such possibilities." Kidder, "Parkour, the Affective Appropriation of Urban Space," 246.

65. Michael Atkinson, "Parkour, Anarcho-Environmentalism, and Poiesis," *Journal of Sport and Social Issues* 33, no. 2 (2009): 169.

66. Matthew Lamb, "Self and the City: Parkour, Architecture, and the Interstices of the 'Knowable' City," *Liminalities* 10, no. 2 (2014): 12.

67. Lauren Elkin, *Flâneuse: Women Walk the City in Paris, New York, Tokyo, Venice and London* (London: Chatto and Windus, 2016), 286.

68. Joan Tumblety, *Remaking the Male Body: Masculinity and the Uses of Physical Culture in Interwar and Vichy France* (Oxford: Oxford University Press, 2012), 183–186.

69. Tumblety, *Remaking the Male Body*, 208–209, 216.

70. John Hellman, *The Knight-Monks of Vichy France: Uriage, 1940–1945* (Montreal: McGill-Queen's University Press), 74.

71. Michael Atkinson and Kevin Young, *Deviance and Social Control in Sport* (Champaign, IL: Human Kinetics, 2008), 61–62.

72. Jeffrey Kidder, "Parkour, Masculinity, and the City," *Sociology of Sport Journal* 30, no. 1 (2013): 2.

73. In an interview with the author, they also described their good relationship with Paris's municipal government: "We maintain excellent relationships with several *mairies* including the Paris mayor's office, which solicited our expertise for a variety of projects that have already been realized or that are in the works, and at the same time we've never had to compromise our beliefs."

74. Nathan Hulsey and Joshua Reeves, "The Gift That Keeps On Giving: Google, Ingress, and the Gift of Surveillance," *Surveillance and Society* 12, no. 3 (2014): 391.

75. Hulsey and Reeves, "The Gift That Keeps On Giving," 397.

76. Luciana Parisi, *Contagious Architecture: Computation, Aesthetics, and Space* (Cambridge, MA: MIT Press, 2013), 17.

77. Parisi, *Contagious Architecture,* ix.

78. Parisi, *Contagious Architecture,* xiii–xv.

79. Michel Serres, *The Parasite,* trans. Lawrence W. Schehr (Minneapolis: University of Minnesota Press, 2007), 182. This is my translation. Schehr renders "écart" [gap] as "difference," and leaves out the phrase "Il dérive."

80. The statue remained altered by these interventions for a year and a half following the march. A monument that once formed the ceremonial backdrop to De Gaulle's coup was regularly used as a channel for dissident political messages in support of causes entirely unrelated to the *Charlie Hebdo* attacks.

81. "4 millions de personnes en France pour la marche républicaine," *L'Obs,* 11 January 2015, www.nouvelobs.com/charlie-hebdo/20150111.OBS9715/4-millions-de-personnes-en-france-pour-la-marche-republicaine.html.

82. Avec l'aimable autorisation de la RATP (Courtesy of RATP © RATP).

83. Manuel Cebrian, Iyad Rahwan, and Alex "Sandy" Pentland, "Beyond Viral," *Communications of the ACM* 59, no. 4 (2016): 36.

84. Jisun An, Haewoon Kwak, Yelena Mejova, Sonia Alonso Saenz De Oger, and Braulio Gomez Fortes, "Are You Charlie or Ahmed? Cultural Pluralism in Charlie Hebdo Response on Twitter," *Proceedings of the 10th International Conference on Web and Social Media* (2016): 2–11.

85. This internal division was aggravated by disputes over who should be allowed to participate in the unity march. Marine Le Pen, the leader of France's far-right Front National party, was not invited to join other political leaders at the head of the march. Jean-Luc Mélenchon, the leader of France's far-left party, La France Insoumise, led his own march.

86. Jacques Rancière, *On the Shores of Politics,* trans. Liz Heron (London: Verso, 1995), 68. In *Figures of History,* Rancière again underlines the preeminence of the voice

and the speech act in his thought: "Against tell-all Romantic poetics and the see-all information-world machine, we must pit the loneliness of the voice, its resonance alone confronting the mutism of the earth that says and shows nothing." Jacques Rancière, *Figures of History*, trans. Julie Rose (Cambridge, UK: Polity, 2014), 42.

87. Rancière, *On the Shores of Politics*, 65.

88. Moisés Naím, *The End of Power: From Boardrooms to Battlefields and Churches to States, Why Being in Charge Isn't What It Used to Be* (New York: Basic Books, 2013); Clay Shirky, *Here Comes Everybody: The Power of Organizing without Organizations* (New York: Penguin, 2008).

89. Cebrian et al., "Beyond Viral," 36.

90. Michael Conover, Emilio Ferrara, Filippo Menczer, and Alessandro Flammini, "The Digital Evolution of Occupy Wall Street," *PLOS ONE* 8, no. 5 (2013): 4.

91. Serres, *The Parasite*, 191, 193.

92. Zeynep Tufekci, *Twitter and Tear Gas: The Power and Fragility of Networked Protest* (New Haven: Yale University Press, 2017), xiv.

Chapter 5

1. David Harvey, *Paris, Capital of Modernity* (New York: Routledge, 2006), 59–90.

2. Ed Cohen, *A Body Worth Defending: Immunity, Biopolitics, and the Apotheosis of the Modern Body* (Durham: Duke University Press, 2009), 6–7.

3. John Farley, "Parasites and the Germ Theory of Disease," *Millbank Quarterly* 67, no. S1 (1989): 55.

4. Ed Cohen, "The Paradoxical Politics of Viral Containment; Or, How Scale Undoes Us One and All," *Social Text* 106, no. 1 (2011): 20.

5. Cohen, "Paradoxical Politics," 24.

6. Roberto Esposito, *Immunitas: The Protection and Negation of Life*, trans. Zakiya Hanafi (Cambridge, UK: Polity Press, 2011), 8.

7. "Things are different now that the technological networks are in place and that many of the arguments of Tarde can be turned into sound empirical use." Bruno Latour, "Gabriel Tarde and the End of the Social," in *The Social in Question: New Bearings in History and the Social Sciences*, ed. Patrick Joyce (New York: Routledge, 2002), 118. "The spread of the internet has produced both a new medium and a means of getting much closer to what Tarde was trying to study." Nigel Thrift, "Pass It On: Towards a Political Economy of Propensity," *Emotion, Space, and Society* 1, no. 2 (2008): 88.

8. Gabriel Tarde, *L'Opinion et la foule* (Paris: Éditions Félix Alcan, 1901), 2.

9. Tarde, *L'Opinion et la foule*, 176.

10. Gustave Le Bon, *La Psychologie des foules* (Paris: Éditions Félix Alcan, 1895), 6. Le Bon believed that the bigger a crowd was, the more it suppressed the intellect of each of its members, and that crowds could only destroy.

11. Jules Romains, *Puissances de Paris* (Paris: Éditions Gallimard, 1919), 91.

12. Quoted in Rosalind Williams, "Jules Romains, *Unanimisme*, and the Poetics of Urban Systems," in *Literature and Technology*, ed. Mark L. Greenberg and Lance Schachterle (Bethlehem, PA: Lehigh University Press, 1992), 186.

13. Romains, *Puissances de Paris*, 18, 20, 128.

14. Jules Romains, *Mort de quelqu'un* (Paris: Éditions Gallimard, 1923), 27–31.

15. Williams, "Jules Romains," 192.

16. Romains, *Mort de quelqu'un*, 21–22, 65.

17. Romains, *Mort de quelqu'un*, 37–38.

18. Georges Perec, *Espèces d'espaces*, new ed. (Paris: Éditions Galilée, 2000), 76.

19. Romains, *Mort de quelqu'un*, 28–30.

20. Romains, *Mort de quelqu'un*, 138–148, 12.

21. Jules Romains, *La Vie unanime, poème 1904–1907* (Paris: Éditions Gallimard, 1983), 31.

22. Romains, *Mort de quelqu'un*, 15, 28, 48, 93.

23. Romains, *Mort de quelqu'un*, 42, 116–117.

24. Romains, *Mort de quelqu'un*, 119.

25. Cohen, *A Body Worth Defending*, 6.

26. Avner Ben-Amos, *Funerals, Politics, and Memory in Modern France, 1789–1996* (Oxford: Oxford University Press, 2000).

27. Jules Romains, *Problèmes d'aujourd'hui* (Paris: Éditions Kra, 1931), 178.

28. Leland Thielemann, "The Problem of Unity and Individualism in Romains' Social Philosophy," *Modern Language Quarterly* 2 (1941): 236.

29. Jules Romains, *Problèmes européens* (Paris: Flammarion, 1933), 183. The "*chacun à leur place*" is a grammatical error that reflects a plural [*leur*] thinking of the individual [*chacun*].

30. Romains, *Problèmes d'aujourd'hui*, 178.

31. Thielemann, "The Problem of Unity," 253.

32. Jules Romains, *Une vue des choses* (Paris: Éditions de la Maison Française, 1945), 43.

33. Thielemann, "The Problem of Unity," 257–258.

34. Tony Sampson, *Virality: Contagion Theory in the Age of Networks* (Minneapolis: University of Minnesota Press, 2012), 91.

35. Sampson, *Virality*, 46.

36. His inspiration is Nigel Thrift, who quotes Jack Katz saying, "If there is anything distinctive about emotions, it is that, even if they commonly occur in the course of speaking, they are not talk, not even just forms of expression, they are ways of expressing that something is going on that talk cannot grasp." Thrift essentially reads this statement as its converse: if something in collective intrarelation is outside language, then it is affect. Nigel Thrift, *Non-Representational Theory: Space/Politics/Affect* (New York: Routledge, 2007).

37. They associate a less noisy and more "reliable" collective with rationality: "Social media has been much better at providing the fuel for unpredictable, bursty mobilization than at steady, thoughtful construction of social change." Manuel Cebrian, Iyad Rahwan, and Alex "Sandy" Pentland, "Beyond Viral," *Communications of the ACM* 59, no. 4 (2016): 36.

38. Speakers were introduced by first name only, *sans* titles or qualifications. The group's commitment to parity and openness was tested by the case of Alain Finkielkraut. The conservative intellectual was effectively expelled from a meeting of the movement in the Place de la République. A video of the event showed multiple protestors accusing Finkielkraut of fascism, with the philosopher responding that the members of Nuit Debout were themselves fascists for refusing to allow people on the right to speak during general assemblies.

39. Sophie Wahnich, "Nuit Debout," *L'Homme et la société* 200, no. 2 (2016): 9.

40. Josh Lowe, "What Is France's 'Nuit Debout' Protest Movement?" *Newsweek*, 11 April 2016, http://www.newsweek.com/nuit-debout-france-david-graeber-place-de-la-republique-446400.

41. John Spitzer and Neil Zaslaw, *The Birth of the Orchestra: History of an Institution, 1650–1815* (Oxford: Oxford University Press, 2004), 514.

42. This characterization of the classical concert hall is not entirely accurate. As Le Corbusier warns and as John Cage demonstrated, the concert hall experience, while it might be designed to focus all attention on the musicians, is also the experience of noise as it is inevitably produced by the other people in the room.

43. Service Infographie du Parisien, "Infographie animée. Nuit Debout, ils communiquent par signes," *Le Parisien*, 8 April 2016, https://www.leparisien.fr/societe/infographie-animee-nuit-debout-ils-communiquent-par-signes-08-04-2016-5697907.php.

44. Éric Aeschimann, "À Nuit Debout, les intellos apprennent la discrétion," *Bibliobs*, 15 May 2016, bibliobs.nouvelobs.com/idees/20160511.OBS0268/a-nuit-debout-les-intellos-apprennent-la-discretion.html.

45. "The movement was founded on the irresponsible idea that you mustn't demand anything. One is almost tempted to say that this movement is made up of people who demand nothing because they want for nothing." Geoffroy Lagasnerie, "Nuit debout a attiré ceux qui pensent leurs intérêts particuliers comme universels, et a exclu les dominés," *Le Monde*, 26 April 2016, www.lemonde.fr/idees/article/2016/04/26/nuit-debout-releve-d-une-conception-traditionnelle-de-la-politique_4909223_3232.html.

46. Olivier Cahn, "La Répression des 'black blocs', prétexte à la domestication de la rue protestataire," *Archives de Politique Criminelle* 32, no. 1 (2010): 165–218.

47. "Revivez la journée du 1er mai et ses défilés sous tension," *Libération*, 1 May 2016, www.liberation.fr/france/2016/05/01/revivez-la-journee-du-1er-mai-et-ses-defiles-sous-tension_1449759.

48. Zeynep Tufekci, *Twitter and Tear Gas: The Power and Fragility of Networked Protest* (New Haven: Yale University Press, 2017), xxix.

49. Alfred Tauber, *Immunity: The Evolution of an Idea* (Oxford: Oxford University Press, 2017), 25, 38, 2.

50. Tauber, *Immunity*, 2, 14.

51. Tauber, *Immunity*, 124; original emphasis.

52. Tauber, *Immunity*, 125.

53. "Nucleic acid analysis, especially genomic sequencing and high-throughput RNA techniques, has challenged traditional definitions of individuality by finding significant interactions of animals and plants with symbiotic microorganisms that disrupt the boundaries that heretofore had characterized the biological organism." Tauber, *Immunity*, 91.

54. Tauber, *Immunity*, 101.

55. Quoted in Tauber, *Immunity*, 98.

56. Tauber, *Immunity*, 129.

57. Jacques Derrida, *Limited Inc*, trans. Samuel Weber (Evanston: Northwestern University Press, 1988), 90.

58. The sentence in question acts out Derrida's argument in more than one way. The context in which Derrida advanced his theory of hosts discursively producing parasites was a discussion of the use of the term "parasites" in speech act theory, where it had come to be applied to "non-serious" speech acts like quotation. The phrase "host organism" has its discursive quality foregrounded in Tauber's text by the quotation marks around it. These quotation marks redirect us to a private conversation, that is to say, to an originary *logos* that can never be recovered by the reader. The "host organism" thus enters Tauber's text as a linguistic parasite.

59. Tauber, *Immunity*, 151, 203.

60. "[Systems biology] has been defined as the effort of placing the various levels of semantic elements into a syntax of organization. But how is information conceived in this research program?" Tauber, *Immunity*, 206.

61. Tauber, *Immunity*, 112, 124, 202, 206.

62. Tauber, *Immunity*, 77; emphasis added.

63. Tauber, *Immunity*, 95, 14–16.

64. Rosi Braidotti, *Transpositions: On Nomadic Ethics* (Cambridge, UK: Polity, 2006), 5.

Chapter 6

1. Jacques Derrida, *Cosmopolites de tous les pays, encore un effort!* (Paris: Galilée, 1997), 42.

2. Jacques Derrida and Anne Dufourmantelle, *Of Hospitality* (Stanford, CA: Stanford University Press, 2000), 25.

3. Derrida and Dufourmantelle, *Of Hospitality*, 55. Earlier in the text, he writes that hospitality requires the ability to produce and enforce frontiers: "Nowadays, a reflection on hospitality presupposes, among other things, the possibility of a rigorous delimitation of thresholds or frontiers: between the familial and the non-familial, between the foreign and the non-foreign, the citizen and the non-citizen, but first of all between the private and the public, private and public law, etc.," 47–49.

4. Derrida and Dufourmantelle, *Of Hospitality*, 23–25.

5. Hospitality implies injustice: "Injustice, a certain injustice, and even a certain perjury, begins right away, from the very threshold of the right to hospitality." Derrida and Dufourmantelle, *Of Hospitality*, 55.

6. Jacques Derrida, *Limited Inc*, trans. Samuel Weber (Evanston: Northwestern University Press, 1988), 90.

7. Mark Wigley, *The Architecture of Deconstruction: Derrida's Haunt*, 2nd ed. (Cambridge, MA: MIT Press, 2002), 182–183.

8. Serres, *The Parasite*, 187.

9. Giovanna Borradori, *Philosophy in a Time of Terror: Dialogues with Jürgen Habermas and Jacques Derrida* (Chicago: University of Chicago Press, 2004), 129.

10. Derrida, *Limited Inc*, 76.

11. Derrida, *Limited Inc*, 48.

12. Derrida, *Limited Inc*, 17.

13. Derrida, *Limited Inc*, 103.

14. Derrida and Dufourmantelle, *Of Hospitality*, 135.

15. Wigley, *The Architecture of Deconstruction*, 79, 73, 186.

16. William Paulson, *The Noise of Culture: Literary Texts in a World of Information* (Ithaca, NY: Cornell University Press, 1988), 83.

17. Elsewhere he says that the reader is "always fundamentally anonymous. He is any reader, none in particular [n'importe quel lecteur], unique but transparent." Maurice Blanchot, *L'Espace littéraire* (Paris: Éditions Gallimard, 1955), 194–198.

18. Blanchot, *L'Espace littéraire*, 191.

19. Gilles Deleuze, *Essays Clinical and Critical* (London: Verso, 1998), 1–5.

20. Deleuze, *Essays Clinical and Critical*, 3.

21. Roberto Esposito, *Third Person: Politics of Life and Philosophy of the Impersonal*, trans. Zakiya Hanafi (Cambridge, UK: Polity Press, 2012), 151.

22. Ross Chambers, *An Atmospherics of the City: Baudelaire and the Poetics of Noise* (New York: Fordham University Press, 2015), 48.

23. Deleuze, *Essays Clinical and Critical*, 5.

24. Derrida, *Limited Inc*, 34.

25. Wigley, *The Architecture of Deconstruction*, 154, 201.

26. Victor Hugo, *Les Misérables*, trans. Isabel F. Hapgood (Minneapolis: Lerner Publishing Group, 2015), 1141.

27. Hugo, *Les Misérables*, 1142.

28. Marc Augé, *In the Metro*, trans. Tom Conley (Minneapolis: University of Minnesota Press, 1986), 35.

29. Camara Laye, *L'Enfant noir* (Paris: Presses Pocket, 1976), 187.

30. Rachid Boudjedra, *Topographie idéale pour une agression caractérisée* (Paris: Folio, 1986), 222.

31. Right before he is murdered, the protagonist is coded as a biological parasite as well. His killers say his suitcase is stuffed with "nonsense stinking of voracious microbes and subversive brochures threatening the very foundations of their civilization." Boudjedra, *Topographie*, 158.

32. "It is almost impossiblc to decide where to begin and where to stop, as if we had embarked on a journey with no planned layover. Even worse, the lack of distinction between what may be important for the plot and what is not, what is a detail and what is pertinent, transforms the text into a city without landmarks. And since quoting from a book would be the equivalent of giving directions, in the absence of such orienting devices, readers are likely to share the traveller's extreme fatigue, his sense of helplessness and despair." Mireille Rosello, "Disorientation and Accompaniment: Paris, the Metro and the Migrant," *Culture, Theory and Critique* 57, no. 1 (2016): 79.

33. Boudjedra, *Topographie*, 174.

34. "He'd been seized with fright for a moment because no one had told him about that, not even the lascars (from the Arabic ASKAR: soldier. Meaning changed in 1830, Familiar. Man who is brave, adventurous, resolute, and clever. By extension: individual with a nuance of admiration or bemused reprobation)." Boudjedra, *Topographie*, 37. Boudjedra's definition emphasizes the positive qualities of the *lascar*, implicitly critiquing the racism that led an Arabic word for soldier to become a French pejorative with a meaning similar to scallywag or rascal (the latter, despite being an anagram, shares no etymology with lascar). By making these subtleties explicit, Boudjedra's definition orients the reader, whether or not he or she was familiar with *lascar* before encountering it in this text.

35. "Moreover, if anyone at all is literate enough to appreciate modernist experiments, *nouveau romans* [*sic*], baroque enumerations and excessive texts, it should be the Western reader. There is such a thing as welcoming textual disorientation. And welcoming disorientation is not the same as suffering from it. If we read that text, after all, we have agency. I would rather not fetishise a universalized form of disorientation." Rosello, "Disorientation and Accompaniment," 86–87.

36. Jacques Derrida, *Monolingualism of the Other, or, The Prosthesis of Origin* (Stanford, CA: Stanford University Press, 1998), 60–61.

37. Derrida and Dufourmantelle, *Of Hospitality*, 75.

38. "My book is first and foremost addressed to North Africans in so much as the urgency of the problem demands a new approach to the politics of emigration." Salim Jay, "Interview avec Rachid Boudjedra," *L'Afrique littéraire et artistique* (1975): 35.

39. Mireille Rosello, *Postcolonial Hospitality: The Immigrant as Guest* (Stanford, CA: Stanford University Press, 2001).

40. Rosello, "Disorientation and Accompaniment," 87.

41. Rosello, "Disorientation and Accompaniment," 81.

42. Boudjedra, *Topographie*, 174–175.

43. Boudjedra, *Topographie*, 176.

44. Deleuze, *Essays Clinical and Critical*, 5.

45. "A great writer is always like a foreigner in the language in which he expresses himself, even if this is his native tongue." Deleuze, *Essays Clinical and Critical*, 109.

46. Boudjedra, *Topographie*, 87.

47. "Resenting themselves for having hesitated for a second before the temptation to have a little daydream, to transcend themselves, to propel themselves toward forbidden spaces, crushed as they were and worked from the inside by the diffuse feeling of sin they dragged around always, as soon as they had an urge to let go of mathematical structures, mechanical speeds, telephone directories, address books, and day planners." Boudjedra, *Topographie*, 120–121.

48. Boudjedra, *Topographie*, 24, 17.

49. Gilles Deleuze and Félix Guattari, *A Thousand Plateaus: Capitalism and Schizophrenia*, trans. Brian Massumi (Minneapolis: University of Minnesota Press, 1987), 479.

50. Boudjedra, *Topographie*, 148–149.

51. Deleuze and Guattari, *A Thousand Plateaus*, 30.

52. Deleuze and Guattari, *A Thousand Plateaus*, 160. The Body without Organs should not be understood simply as desire, flow, or intensity, but as a "connection of desires, conjunction of flows, continuum of intensities," 161.

53. Deleuze and Guattari, *A Thousand Plateaus*, 153.

54. Rosi Braidotti, *The Posthuman* (Cambridge, UK: Polity, 2013), 65, 82, 100.

55. Braidotti, *The Posthuman*, 102; original emphasis.

56. Describing her vision for posthuman universities, for instance, she writes: "we need a university that looks like the society it both reflects and serves, that is to say a globalized, technologically mediated, ethnically and linguistically diverse society that is still in tune with basic principles of social justice, the respect for diversity, the principles of hospitality and conviviality. I am aware [of] but do not mind the residual Humanism of such aspirations." Braidotti, *The Posthuman*, 183.

57. Braidotti, *The Posthuman*, 187; Rosi Braidotti, *Transpositions: On Nomadic Ethics* (Cambridge, UK: Polity, 2006), 7.

58. Braidotti, *The Posthuman*, 82.

59. "More Internet-backed interactivity will allow citizens to participate in all forms of planning, managing and assessing their urban environment. The key words are: open source, open governance, open data and open science, granting free access by the public to all scientific and administrative data." Braidotti, *The Posthuman*, 180.

60. Jacques Derrida, "Il faut bien manger, ou le calcul du sujet," interview by Jean-Luc Nancy, *Cahiers Confrontation* 20 (Winter 1989).

61. Rosello, "Disorientation and Accompaniment," 87.

62. Quoted in Denis Hollier, "Bloody Sundays," *Representations* 28 (Autumn 1989): 80.

63. Quoted in Hollier, "Bloody Sundays," 79.

64. Jacques Derrida and Peter Eisenman, *Chora L Works*, ed. Jeffrey Kipnis and Thomas Leeser (New York: Monacelli Press, 1997), 136.

65. Derrida and Eisenman, *Chora L Works*, 9–10.

66. Julia Kristeva, "The Subject in Process," in *The Tel Quel Reader*, ed. Patrick ffrench and Roland-François Lack (London: Routledge, 1998), 142.

67. Brendan Wocke, "Derrida at Villette: (An)aesthetic of Space," *University of Toronto Quarterly* 83, no. 3 (2014): 744.

68. "I perceive myself as writing in a discursive form which is analogous to the architecture of which I dream, an architecture which has been both repressed and forbidden. How can I begin to describe this architecture which I know of, but do not yet know?" Derrida and Eisenman, *Chora L Works*, 167.

69. Derrida and Eisenman, *Chora L Works*, 167.

70. Derrida and Eisenman, *Chora L Works*, 105.

71. Jennifer Bloomer, *Architecture and the Text: The (S)crypts of Joyce and Piranesi* (New Haven: Yale University Press, 1993), 173.

72. Deleuze, *Essays Clinical and Critical*, 5.

73. Borradori, *Philosophy in a Time of Terror*, 129.

Bibliography

"4 millions de personnes en France pour la marche républicaine." *L'Obs*, 11 January 2015, www.nouvelobs.com/charlie-hebdo/20150111.OBS9715/4-millions-de-personnes-en-france-pour-la-marche-republicaine.html.

Abaza, Mona. "Walls, Segregating Downtown Cairo and the Mohammed Mahmud Street Graffiti." *Theory, Culture and Society* 30, no. 1 (2012): 122–139.

Aeschimann, Éric. "À Nuit Debout, les intellos apprennent la discrétion." *Bibliobs*, 15 May 2016, bibliobs.nouvelobs.com/idees/20160511.OBS0268/a-nuit-debout-les-intellos-apprennent-la-discretion.html.

Alessandrin, Patrick, dir. *Banlieue 13: Ultimatum*. Saint-Denis: EuropaCorp, 2009.

Ambiciti SAS. "Ambiciti." Google Play Store, Vers. 2.4 (2019), play.google.com/store/apps/details?id=fr.inria.mimove.quantifiedself&hl=fr.

Ameel, Lieven, and Sirpa Tani. "Parkour: Creating Loose Spaces?" *Geografiska Annaler: Series B, Human Geography* 94, no. 1 (2012): 17–30.

An, Jisun, Haewoon Kwak, Yelena Mejova, Sonia Alonso Saenz De Oger, and Braulio Gomez Fortes. "Are You Charlie or Ahmed? Cultural Pluralism in Charlie Hebdo Response on Twitter." *Proceedings of the 10th International Conference on Web and Social Media* (2016): 2–11.

Anyinefa, Koffi. "Le Métro parisien: Figure de l'exotisme postcolonial." *French Forum* 28, no. 2 (2003): 77–98.

Archer, Neil. "Visual Poaching and Altered Space: Reading Parkour in French Visual Culture." *Modern and Contemporary France* 18, no. 1 (2010): 93–107.

Armstrong, Joshua. "Empiritexts: Mapping Attention and Invention in Post-1980 French Literature." *French Forum* 40, no. 1 (Winter 2015): 93–108.

Armstrong, Joshua. *Maps and Territories: Global Positioning in the Contemporary French Novel*. Liverpool: Liverpool University Press, 2019.

Atkinson, Michael. "Parkour, Anarcho-Environmentalism, and Poiesis." *Journal of Sport and Social Issues* 33, no. 2 (2009): 169–194.

Atkinson, Michael, and Kevin Young. *Deviance and Social Control in Sport.* Champaign, IL: Human Kinetics, 2008.

Augé, Marc. *In the Metro.* Translated by Tom Conley. Minneapolis: University of Minnesota Press, 1986.

Barthes, Roland. *The Eiffel Tower and Other Mythologies.* Translated by Richard Howard. Berkeley: University of California Press, 1997.

Bartholl, Aram. *Dead Drops.* 2018, deaddrops.com/.

Baudelaire, Charles. *Le Spleen de Paris: Petits poèmes en prose.* Paris: Librairie Générale Française, 2003.

Ben-Amos, Avner. *Funerals, Politics, and Memory in Modern France, 1789–1996.* Oxford: Oxford University Press, 2000.

Bénard, Clélia. "Ils collent des parapluies sur les murs pour rapprocher les parisiens." *Cheek Magazine,* 8 November 2014, cheekmagazine.fr/culture/le-mouvement-ils-collent-des-parapluies-sur-les-murs-pour-rapprocher-les-parisiens/.

Benjamin, Walter. *The Arcades Project.* 2nd ed. Translated by Howard Eiland and Kevin McLaughlin. Cambridge, MA: Harvard University Press, 1999.

Benjamin, Walter. *Reflections.* Edited by Peter Demetz. New York: Schocken, 1986.

Benveniste, Émile. *Le Vocabulaire des institutions indo-européens.* Paris: Éditions de Minuit, 1969.

Berger, Jonah, and Katherine Milkman. "What Makes Online Content Viral?" *Journal of Marketing Research* 49, no. 2 (2012): 192–205.

Biggs, Michael. "Putting the State on the Map: Cartography, Territory, and European State Formation." *Comparative Studies in Society and History* 41, no. 2 (1999): 374–405.

Blanchot, Maurice. *L'Espace littéraire.* Paris: Éditions Gallimard, 1955.

Bloomer, Jennifer. *Architecture and the Text: The (S)crypts of Joyce and Piranesi.* New Haven: Yale University Press, 1993.

Bolter, Jay David, and Richard Grusin. *Remediation: Understanding New Media.* Cambridge, MA: MIT Press, 2000.

Borges, Jorge Luis. *Dreamtigers.* Translated by Mildred Boyer and Harold Morland. Austin, TX: University of Texas Press, 2014).

Borradori, Giovanna. *Philosophy in a Time of Terror: Dialogues with Jürgen Habermas and Jacques Derrida.* Chicago: University of Chicago Press, 2004.

Boudjedra, Rachid. *Topographie idéale pour une agression caractérisée.* Paris: Folio, 1986. First published 1973 by Denoël (Paris).

Boutin, Aimée. *City of Noise: Sound and Nineteenth-Century Paris.* Urbana: University of Illinois Press, 2015.

Braidotti, Rosi. *The Posthuman.* Cambridge, UK: Polity, 2013.

Braidotti, Rosi. *Transpositions: On Nomadic Ethics.* Cambridge, UK: Polity, 2006.

Brassaï. *Graffiti.* Paris: Flammarion, 2002.

Brennan, Teresa. *The Transmission of Affect.* Ithaca, NY: Cornell University Press, 2004.

Bressani, Martin, and Marc Grignon. "Henri Labrouste and the Lure of the Real: Romanticism, Rationalism, and the Bibliothèque Sainte-Geneviève." *Art History* 28, no. 5 (2005): 712–751.

Breton, André. *Nadja.* Paris: Éditions Gallimard, 1964.

Brott, Simone. "The Le Corbusier Scandal, or, was Le Corbusier a Fascist?" *Fascism* 6, no. 2 (December 2017): 196–227.

Bucky Turco, and Invader. "From the Streets to the Stratosphere: An Interview with 'Space Artist' Invader." *Animal,* 4 November 2013, web.archive.org/web/20170910174129/http://animalnewyork.com/2013/streets-stratosphere-interview-space-artist-invader/.

Burggraf, Vanessa, presenter. *Le Débat.* "Charlie Hebdo, un an après: que reste-t-il de l'esprit Charlie? (Partie 1)." Aired 12 January 2016 on France 24. www.france24.com/fr/20160111-le-debat-france-24-marche-republicaine-charlie-hebdo-an-apres-partie1.

Cahn, Olivier. "La Répression des 'black blocs', prétexte à la domestication de la rue protestataire." *Archives de Politique Criminelle* 32, no. 1 (2010): 165–218.

Camara Laye. *L'Enfant noir.* Paris: Presses Pocket, 1976. First published 1953 by Plon (Paris).

Campbell, Martin, dir. *Casino Royale.* London: Eon Productions, 2006.

Carroll, Lewis. *Alice's Adventures in Wonderland and Through the Looking Glass.* London: Puffin Books, 1997.

Carvin, Andy. "The 'Standing Man' of Turkey: Act of Quiet Protest Goes Viral." *NPR,* 18 June 2013, www.npr.org/sections/thetwo-way/2013/06/18/193183899/the-standing-man-of-turkey-act-of-quiet-protest-goes-viral.

Castigliano, Federico. "Le Divertissement du texte: écriture et flânerie chez Jacques Réda." *Poétique* 4, no. 164 (2010): 461–476.

Cebrian, Manuel, Iyad Rahwan, and Alex "Sandy" Pentland. "Beyond Viral." *Communications of the ACM* 59, no. 4 (2016): 36–39.

Chambers, Ross. *An Atmospherics of the City: Baudelaire and the Poetics of Noise*. New York: Fordham University Press, 2015.

Chaslin, François. *Un Corbusier*. Paris: Éditions du Seuil, 2015.

Chenal, Pierre, dir. *Architecture d'aujourd'hui*. Paris: Architecture d'aujourd'hui, 1930.

Chevallier, Fabienne. *Le Paris moderne: histoire des politiques d'hygiène, 1855–1898*. Rennes: Presses Universitaires de Rennes, 2010.

Chombart de Lauwe, Paul-Henry. *Paris et l'agglomération parisienne*. Paris: Presses Universitaires de France, 1952.

Christian, Marie. *La Mémoire des murs: le street art et Charlie*. Paris: Omniscience, 2015.

Clark, T. J. *The Painting of Modern Life: Paris in the Art of Manet and His Followers*. Princeton: Princeton University Press, 1999.

Clermont-Tonnerre, Claire de. "Intervention de Claire de Clermont-Tonnerre sur le Plan de Prévention du Bruit." *Délibération 2015 DEVE 123: Approbation du PPBE de la Ville de Paris*, groupelesrepublicains.paris/intervention/intervention-de-claire-de-clermont-tonnerre-sur-le-plan-de-prevention-du-bruit-septembre-2015/.

Clet, Abraham. "Florence Street Sign Art by Clet." *Visit Tuscany*. Accessed 4 April 2020, https://www.visittuscany.com/en/ideas/florence-street-sign-art-by-clet/.

Cohen, Ed. *A Body Worth Defending: Immunity, Biopolitics, and the Apotheosis of the Modern Body*. Durham: Duke University Press, 2009.

Cohen, Ed. "The Paradoxical Politics of Viral Containment; Or, How Scale Undoes Us One and All." *Social Text* 106, no. 1 (2011): 15–35.

Cohen, Jean-Louis. "A Dialogue with Jean-Louis Cohen." *Design Book Review* 14 (1988): 15–18.

Cohen, Jean-Louis. *France*. London: Reaktion Books, 2015.

Cohen, Jean-Louis, and Monique Eleb. *Paris Architecture 1900–2000*. Paris: Éditions NORMA, 2000.

Colomina, Beatriz. *Privacy and Publicity: Modern Architecture as Mass Media*. Cambridge, MA: MIT Press, 1996.

Colon, Églantine. "Neither *lieux-de-mémoire* nor *non-lieux*: Towards a Concept of Precarious Spaces in Philippe Vasset's *Un livre blanc*." *French Studies* 71, no. 1 (2017): 66–83.

Conover, Michael, Emilio Ferrara, Filippo Menczer, and Alessandro Flammini. "The Digital Evolution of Occupy Wall Street." *PLOS ONE* 8, no. 5 (2013).

"Contribution à une définition situationniste du jeu." *Internationale Situationniste*, no. 1 (1958): 9–10.

Cowan, Michael. "Between the Street and the Apartment: Disturbing the Space of Fortress Europe in Michael Haneke." *Studies in European Cinema* 5, no. 2 (2008): 117–129.

Cuisenier, André. *Jules Romains et l'unanimisme*. Paris: Flammarion, 1935.

Dawkins, Richard. *The Selfish Gene*. Oxford: Oxford University Press, 1976.

De Certeau, Michel. *L'Invention du quotidien, I: arts de faire*. Paris: Éditions Gallimard, 1990.

De Lange, Michiel, and Martijn de Waal, eds. *The Hackable City: Digital Media and Collaborative City-Making in the Network Society*. Singapore: Springer, 2019.

De Waal, Martijn. *The City as Interface: How New Media Are Changing the City*. Rotterdam: Nai010 Publishers, 2014.

Debord, Guy. *La Société du spectacle*. Paris: Éditions Buchet-Chastel, 1967.

Debord, Guy. "Théorie de la dérive." *Les Lèvres nues*, no. 9 (1956).

Deibert, Ron. "Cyberspace under Siege." *Journal of Democracy* 26, no. 3 (2015): 64–78.

Deleuze, Gilles. *Essays Clinical and Critical*. London: Verso, 1998.

Deleuze, Gilles, and Félix Guattari. *A Thousand Plateaus: Capitalism and Schizophrenia*. Translated by Brian Massumi. Minneapolis: University of Minnesota Press, 1987.

Delvau, Alfred. *Les Murailles révolutionnaires*. Paris: Joubert, 1851.

Dennett, Daniel. *Consciousness Explained*. New York: Little, Brown, 1991.

Département des Hauts-de-Seine. *Projet de plan de prévention du bruit dans l'environnement*. Compiègne: Imprimerie de Compiègne, 2016.

Derrida, Jacques. *Cosmopolites de tous les pays, encore un effort!* Paris: Galilée, 1997.

Derrida, Jacques. *Dissemination*. Translated by Barbara Johnson. London: Continuum, 2004.

Derrida, Jacques. "Il faut bien manger, ou le calcul du sujet." Interview by Jean-Luc Nancy. *Cahiers Confrontation* 20 (Winter 1989).

Derrida, Jacques. *Limited Inc*. Translated by Samuel Weber. Evanston: Northwestern University Press, 1988.

Derrida, Jacques. *Monolingualism of the Other, or, The Prosthesis of Origin*. Stanford, CA: Stanford University Press, 1998.

Derrida, Jacques. *Of Grammatology*. Corrected ed. Translated by Gayatri Chakravorty Spivak. Baltimore: Johns Hopkins University Press, 1997.

Derrida, Jacques, and Anne Dufourmantelle. *Of Hospitality*. Translated by Rachel Bowlby. Stanford, CA: Stanford University Press, 2000.

Derrida, Jacques, and Peter Eisenman. *Chora L Works*. Edited by Jeffrey Kipnis and Thomas Leeser. New York: Monacelli Press, 1997.

Duclos, Jean-François Rémy. "La Revanche du flou: Jacques Réda à l'épreuve de la cartographie dans *Le Méridien de Paris*." *French Studies* 68, no. 1 (2014): 48–60.

Durm, Josef, Hermann Ende, Eduard Schmitt, and Heinrich Wagner. *Handbuch der Architektur*. Darmstadt: Arnold Bergsträsser, 1880.

Dunnett, James. "The Architecture of Silence." *Architectural Review* 178, no. 1064 (1985): 69–72.

Eleb, Monique, and Anne Debarre. *L'Invention de l'habitation moderne, Paris, 1880–1914*. Paris: Éditions Hazan, 2000.

Elkin, Lauren. *Flâneuse: Women Walk the City in Paris, New York, Tokyo, Venice and London*. London: Chatto and Windus, 2016.

Esposito, Roberto. *Communitas: The Origin and Destiny of Community*. Translated by Timothy Campbell. Stanford, CA: Stanford University Press, 2010.

Esposito, Roberto. *Immunitas: The Protection and Negation of Life*. Translated by Zakiya Hanafi. Cambridge, UK: Polity Press, 2011.

Esposito, Roberto. *Terms of the Political: Community, Immunity, Biopolitics*. Translated by Rhiannon Noel Welch. New York: Fordham University Press, 2013.

Esposito, Roberto. *Third Person: Politics of Life and Philosophy of the Impersonal*. Translated by Zakiya Hanafi. Cambridge, UK: Polity Press, 2012.

Farley, John. "Parasites and the Germ Theory of Disease." *Millbank Quarterly* 67, no. S1 (1989): 50–68.

Faye, Olivier. "Marche républicaine: la gauche radicale fait bande à part." *Le Monde*, 12 January 2015, www.lemonde.fr/politique/article/2015/01/12/marche-republicaine-la-gauche-radicale-fait-bande-a-part_4554341_823448.html.

Fierro, Annette. *The Glass State: The Technology of the Spectacle, Paris, 1981–1998*. Cambridge, MA: MIT Press, 2003.

Figueiredo, Sergio M., Sukanya Krishnamurthy, and Torsten Schroeder. *Architecture and the Smart City*. London: Routledge, 2019.

Fischer, Peter, Stephanie Guter, and Dieter Frey. "The Effects of Risk-Promoting Media on Inclinations Towards Risk Taking." *Basic and Applied Social Psychology* 30, no. 230 (2008): 230–240.

Fischer, Peter, Evelyn Vingilis, Tobias Greitmeyer, and Claudia Vogrincic. "Risk-Taking and the Media." *Risk Analysis* 31, no. 5 (2011): 699–705.

Foucault, Michel. *The Archaeology of Knowledge*. Translated by Alan Sheridan. New York: Vintage Books, 2010.

Foucault, Michel. *Discipline and Punish: The Birth of the Prison*. Translated by Alan Sheridan. New York: Vintage Books, 1995.

Foucault, Michel. *The Order of Things: An Archaeology of the Human Sciences*. New York: Vintage Books, 1994.

Frumkin, Kenneth. "Bilateral Calcaneal Fractures and 'Free Running': A Dangerously Cool Emerging 'Sport.'" *Annals of Emergency Medicine* 46, no. 3 (2005): 300.

Gallagher, Brianne. "Policing Paris: Private Publics and Architectural Media in Michael Haneke's *Caché*." *Journal for Cultural Research* 12, no. 1 (2008): 19–38.

Geinoz, Philippe. "Lecture unanimiste des espaces urbains—Jules Romains et les *Puissances de Paris*." In *Metropolen der Avantgarde*, edited by Thomas Hunkeler and Edith Anna Kuntz, 49–62. Pieterlen and Bern: Peter Lang, 2011.

Godard, Jean-Luc, dir. *2 ou 3 choses que je sais d'elle*. Paris: Argos Films, 1970.

Goncourt, Edmond de and Jules de Goncourt. *Journal des Goncourt* 1. Paris: Bibliothèque-Charpentier, 1888.

González-Bailón, Sandra, Javier Borge-Holthoefer, Alejandro Rivero, and Yamir Moreno. "The Dynamics of Protest Recruitment through an Online Network." *Scientific Reports* 1, no. 197 (2011): 1–7.

Graham, Stephen, ed. *Cybercities Reader*. New York: Routledge, 2003.

Gravier, Jean-François. *Paris et le désert français*. Paris: Éditions du Portulan, 1947.

Haneke, Michael, dir. *Caché*. Paris: Les Films du Losange, 2005.

Harley, J. B. *New Nature of Maps: Essays in the History of Cartography*. Baltimore: Johns Hopkins University Press, 2001.

Haraway, Donna J. *Simians, Cyborgs, and Women: The Reinvention of Nature*. New York: Routledge, 1991.

Haraway, Donna J. *Staying with the Trouble: Making Kin in the Chthulucene*. Durham: Duke University Press, 2016.

Harvey, David. *Paris, Capital of Modernity*. New York: Routledge, 2006.

Haussmann, Georges-Eugène. *Mémoires du Baron Haussmann* 2. Paris: Victor-Havard, 1890.

Hazan, Éric. *L'Invention de Paris*. Paris: Éditions du Seuil, 2002.

Hazan, Éric. *Paris sous tension*. Paris: La Fabrique Éditions, 2011.

Hazan, Éric. *A Walk through Paris*. London: Verso, 2018.

Heidegger, Martin. *Poetry, Language, Thought*. New York: HarperCollins, 1971.

Heidegger, Martin. *The Principle of Reason*. Translated by Reginald Lilly. Bloomington: Indiana University Press, 1991.

Hellman, John. *The Knight-Monks of Vichy France: Uriage, 1940–1945*. Montreal: McGill-Queen's University Press, 1993.

Hemsley, Jeff, and Robert M. Mason. "The Nature of Knowledge in the Social Media Age: Implications for Knowledge Management Models." *Journal of Organizational Computing and Electronic Commerce* 23, no. 1–2 (2013): 138–176.

Higonnet, Patrice. *Paris, Capital of the World*. Cambridge, MA: Harvard University Press, 2002.

Hobbes, Thomas. *Leviathan*. New York: E. P. Dutton, 1914.

Hollier, Denis. "Bloody Sundays." *Representations* 28 (Autumn 1989): 77–89.

Hugo, Victor. *Les Misérables*. Translated by Isabel F. Hapgood. Minneapolis: Lerner Publishing Group, 2015.

Hugo, Victor. *Notre-Dame of Paris*. Translated by John Sturrock. New York: Penguin, 1978.

Hulsey, Nathan, and Joshua Reeves. "The Gift That Keeps on Giving: Google, Ingress, and the Gift of Surveillance." *Surveillance and Society* 12, no. 3 (2014): 389–400.

Internationale Lettriste. "Projets d'embellissement rationnels de la ville de Paris." *Potlatch*, no. 23 (1955).

Invader. *L'Invasion de Paris* 2. Paris: CTRL + P, 2012.

Ivain, Gilles. "Formulaire pour un urbanisme nouveau." *Internationale Situationniste*, no. 1 (1958): 15–20.

Jacobs, Jane. *The Death and Life of Great American Cities*. New York: Random House, 1961.

Jarcy, Xavier de. *Le Corbusier, un fascisme français*. Paris: Albin Michel, 2015.

Jay, Salim. "Interview avec Rachid Boudjedra." *L'Afrique littéraire et artistique* (1975): 35–38.

Jeunet, Jean-Pierre, and Marc Caro, dirs. *Delicatessen*. Neuilly-sur-Seine: UGC Films, 1991.

Jones, Colin. *Paris: Biography of a City*. New York: Penguin, 2006. First published 2004 by Allen Lane (New York).

JR. "Group Action Guidelines." *Inside Out Project*. Accessed 2 April 2020, http://www.insideoutproject.net/sites/all/themes/insideout/documents/Group_Action_Guidelines.pdf.

JR. "Use Art to Turn the World Inside Out." *TED*. YouTube Video, 24:09. 5 March 2011. https://www.youtube.com/watch?v=0PAy1zBtTbw.

Keck, Frédéric. "Space Invader rencontre King of Kowloon." *Esprit* 8 (August/September 2011): 175–178.

Kidder, Jeffrey. "Parkour: Adventure, Risk, and Safety in the Urban Environment." *Qualitative Sociology* 36 (2013): 231–250.

Kidder, Jeffrey. "Parkour, Masculinity, and the City." *Sociology of Sport Journal* 30, no. 1 (2013): 1–23.

Kidder, Jeffrey. "Parkour, the Affective Appropriation of Urban Space, and the Real/Virtual Dialectic." *City and Community* 11, no. 3 (2012): 229–253.

Kittler, Friedrich, and Matthew Griffin. "The City Is a Medium." *New Literary History* 27, no. 4 (1996): 717–729.

Knabb, Ken, ed. and trans. *Situationist International Anthology*. Revised ed. Berkeley: Bureau of Public Secrets, 2006.

Kristeva, Julia. "The Subject in Process." In *The Tel Quel Reader*, edited by Patrick ffrench and Roland-François Lack, 142–143. London: Routledge, 1998.

Kunstmann, Lazar. *La Culture en clandestins, les UX*. Paris: Éditions Hazan, 2009.

"L'Invasion des 'Space Invaders' se poursuit, Le 1.000e installé à Paris." *Le Parisien*, 8 June 2011, www.leparisien.fr/flash-actualite-culture/l-invasion-des-space-invaders-se-poursuit-le-1-000e-installe-a-paris-08-06-2011-1485931.php.

Lack, Roland-François. "Three Filmmakers in Romainville: Haneke, Bosetti, Feuillade." *The Cine-Tourist*, www.thecinetourist.net/three-filmmakers-in-romainville.html.

Lagasnerie, Geoffroy de. "Nuit debout a attiré ceux qui pensent leurs intérêts particuliers comme universels, et a exclu les dominés." *Le Monde*, 26 April 2016, www.lemonde.fr/idees/article/2016/04/26/nuit-debout-releve-d-une-conception-traditionnelle-de-la-politique_4909223_3232.html.

Lamb, Matthew D. "Self and the City: Parkour, Architecture, and the Interstices of the 'Knowable' City." *Liminalities* 10, no. 2 (2014) 1–20.

Latour, Bruno. "Gabriel Tarde and the End of the Social." In *The Social in Question: New Bearings in History and the Social Sciences*, edited by Patrick Joyce, 117–132. New York: Routledge, 2002.

Le Bon, Gustave. *La Psychologie des foules*. Paris: Éditions Félix Alcan, 1895.

Le Corbusier. *L'Art décoratif d'aujourd'hui*. Paris: G. Crès, 1925.

Le Corbusier. *Toward an Architecture*. Translated by John Goodman. Los Angeles: Getty Publications, 2007.

Le Corbusier. *Urbanisme*. Paris: G. Crès, 1925.

Le Corbusier. *La Ville radieuse: éléments d'une doctrine d'urbanisme pour l'équipement de la civilisation machiniste*. Paris: Éditions de l'architecture d'aujourd'hui, 1935.

Le Corbusier and Amédée Ozenfant. *L'Esprit nouveau*, no. 28 (1925): 2312–2411.

Lee, Min Kyung. "The Bureaucracy of Plans: Urban Governance and Maps in Nineteenth-Century Paris." *Journal of Urban History* 46, no. 2 (2020): 248–269.

Lee, Min Kyung. "Drawing Plans Together: The Administration of Nineteenth-Century Plans of Paris." *Art in Translation* 10, no. 1 (2018): 91–111.

Lefebvre, Henri. *Le Droit à la ville*. Paris: Anthropos, 1968.

Lefebvre, Henri. *The Production of Space*. Translated by Donald Nicholson-Smith. Oxford: Blackwell, 1991.

Lefebvre, Henri. *The Urban Revolution*. Translated by Robert Bononno. Minneapolis: University of Minnesota Press, 2003.

Leroux, Gaston. *Le Fantôme de l'opéra*. Paris: Éditions Pierre Lafitte, 1910.

Levin, Thomas Y. "Five Tapes, Four Halls, Two Dreams: Vicissitudes of Surveillant Narration in Michael Haneke's *Caché*." In *A Companion to Michael Haneke*, edited by Roy Grundmann, 75–90. Malden, MA: Wiley-Blackwell, 2014.

Levine, Neil. "The Book and the Building." In *The Beaux-Arts and Nineteenth-Century French Architecture*, edited by Robin Middleton, 138–173. Cambridge, MA: MIT Press, 1982.

Lieberstein, Paul, dir. *The Office*. Season 6, episode 1, "Gossip." Written by Paul Lieberstein. Aired 17 September 2009. NBC.

Loos, Adolf. *Ornament and Crime*. London: Penguin Classics, 2019.

Lowe, Josh. "What Is France's 'Nuit Debout' Protest Movement?" *Newsweek*, 11 April 2016, http://www.newsweek.com/nuit-debout-france-david-graeber-place-de-la-republique-446400.

Loyer, François. *Paris Nineteenth Century: Architecture and Urbanism*. Translated by Charles Lynn Clark. New York: Abbeville Press, 1988.

Lussato, Céline. "Infographie. 'Charlie Hebdo': les hypocrites de la marche républicaine." *L'Obs*, 21 January 2015, www.nouvelobs.com/monde/20150120.OBS0392/infographie-charlie-hebdo-les-hypocrites-de-la-marche-republicaine.html.

MacDowall, Lachlan John, and Poppy de Souza. "I'd Double Tap That!! Street Art, Graffiti, and Instagram Research." *Media, Culture and Society* 40, no. 1 (January 2018): 3–22.

McLuhan, Marshall. *Understanding Media: The Extensions of Man*. Cambridge, MA: MIT Press, 1994.

McQuire, Scott. *Geomedia: Networked Cities and the Future of Public Space*. Cambridge, UK: Polity Press, 2016.

McQuire, Scott. *The Media City: Media, Architecture and Urban Space*. Thousand Oaks, CA: SAGE Publications, 2010.

Mairie de Paris. *Paris intelligente et durable: Perspectives 2020 et au-delà*. api-site-cdn.paris.fr/images/89758.

Marcus, Sharon. *Apartment Stories: City and Home in Nineteenth-Century Paris and London*. Berkeley: University of California Press, 1999.

Mattern, Shannon. "A City Is Not a Computer." *Places Journal* (February 2017).

Mattern, Shannon. *Code + Clay . . . Data + Dirt: Five Thousand Years of Urban Media*. Minneapolis: University of Minnesota Press, 2017.

Mattern, Shannon. *Deep Mapping the Media City*. Minneapolis: University of Minnesota Press, 2015.

Miller, Jason R., and Sébastien G. Demoiny. "Parkour: A New Extreme Sport and a Case Study." *Journal of Foot and Ankle Surgery* 47, no. 1 (2008): 63–65.

Mitchell, William J. *City of Bits: Space, Place, and the Infobahn*. Cambridge, MA: MIT Press, 2000.

Mitchell, William J. *e-topia: "Urban Life, Jim, But Not as We Know It!"* Cambridge, MA: MIT Press, 1999.

Mitchell, William J. *Me++: The Cyborg Self and the Networked City*. Cambridge, MA: MIT Press, 2004.

Mogli Oak, and SOBR. "An Interview with French Street Artist SOBR." Mogli Oak Berlin, 25 May 2014, web.archive.org/web/20140525211421/http://www.mo-berlin.com/an-interview-with-french-street-artist-sobre/.

Morel, Pierre, dir. *Banlieue 13*. Paris: EuropaCorp, 2004.

Moretti, Franco. "Homo Palpitans: Balzac's Novels and the Urban Personality." In *Signs Taken for Wonders: On the Sociology of Literary Forms*, 109–129. London: Verso, 2005.

Naím, Moisés. *The End of Power: From Boardrooms to Battlefields and Churches to States, Why Being in Charge Isn't What It Used to Be*. New York: Basic Books, 2013.

Nakassis, Constantine. "Para-s/cite, Part 1. The Parasite." *Semiotic Review*, 2013, www.semioticreview.com/ojs/index.php/sr/article/view/33/33.

"Nuit Debout Wiki." Wikimedia Foundation. Accessed 10 April 2018.

Nunes, Mark, ed. *Error: Glitch, Noise, and Jam in New Media Cultures*. New York: Continuum, 2011.

O'Grady, Alice. "Tracing the City—Parkour Training, Play and the Practice of Collaborative Learning." *Theatre, Dance and Performance Training* 3, no. 2 (2012): 145–162.

O'Rourke, Karen. *Walking and Mapping: Artists as Cartographers*. Cambridge, MA: MIT Press, 2013.

Onnela, Jukka-Pekka, et al. "Spontaneous Emergence of Social Influence in Online Systems." *Proceedings of the National Academy of Sciences of the United States of America* 107, no. 43 (2010): 18375–18380.

Palsky, Gilles. *Des chiffres et des cartes: naissance et développement de la cartographie quantitative française au XIX siècle*. Paris: Ministère de l'enseignement supérieur et de la recherche, comité des travaux historiques et scientifiques, 1996.

Parikka, Jussi. *Digital Contagions: A Media Archaeology of Computer Viruses*. 2nd ed. New York: Peter Lang, 2016.

Parikka, Jussi. *Insect Media: An Archaeology of Animals and Technology*. Minneapolis: University of Minnesota Press, 2010.

Parisi, Luciana. *Contagious Architecture: Computation, Aesthetics, and Space*. Cambridge, MA: MIT Press, 2013.

Park, Sun-Young. *Ideals of the Body: Architecture, Urbanism, and Hygiene in Postrevolutionary Paris*. Pittsburgh: University of Pittsburgh Press, 2018.

Pascual, Julia. "Manifestations du 1er-Mai: le discours officiel sur les casseurs contesté par le terrain." *Le Monde*, 2 May 2016, www.lemonde.fr/police-justice/article/2016/05/02/le-maintien-de-l-ordre-a-l-epreuve-des-casseurs_4911784_1653578.html.

Paulson, William. *The Noise of Culture: Literary Texts in a World of Information*. Ithaca, NY: Cornell University Press, 1988.

Peiter, Sebastian, and Goetz Werner, authors and dirs. *Guerilla Art*. London: Laurence King, 2009.

Pennac. *Nemo*. Paris: Éditions Hoëbeke, 2006.

Perec, Georges. *Espèces d'espaces*. New ed. Paris: Éditions Galilée, 2000.

Perelman, Marc. *Le Corbusier, une froide vision du monde*. Paris: Michalon, 2015.

Pettersen, David. "American Genre Film in the French Banlieue: Luc Besson and Parkour." *Cinema Journal* 53, no. 3 (2014): 26–51.

Pinçon, Michel, and Monique Pinçon-Charlot. *Paris mosaïque: promenades urbaines*. Paris: Calmann-Lévy, 2001.

Pinon, Pierre. *Paris, biographie d'une capitale*. Paris: Éditions Hazan, 1999.

"Pour les droits plus protecteurs des salarié-es du privé comme du public pour obtenir le retrait du projet de loi Travail." *SNUDI-FO*, Force Ouvrière, 22 April 2016, www.snudifo13.org/spaw/uploads/files/national/autres/Comm_commun_OS_FP_220416.pdf.

Prendergast, Christopher. *Paris and the Nineteenth Century*. Oxford: Blackwell, 1992.

Prou, Xavier. Interview by Mark Jenkins. *UK Street Art*. 29 July 2008. www.ukstreetart.co.uk/blek-le-rat-interview/.

Rancière, Jacques. *Dissensus: On Politics and Aesthetics*. Translated by Steve Corcoran. London: Continuum, 2010.

Rancière, Jacques. *Figures of History*. Translated by Julie Rose. Cambridge, UK: Polity, 2014.

Rancière, Jacques. *On the Shores of Politics*. Translated by Liz Heron. London: Verso, 1995.

Rancière, Jacques. "Onze thèses sur la politique." *Filozofski vestnik* 2 (1997): 91–106.

Réda, Jacques. *L'Adoption du système métrique*. Paris: Éditions Gallimard, 2004.

Réda, Jacques. *La Liberté des rues*. Paris: Éditions Gallimard, 1997.

Réda, Jacques. *Le Méridien de Paris*. Paris: Fata Morgana, 1997.

Réda, Jacques. *Les Ruines de Paris*. Paris: Éditions Gallimard, 1977.

Reiss, Jon, and Xavier Prou. "Interview with Blek in Swindle Magazine." *Jon Reiss*. 23 May 2007, jonreiss.com/2007/05/interview-with-blek-in-swindle-magazine/.

"Revivez la journée du 1er mai et ses défilés sous tension." *Libération*, 1 May 2016, www.liberation.fr/france/2016/05/01/revivez-la-journee-du-1er-mai-et-ses-defiles-sous-tension_1449759.

Richards, Simon. "The Antisocial Urbanism of Le Corbusier." *Common Knowledge* 13, no. 1 (2007): 50–66.

Richards, Simon. *Le Corbusier and the Concept of Self.* New Haven: Yale University Press, 2003.

Rochefort, Christiane. *Les Petits Enfants du siècle.* Paris: Grasset, 1961.

Romains, Jules. *Mort de quelqu'un.* Paris: Éditions Gallimard, 1923. First published 1911 by Eugène Figuière (Paris).

Romains, Jules. *Problèmes d'aujourd'hui.* Paris: Éditions Kra, 1931.

Romains, Jules. *Problèmes européens.* Paris: Flammarion, 1933.

Romains, Jules. *Puissances de Paris.* Paris: Éditions Gallimard, 1919.

Romains, Jules. *Une vue des choses.* Paris: Éditions de la Maison Française, 1945.

Romains, Jules. *La Vie unanime, poème 1904–1907.* Paris: Éditions Gallimard, 1983.

Rosello, Mireille. "Disorientation and Accompaniment: Paris, the Metro and the Migrant." *Culture, Theory and Critique* 57, no. 1 (2016): 77–91.

Rosello, Mireille. *Postcolonial Hospitality: The Immigrant as Guest.* Stanford, CA: Stanford University Press, 2001.

Roubaud, Jacques. *The Great Fire of London: A Story with Interpolations and Bifurcations.* Champaign, IL: Dalkey Archive Press, 1991.

Rowe, Colin, and Robert Slutzky. "Transparency: Literal and Phenomenal." *Perspecta* 8 (1963): 45–54.

Ruest, Nick. "An Exploratory Look at 13,968,293 #JESUISCHARLIE, #JESUISAHMED, #JESUISJUIF, and #CHARLIEHEBDO Tweets." *Nick Ruest,* 2 March 2015, web.archive.org/web/20161106020247/http://ruebot.net/tag/charliehebdo.

Rutherford, Alex, Manuel Cebrian, Sohan Dsouza, Esteban Moro, Alex "Sandy" Pentland, and Iyad Rahwan. "Limits of Social Mobilization." *Proceedings of the National Academy of Sciences of the United States of America* 110, no. 16 (2013): 6281–6286.

Said, Edward. *Orientalism.* New York: Pantheon Books, 1978.

Sampson, Tony. *Virality: Contagion Theory in the Age of Networks.* Minneapolis: University of Minnesota Press, 2012.

Sassen, Saskia. *The Global City: New York, London, Tokyo.* Princeton: Princeton University Press, 1991.

Savile, Stephen John. "Playing with Fear: Parkour and the Mobility of Emotion." *Social and Cultural Geography* 9, no. 8 (2008): 891–914.

Sénécat, Adrien, and Samuel Laurent. "Alain Finkielkraut expulsé de Nuit Debout: les faits." *Le Monde*, 18 April 2016, www.lemonde.fr/les-decodeurs/article/2016/04/18/alain-finkielkraut-expulse-de-nuit-debout-les-faits_4904275_4355770.html.

Serres, Michel. *Le Mal propre: Polluer pour s'approprier?* Paris: Éditions Le Pommier, 2012.

Serres, Michel. *The Parasite*. Translated by Lawrence R. Schehr. Minneapolis: University of Minnesota Press, 2007. First published 1982 by Johns Hopkins University Press (Baltimore).

Service Infographie du Parisien. "Infographie animée. Nuit Debout, ils communiquent par des signes." *Le Parisien*, 8 April 2016.

Shifman, Limor. *Memes in Digital Culture*. Cambridge, MA: MIT Press, 2014.

Shirky, Clay. *Here Comes Everybody: The Power of Organizing without Organizations*. New York: Penguin, 2008.

Shonfield, Katherine. *Walls Have Feelings: Architecture, Film, and the City*. London: Routledge, 2000.

Simmel, Georg. "The Metropolis and Mental Life." In *The Blackwell City Reader*, edited by Gary Bridge and Sophie Watson. Oxford: Wiley-Blackwell, 2002.

Solesbury, William. *World Cities, City Worlds: Explorations with Metaphors, Icons, and Perspectives*. Kibworth Beauchamp: Matador, 2013.

Spitzer, John, and Neil Zaslaw. *The Birth of the Orchestra: History of an Institution, 1650–1815*. Oxford: Oxford University Press, 2004.

Spivak, Gayatri Chakravorty. "Can the Subaltern Speak?" In *Marxism and the Interpretation of Culture*, edited by Cary Nelson and Lawrence Grossberg, 271–313. Basingstoke: Macmillan Education, 1988.

Stagi, Luisa. "Crossing the Symbolic Boundaries: Parkour, Gender and Urban Spaces in Genoa." *Modern Italy* 20, no. 3 (2015): 295–305.

"Stations fantômes à Paris." *Oxo Architecture*, 2014, www.oxoarch.com/front/project/stations-fantomes-a-paris.

Stoehr, Kevin L. "Haneke's Secession: Perspectivism and Anti-Nihilism in *Code Unknown* and *Caché*." In *A Companion to Michael Haneke*, edited by Roy Grundmann. Oxford: Wiley-Blackwell, 2010.

Sucker Punch Productions. *Infamous*. Tokyo: Sony Computer Entertainment, 2009.

"Suivez en direct les défilés du 1er mai." *Le Monde*, 1 May 2016, www.lemonde.fr/politique/live/2016/05/01/suivez-en-direct-les-defiles-du-1er-mai_4911626_823448.html.

Sutcliffe, Anthony. *Paris: An Architectural History*. New Haven: Yale University Press, 1993.

Tarde, Gabriel. *Les Lois de l'imitation*. 2nd ed. Paris: Éditions Félix Alcan, 1895.

Tarde, Gabriel. *L'Opinion et la foule*. Paris: Éditions Félix Alcan, 1901.

Tauber, Alfred. *Immunity: The Evolution of an Idea*. Oxford: Oxford University Press, 2017.

Taunton, Matthew. *Fictions of the City: Class, Culture and Mass Housing in London and Paris*. London: Palgrave Macmillan, 2009.

Techland. "Dying Light." Burbank, CA: Warner Bros. Interactive Entertainment, 2015.

Théobald, Marie. "Défilés du 1er mai: faible mobilisation et débordements à Paris." *Le Figaro,* 1 May 2016, www.lefigaro.fr/conjoncture/2016/05/01/20002-20160501ART FIG00071-les-defiles-du-1er-mai-reunissent-les-opposants-a-la-loi-travail.php.

Thacker, Eugene. *Biomedia*. Minneapolis: University of Minnesota Press, 2004.

Thiec, Yvon J. "Gustave Le Bon, prophète de l'irrationalisme de masse." *Revue Française de Sociologie* 22, no. 3 (1981): 409–428.

Thielemann, Leland. "The Problem of Unity and Individualism in Romains' Social Philosophy." *Modern Language Quarterly* 2 (1941): 249–262.

Thrift, Nigel. *Non-Representational Theory: Space/Politics/Affect*. New York: Routledge, 2007.

Thrift, Nigel. "Pass It On: Towards a Political Economy of Propensity." *Emotion, Space, and Society* 1, no. 2 (2008): 83–96.

Tonkonoff, Sergio. *From Tarde to Deleuze and Foucault: The Infinitesimal Revolution*. London: Palgrave Macmillan, 2017.

Tosoni, Simone, Matteo Tarantino, and Chiara Giaccardi, eds. *Media and the City: Urbanism, Technology, and Communication*. Cambridge, UK: Cambridge Scholars Publishing, 2013.

Tufekci, Zeynep. *Twitter and Tear Gas: The Power and Fragility of Networked Protest*. New Haven: Yale University Press, 2017.

Tumblety, Joan. *Remaking the Male Body: Masculinity and the Uses of Physical Culture in Interwar and Vichy France*. Oxford: Oxford University Press, 2012.

Ubisoft Montreal. "Assassin's Creed." Montreuil: Ubisoft, 2007.

Vadelorge, Loïc, ed. *Habiter les villes nouvelles*. Paris: Éditions Le Manuscrit, 2006.

Van Eeckhout, Laetitia. "Paris part en guerre contre le bruit." *Le Monde*, 10 March 2015, www.lemonde.fr/planete/article/2015/03/10/paris-part-en-guerre-contre-le-bruit_4590463_3244.html.

Vasset, Philippe. *La Conjuration*. Paris: Librairie Arthème Fayard, 2013.

Vasset, Philippe. *Un livre blanc*. Paris: Librairie Arthème Fayard, 2007.

Vidler, Anthony. *The Architectural Uncanny: Essays in the Modern Unhomely*. Cambridge, MA: MIT Press, 1992.

Vidler, Anthony. "Books in Space: Tradition and Transparency in the Bibliothèque de France." *Representations*, no. 12 (1993): 115–134.

Vidler, Anthony. *The Scenes of the Street and Other Essays*. New York: Monacelli Press, 2011.

Vidler, Anthony. *Warped Space: Art, Architecture, and Anxiety in Modern Culture*. Cambridge, MA: MIT Press, 2001.

Vijgen, Richard. "The Deleted City 3.0." *The Deleted City 3.0*, 2017, deletedcity.net.

Wahnich, Sophie. "Nuit Debout." *L'Homme et la société* 200, no. 2 (2016): 7–12.

Walter, Felix. "Unanimism and the Novels of Jules Romains." *PMLA* 51, no. 3 (1936): 863–871.

Whitehead, Tom. "Paris Charlie Hebdo Attack: Je Suis Charlie Hashtag One of Most Popular in Twitter History." *The Telegraph*, 9 January 2015, www.telegraph.co.uk/news/worldnews/europe/france/11336879/Paris-Charlie-Hebdo-attack-Je-Suis-Charlie-hashtag-one-of-most-popular-in-Twitter-history.html.

Wigley, Mark. *The Architecture of Deconstruction: Derrida's Haunt*. Cambridge, MA: MIT Press, 1993.

Williams, Rosalind. "Jules Romains, *Unanimisme*, and the Poetics of Urban Systems." In *Literature and Technology*, edited by Mark L. Greenberg and Lance Schachterle, 177–205. Bethlehem, PA: Lehigh University Press, 1992.

Wocke, Brendon. "Derrida at Villette: (An)aesthetic of Space." *University of Toronto Quarterly* 83, no. 3 (2014): 739–755.

Zakavati, Nioucha. "Street art féministe: Visite guidée à la Butte-aux-Cailles, un 'musée à ciel ouvert.'" *TV5Monde*. 9 August 2019, https://information.tv5monde.com/terriennes/street-art-feministe-visite-guidee-la-butte-aux-cailles-un-musee-ciel-ouvert-313316.

Zanghi, Filippo. *Zone indécise: Périphéries urbaines et voyage de proximité dans la littérature contemporaine*. Villeneuve d'Ascq: Presses universitaires du Septentrion, 2014.

ZEVS. "ZEVS: Visual Kidnapping." *Ping Mag*, 11 August 2008, http://pingmag.jp/2008/08/11/zevs-visual-kidnapping/.

Zillman, Dolf. "Excitation Transfer in Communication-Mediated Aggressive Behavior." *Journal of Experimental Social Psychology* 7 (1971): 419–434.

Zola, Émile. *La Curée*. Paris: Pocket, 1990.

Zuboff, Shoshana. *The Age of Surveillance Capitalism*. London: Profile Books, 2019.

Index